THE EARLY CAREER RESEARCHER'S TOOLBOX:

Insights into Mentors, Peer Review, and Landing a Faculty Job

ANDRES DE LOS REYES, PH.D.

Copyright © by Andres De Los Reyes
All rights reserved.

Except as permitted by the United States Copyright Act of 1976, no part of this publication may be reproduced or distributed in any form or by any means, including, but not limited to, the process of scanning and digitization, or stored in a database or retrieval system, without the prior written permission of the author.

Cover Design: Mary Ann Smith
Back Cover Photo: Ronald Flores
Copy Editing: Caitlin Panarella
Interior Design and Typesetting: Asya Blue
Indexing: Heather Pendley

Library of Congress Cataloging-in-Publication Data
De Los Reyes, Andres, 1978-
The early career researcher's toolbox: insights into mentors, peer review, and landing a faculty job / by Andres De Los Reyes. — 1st ed.
p. cm.
Includes bibliographical references and index.
LCCN: 2019921284
Print ISBN: 978-1-7344425-0-2
Ebook ISBN: 978-1-7344425-1-9
BISAC: 1. STU015000   2. EDU046000   3. STU021000
Printed in the United States of America

The Center for Reinforcing Early Academic Training and Enhancement (CREATE)
2300 18th St NW Lbby #21255
Washington, DC 20009
CREATE.DeLosReyes@gmail.com

Leading Scholars Praise *The Early Career Researcher's Toolbox*

"'How did I get here? Do I really belong? What on earth do I do next?' Such are the questions that huge numbers of young researchers constantly ask themselves. In *The Early Career Researcher's Toolbox,* De Los Reyes provides vivid and cogent answers to these compelling professional, even existential, questions. Using metaphors from film and contemporary media, he lays out 'three acts' of actionable objectives around which emerging investigators can make progress to embark upon their careers. Replete with vignettes and actual early-researcher questions and experiences, this book will provide both inspiration and concrete tools for trainees and early-career researchers across the sciences."

—Stephen P. Hinshaw, Ph.D. Professor of Psychology, UC Berkeley and Professor of Psychiatry, UC San Francisco; Editor, *Psychological Bulletin* (2009-2014); Recipient, American Psychological Association Distinguished Scientific Contribution Award (2020)

"The old adage 'publish or perish' has not changed, but it now has valuable nutrition attached to its fragile bones. De Los Reyes, feeding from his annual *Future Directions Forum,* provides the diet for success. In sage and readable style, De Los Reyes leads the novice to discover what drives them, to learn how to manage the publishing world, and to tell a compelling story about their work. Using classic and recent film as a parallel set of illustrations, and laced with personal experiences, De Los Reyes' guidance in *The Early Career Researcher's Toolbox* is both general and individually germane. This readable, useful, and valuable book

demystifies early career tasks for future emerging academics."
—Philip C. Kendall, Ph.D. Distinguished University Professor and Laura H. Carnell Professor of Psychology, Temple University; President, Association for the Behavioral and Cognitive Therapies (1989-1990); Editor, *Clinical Psychology: Science and Practice* (2003-2010)

"Dr. De Los Reyes' *The Early Career Researcher's Toolbox* is a true gift to our field's future. Too often, students receive high-quality guidance on how to gain admission to competitive doctoral programs, only to face the more opaque challenge of 'succeeding' as a scientist—and determining what 'success' really means!—upon arrival. This book offers a roadmap for students and early-career researchers as they navigate this complex task. Its chapters demystify academic systems and structures, from navigating peer reviews to crafting job talks, and offer wise guidance on developing a 'research identity' and finding awe and meaning in one's work. Its inclusion of anonymous scientists' own stories and experiences, from graduate students to early-career faculty, renders content all the more motivating and relatable. I will be thrilled to share this resource with my own doctoral trainees for years to come!"
—Jessica L. Schleider, Ph.D. Assistant Professor of Psychology, Stony Brook University; Selected as one of Forbes' 30 Under 30 in Healthcare (2020); Recipient, National Institutes of Health Director's Early Independence Award (2019)

"De Los Reyes has translated his careful observations of how to thrive in academia with humor, generosity, and a wealth of real-world examples in *The Early Career Researcher's Toolbox*. We are lucky he has used his talents to develop and support emerging academics and I am thrilled that he has turned many of the ideas previously shared at the *Future Directions Forum* into a book

THE EARLY CAREER RESEARCHER'S TOOLBOX

to aid early career scholars. This book is ideal for new scholars and their mentors alike! I plan to cover this chapter by chapter with my students and trainees as they learn both the basics on writing scientific articles and responding to peer reviews as well as framing their larger questions and motivations for their work."

—Kathryn L. Humphreys, Ph.D., Ed.M. Assistant Professor of Psychology and Human Development, Vanderbilt University; Recipient, Association for Psychological Science Janet Taylor Spence Award for Transformative Early Career Contributions (2020)

"For years, De Los Reyes has built a reputation providing unparalleled professional mentorship and sage career guidance to the next generation of researchers. With *The Early Career Researcher's Toolbox*, he has finally consolidated his expertise on this front into a highly engaging book that's overflowing with invaluable wisdom, direction, and practical tools—all while drawing on effective metaphors and captivating references to superheroes, villains, and Hollywood magic. I wish there had been a book like this when I was starting out. Any emerging academic who is not reading this remarkable work is launching their career at a significant disadvantage."

—Jonathan S. Comer, Ph.D. Professor of Psychology, Florida International University; President, Society of Clinical Psychology (2019); Recipient, American Psychological Association Early Career Award for Outstanding Contributions to Benefit Children, Youth and Families (2015)

"De Los Reyes has outdone himself in this compendium of resources for the early-career academic. He draws on a wealth of knowledge and expertise on establishing one's research program to provide a much-needed and easy-to-use resource. Reading this book early in one's training will no doubt help students increase their productivity and have an impact on the field. It will surely be the dog-eared book on many desks around the country!"

—Susan W. White, Ph.D. Doddridge Saxon Chairholder in Clinical Psychology, University of Alabama; Director, Center for Youth Development and Intervention; Associate Editor, *Journal of Autism and Developmental Disorders* (2014-2019)

"Dr. De Los Reyes is one of the most dedicated and successful mentors of his generation. He's facilitated the careers of countless trainees in psychology, and we are incredibly fortunate for his commitment to mentoring. This book is chock-full of wisdom about how to succeed in academic psychology. It is a must-read for young scholars!"

—Gregory E. Miller, Ph.D. Professor of Psychology, Northwestern University; President, Academy of Behavioral Medicine Research (2015-2016); Associate Editor, *Psychosomatic Medicine* (2008-2011)

"If only this book had been around when I launched my career! It could have spared me many blind alleys and clueless moments. This book answers questions a budding academic might feel too naïve (you aren't!) to ask and provides information you might not even know you need (until you read this critical compendium). Dr. De Los Reyes' writing is captivating, clever, comprehensive, and contains all the elements needed to prepare for academic success. I plan to share this book with all my mentees!"

—Mary A. Fristad, Ph.D. Professor of Psychiatry and Behavioral Health, The Ohio State University; President, Society of Clinical Child and Adolescent Psychology (2009, 2012); President, American Board of Clinical Child and Adolescent Psychology (2011-2013)

Table of Contents

Acknowledgements 1
Chapter 1: An Introduction to Emerging
Academics, Stories, and Tools 3
Act I: Your Burning Question 17
   Chapter 2: When You Learn One Tool, You Stumble
   onto New Tools 18
   Chapter 3: A Mentor's Work Exists in a Scholarly Universe . 30
   Chapter 4: The Shared Universe Tool 40
   Chapter 5: Selecting a Mentor 61
   Chapter 6: Optimizing Your Relationship with Your Mentor ... 95
Act II: Your Combat Tools 111
   Chapter 7: Basic Training for Peer Review 112
   Chapter 8: Peer Review Tools When the System
   Treats You Fairly 133
   Chapter 9: Peer Review Tools When the System
   Treats You Unfairly 157
Act III: Your Research Program 173
   Chapter 10: Basic Training for the Job Talk 174
   Chapter 11: Selecting Scholarship for the Job Talk 184
   Chapter 12: The Trilogy Tool 195
   Chapter 13: Trilogy: Part 1 204
   Chapter 14: Trilogy: Part 2 217
   Chapter 15: Trilogy: Part 3 226
   Chapter 16: Trilogy: Epilogue 240
Chapter 17: How Your Research Program Serves You
and Your Scholarly Universe 249
Glossary 256
About the Author 260
References 261
Index 278

Acknowledgments

To attendees of our *Future Directions Forum* (www.jccapfuturedirectionsforum.com): Each year, your feedback provides us with resources for improving our efforts at providing the next generation of researchers the tools to succeed in academia. Thank you so much for your ideas and support. In fact, the motivation to prepare this book came from the following comment by an anonymous attendee of our 2018 *Forum*: "[S]omething like 'developing your research program' would be cool, to help students think about each project in a more programmatic long-term way." Whoever you are, you started this.

CHAPTER 1
An Introduction to Emerging Academics, Stories, and Tools

This book begins and ends with stories. Stories about research. It may seem like a foreign concept to think about research in the form of a story. But think about it: Any of us in academia take anywhere from five to 10 years to complete our formative doctoral training. For some of us, the training continues after that and we complete one or more post-doctoral fellowships before we build the scholarly record that prepares us for the job market. For all of us, we don't just live through our years of training. We navigate these years, and overcome them. The long hours and sleepless nights. The setbacks and rejections. The years invested in building the foundation for a career in research. If you picked up this book, I would bet that, on occasion, you ask yourself: *Why am I doing this?* This question strikes at the core of why each of us choose to pursue a research career, and one tool can help you answer this question: story. You deliver your research to an audience of colleagues through various formats like talks and manuscripts. If you deliver your research clearly to an audience, story is the active ingredient; it is the reason why your audience understands you. Delivering your scholarly work in the form of a story allows you to make plain to your audience what keeps you up at night and gets you out of bed in the morning. During our time together, you will learn to leverage story as a tool for delivering your own compelling account of your work. You will learn about discovering the burning question that drives your work. On the road to disseminating your work, you will encounter struggles, namely with the peer review system that governs the publication of scholarly work. And so you will acquire tools for conquering this system and publishing your work. In the end, I will teach you how to use story to build your research program. If you master the tools described in this book and learn to tell a compelling story about your work, scholars with little to no background in what you do will nonetheless understand what your research program has to offer.

Emerging Academics: Defined

This book contains stories for those in their formative years of academic training, a group that includes those who seek admission to a doctoral program, those enrolled in doctoral programs, and scholars in post-doctoral fellowship programs. This group accounts for a large part of academia that, in the United States alone, numbers in the hundreds of thousands (National Center for Science and Engineering Statistics, 2018; Okahana & Zhou, 2018). In this book I use the term *Emerging Academic* to collectively refer to these various training stages in academics' careers. What do I mean by this term? I am a clinical psychologist by training, and I direct a laboratory where I train students enrolled in a doctoral program in the discipline of Clinical Psychology. Much of my research deals with how to measure and understand the thoughts, feelings, and behaviors of children and adolescents. As many of us know from our own lives and those of our loved ones, in your youth the way you think, feel, and react to the world around you profoundly shapes your path to developing into an adult. But we all know that we don't stop developing when we graduate high school or start our first job. And so in recent years many of my colleagues and I began using a term to encapsulate that period after adolescence when we are sure that people continue to develop at a furious pace: emerging adulthood (Fincham & Lucier-Greer, 2018).

The lived experience of an Emerging Academic differs from that of an emerging adult. Clearly, Emerging Academics exert a considerable degree of independence in selecting their discipline and the training programs in which they enroll. At the same time, an Emerging Academic kind of feels like they are reliving all of the developmental periods that precede adulthood, and on a much shorter timescale. In just a few years, an Emerging Academic lives through the good (and bad) of all of the developmental periods that allow someone to "gear up" for life as an independent scholar. The beginning of doctoral training at times feels like early childhood: a developmental period typified by rapid changes across numerous biological, cognitive, behavioral, social, and emotional systems (Rao & Wong, 2018). Professors in doctoral programs expect Emerging Academics in their programs to undergo a swift metamorphosis, learn the lingo of their discipline, and become a card-carrying member of this discipline. This often takes the form of ingesting material from copious amounts of coursework. Make no mistake, this is an exciting time! We share new ideas. We learn what it's like to collaborate with like-minded individuals. And these experiences manifest in intimate settings: one-on-one and small-group meetings that look nothing like the relatively large classrooms from our undergraduate days. We also find this to be a stressful time. Professors expect you to meet degree milestones, and quickly. Throughout the process of proposing and defending a master's thesis, sometimes it feels like you have to sprint before you learn to walk!

Before you know it, the formative years of an Emerging Academic beget even more advanced stages of development. When I was an Emerging Academic, at times I felt like I was in a perpetual loop reliving my first day of sophomore year in high school. The rapid pace of graduate training, coupled with the exceedingly high expectations held by graduate programs, often felt quite overwhelming. Wait, a short while ago I learned a bunch of stuff. Now, you want me to develop an identity, an expertise, based on the stuff I just learned? You want me to: (a) read, understand, and interpret a body of literature; (b) identify gaps in its knowledge base; and (c) cogently tease out an area of expertise that both fills those knowledge gaps and forms the basis of huge portions of my doctoral training, like my dissertation? I am feeling all the feels here, can I have a moment, please?

Much of the Emerging Academic period feels like being stuck in adolescence for much longer than you want to be. During adolescence, in addition to continued development in all aspects of our bodily, cognitive, behavioral, and emotional functioning, we encounter a bounty of novel social experiences typified by confusion, frustration, and uncertainty (Benner, 2018). Emerging Academics encounter novel social experiences of their own. The confusion you encounter when someone provides feedback on your paper that you do not understand and get stuck trying to address. The frustration you experience the first time—and the second time, and the third time—a manuscript of yours receives a rejection notice from a scholarly outlet like a journal or book publisher. The uncertainty you feel when someone asks you to complete a task that you have never been asked to complete, but you receive little guidance on how to do so. It's these "adolescent issues" that embody some of the most crucial elements of the Emerging Academic period. They also encapsulate some of the biggest issues educators encounter in graduate and post-graduate studies. They deal with the production of scholarship. Not term papers written to meet the requirements of courses offered at institutions of higher learning, but pieces of scholarly work. Work for which the ultimate goal is to disseminate its contents to those who reside well outside the campus walls where Emerging Academics receive training.

The Tools to Produce Scholarship and Launch Your Career

Scholarship—both the amount we produce and the quality of what we produce—is what makes or breaks research careers. Producing multiple, high-quality pieces of scholarship and building the record for a research career requires an academic toolbox. This toolbox contains tools for effectively communicating ideas and scholarly findings. For making time to produce scholarship. For securing funding for scholarly work. For identifying where and when scholarly job opportunities arise. For getting the offers to start a job and building the record to keep that job. And the perennial barrier is that at institutions of higher learning generally, there simply do not exist methods for building these toolboxes. Why? Because you do not have time. Neither do graduate programs. Program curricula at institutions of higher learning are already stretched beyond their means to cover the coursework necessary to ensure that graduates attain the "book smarts" that all researchers need to become socialized into their respective disciplines. But book smarts only get you so far. You also need the tools—the "street smarts"—to survive in research. Without this training, the most gifted of researchers find the most mundane of research activities—from staying productive to navigating the peer review system—mystifying.

I have grown frustrated by the reality that the next generation of scholars—our current cadre of Emerging Academics—often find themselves mystified by the tasks necessary to get an academic job and keep that job. And I think educators—myself included—often allow this to happen because when we were Emerging Academics, we too found these tasks mystifying. Do we know any better than those who educated us about how to convey professional development tools to our Emerging Academics? I think we do. Some of these tools lie in plain sight. As academics, we use them every day, and what we need to do is describe these tools within consumable formats like books (Olson, 2015; Prinstein & Patterson, 2013; Silvia, 2007, 2018) and workshops (e.g., De Los Reyes, 2018a, b). Sometimes, the process of acquiring a tool for mastering an academic task appears quite opaque. Educators can only demystify such tasks for Emerging Academics and describe the tools for mastering them by thinking outside of the box and turning to industries that have the solutions to perennial problems in scholarship. Informed by narrative tools that have their origins in film, this book provides Emerging Academics with the tools to master the three crucial questions germane to pursuing a research career. To be fair, a research career consists of many tasks and questions for consideration. Yet, if you cannot answer the three questions listed below and outlined in Figure 1.1—where I also list the sections of the book (i.e., Acts) and chapters that focus on each question—I suspect you will encounter difficulty on the path to pursuing a research career:

- *Where do you fit within academia, and what burning question drives your work?*
- *On the path to publishing your work, how do you respond to reviews of your work?*
- *How do you connect pieces of your work to build a research program?*

Why Filmmaking Tools?

Let us tackle a key issue before we proceed. You might have read this previous sentence with a fair degree of skepticism: *"Informed by narrative tools that have their origins in film...."* I began this book by arguing about the importance of communicating scholarly work in the form of a story. Now, I just conveyed the idea that filmmakers have the answers to crucial questions germane to scholarly work? We researchers embrace equations. We strive to make observations of our world that replicate, such that when other scholars follow in our footsteps and conduct scholarly work in the same way we did earlier, they observe things as we did (Schekman, 2016; Schmidt, 2009). We live and die by "active ingredients" that, when installed, applied, or otherwise scaled up and disseminated to the masses, produce predictable results. Permit me to make a bold statement:

- *No other industry on this planet has the capability to reveal robust, replicable storytelling principles than the film industry in its current form.*

To be fair, plenty of other industries know storytelling and do it well. However, the film industry is in a league of its own when it comes to how much it invests in storytelling. Great films tell coherent, compelling stories (e.g., Olson, 2015). Thus, much like the National Institutes of Health invests in science to improve public health, collectively the film industry invests considerable resources in order to optimize use of story as a communication device.

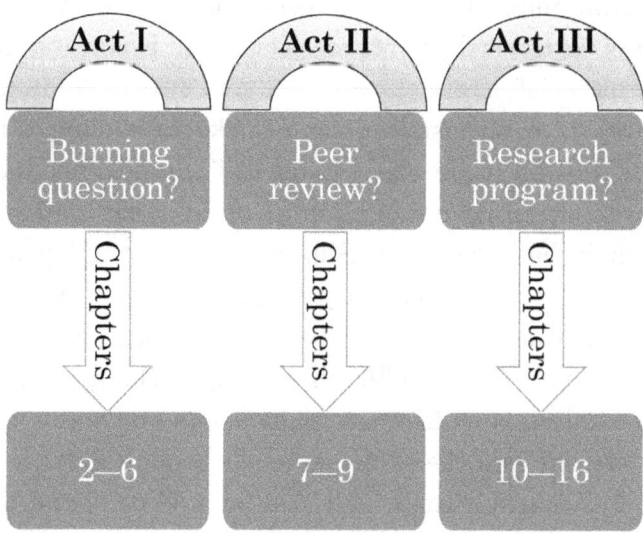

Figure 1.1. Three questions about academia addressed in this book, and the chapters addressing each question.

The money behind producing films ramps up the industry's ability to use storytelling tools to communicate. Granted, we have all seen our share of bad films; the industry isn't perfect. Nevertheless, filmmakers who produce financially successful films leverage story with surgical precision. I suspect some of you might be thinking: *But it's been years since the film industry produced a film that I found memorable, let alone good.* A key reason why you might be thinking this is precisely why tools from filmmaking inform the tools described in this book. Specifically, the film industry in its current form is frustratingly risk-averse. Just about every film you have the option of viewing in brick and mortar theaters has its basis in: (a) previously produced films (e.g., sequel to an earlier film); (b) widely known characters (e.g., from classic animation or comic books); and/or (c) genres with mainstream appeal (e.g., action/adventure, science fiction). These films often generate revenues on gargantuan scales. But here is the thing: These films also require considerable funds to write, cast, direct, produce, and distribute.

The film industry is risk-averse because even low-budget projects are costly, risky ventures. Yet, as an Emerging Academic, the industry's risk aversion works in your favor. Filmmakers use storytelling to avoid risky outcomes, like producing a film that bankrupts the film studio that funded it. The studio needs certainty that their storytelling not only helps them avoid bankruptcy but adds to their bank account. Similarly, you would benefit from certainty in your own scholarly work. You need concrete tools for communicating your scholarly work that achieve predictable, positive outcomes, like publishing your work, nailing your job talk, and landing your first job. Your needs and those of the film industry are one and the same, so why not capitalize on what the industry has learned from all the money they spend to perfect their storytelling?

So, what do filmmakers buy to avoid risky outcomes? They buy data, and lots of it. Sales estimates for previous films within the same genre as a new film project. Focus groups consisting of a sample of a target audience to which filmmakers wish to pitch ideas and solicit feedback on their film project. Test screenings that filmmakers use to make sure that audiences enjoy the latest draft of the film. All of these data serve one boss: the storytelling.

Data help filmmakers understand whether the product of their hard work successfully reproduced the equation of clear, compelling storytelling. If these data come up short of expectations, it's time to revise the product or otherwise risk monumental (and costly) failure. Filmmakers refer to this equation as the three-act structure. In fact, I organized the book using this exact structure, and I do what every memorable film you have ever seen does. In Act I, I create a universe for you to house your scholarly work. In Act II, I upend your newfound scholarly universe by creating a conflict that makes it hard for you to produce scholarly work. Act III serves to resolve the conflict that you encounter in Act II and return your scholarly universe to homeostasis. At its core, you will find in each Act a concrete set of tools. Tools to make sense of your scholarly universe, meet the challenges all researchers invariably encounter, and overcome these challenges to launch your research career.

Which Filmmaking Tools Help You Tell Your Story?

Beginning a research career involves providing solid answers to the questions outlined in Figure 1.1. Indeed, these questions focus on developing your *Research Program*: the story that you tell others who seek to learn more about your work. Your research program is what you show colleagues when you discuss your work at job interviews for faculty positions. You know you answered these questions well if you can tell a cogent, compelling story about your work to other scholars, even when they have little background in what you do. The crucial test of your story manifests as perhaps the most vexing, mystifying, and stress-inducing academic task of them all: the academic job talk.

If you hang around an academic setting long enough, you will attend countless academic talks. You will see great talks by Emerging Academics and seasoned researchers alike. You will also learn that any scholar, regardless of career stage, can deliver an unclear, even cringe-worthy talk. Scholars need a variety of tools to deliver a great academic talk. Yet, all academic talks have a primary objective: to organize multiple pieces of scholarly work into a coherent narrative or story of the speaker's scholarship.

In this book, I chose to describe a particular set of academic tools. I designed these tools to fit the lived experiences of Emerging Academics. In Table 1.1, I summarize their use in this book. Over the course of their training, a successful Emerging Academic produces several pieces of well-thought-out scholarship. This work is not a solo effort. Emerging Academics think about, develop, and complete scholarship under the supervision of a relatively more experienced professional—a *Mentor*. Scholarship in this space tends to occur: (a) in a relatively short period of time, (b) within the confines of an area of study often at the discretion of the mentor, and (c) without a clear view from the outset of how each of the pieces of scholarly work connect with one another thematically. Within this context of scholarship, the approach to scholarly work described in this book has its origins in two filmmaking tools. The first is the tool of the *Shared Universe*: an innovative filmmaking tool that I use as a metaphor for the scholarly relationship between mentor and Emerging Academic. This metaphor allows me to conceptualize for you an adaptive perspective on mentored scholarship. The second is the tool of *Trilogy*: a method for integrating a small number of related yet independent bodies of work into a compelling story. I elaborate on how these tools yield an approach tailor-made for Emerging Academics, who have just a few years to (a) develop an area of expertise; (b) produce scholarly work in this area; and (c) develop a compelling story about this work that positions them well for a career in research.

Table 1.1. Summary of Academic Tools and Strategies Used to Illustrate Their Application to Academic Work	
Academic Tools	*Methods for Illustrating How to Apply Academic Tools*
Shared Universe: Metaphorical device for conceptualizing the relationship between mentor and Emerging Academic	—Cite contemporary and classic examples in film to distill key principles of tools
Trilogy: Method for integrating and organizing multiple pieces of academic work into a compelling story of one's scholarship	—**Modeling Moments:** Illustrate application of academic tools to my own work, and to the work of one of my own graduate students
	—**Anonymous Accounts:** Narratives from current and former Emerging Academics and their experiences with work linked to the three questions in Figure 1.1

Overview of Our Strategies for Success

Throughout the book, I use three strategies to help you successfully master the academic tools described in Table 1.1. First, I cite contemporary and classic examples in film to both distill storytelling principles and connect these principles to scholarly work. Second, I describe elements of both my work and that of one of my own doctoral students, using a feature of the book I refer to as *Modeling Moments*. These Modeling Moments provide you with examples of how to apply the academic tools to produce and refine scholarly work, as well as describe this work to audiences of interest (e.g., faculty at an academic job talk).

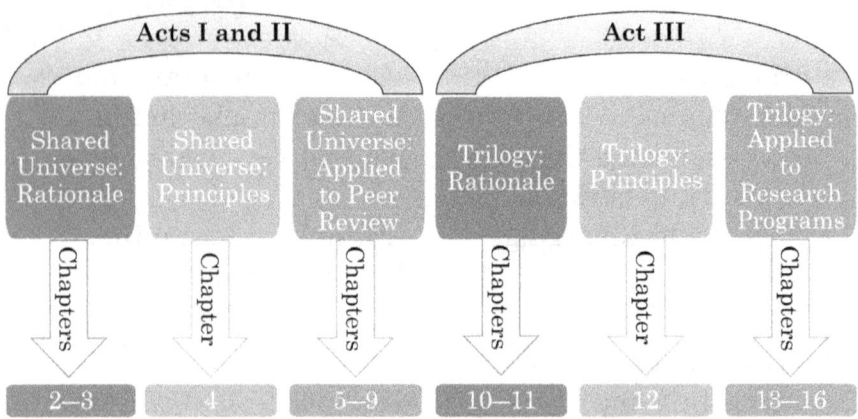

Figure 1.2. Structure of the book by content, chapter, and act.

Third, an additional feature, *Anonymous Accounts*, includes narratives from Emerging Academics and early career professionals. In unique ways, each Anonymous Account details experiences with work linked to the three questions in Figure 1.1. Some accounts provide you with useful tidbits of advice to complement the tools described in the main text. Others detail real-world experiences with struggles that all academics encounter, from those that precede the advent of doctoral training to those encountered during the first years on the job. Still other accounts reveal in lucid detail inspirational experiences that exemplify what makes a research career worth pursuing. Collectively, the three strategies breathe life into the academic tools described in the book, and reveal their functional properties when applied to scholarly work.

Organizational Structure of the Book

In this chapter, we discussed the rationale for the book, our focus on Emerging Academics like you, the academic tools for building a research program, and the strategies to facilitate learning the tools. How do we package all this knowledge to optimize its utility? As seen in Figure 1.2, I organized the book so that each chapter builds on material from previous chapters. Chapters 2 and 3 focus on the rationale for learning the first of the two academic tools revealed in the book, the Shared Universe tool. Chapter 4 covers all of the principles underlying the tool, and in Chapters 5 through 9 we apply these principles to the academic tasks germane to Acts I and II of the book (i.e., mentoring and peer review). With Act III, we repeat this process for the Trilogy tool. Chapters 10 and 11 present the rationale for learning the tool; Chapter 12 covers its underlying principles; and in Chapters 13 through 16 we learn how to apply the tool to developing a compelling account of your work (i.e., research program).

I want to close this chapter with two comments. First, as with all readers of this book, I suspect that some of the tools I reveal to you may be catching you at just the right time. Perhaps you picked up this book as you await the decision on a manuscript you submitted to a publication outlet. You might be on the cusp of beginning your first job search. Some of you might even be at the beginning of your journey in doctoral training, applying to graduate programs for the first time or just starting your graduate program. For each of you, only some of the tools we discuss may be of relevance to your work right now. What this means is that, on occasion, you may feel the need to take a break from our time together and wait for the right moment to return. That is fine, and I constructed the chapters with this possibility in mind. For instance, later chapters include reminders of key concepts presented in earlier chapters, so as to reduce the need to return to earlier material to understand the tools we discussed where you left off.

Second, please read the whole book. A prevailing theme in our time together involves the interconnected nature of scholarly work. If only some of the material is of relevance to you right now, I guarantee you that all of the material will be relevant to people with whom you meet and work during your career. I am asking you to read the whole book because if you find it helpful, my hope is that you will pay it forward. Permit me to explain. I see many of the students I mentor in my academic work—my own Emerging Academics—more often than I see close family and relatives. They comprise key components of my scholarly *Galaxy*: a metaphor I leverage throughout this book to describe mentored scholarship. If you find success in academia and begin a research career that involves raising your own Emerging Academics—creating your own scholarly galaxy—then please impart the tools in this book to your students. Don't wait until they graduate and look for work. To those who will eventually see you as their mentor, reveal these tools to your students early and often. We begin our journey with learning about *Burning Questions*: the topic of inquiry that propels a scholar's research program.

ACT I:
YOUR BURNING QUESTION

CHAPTER 2

When You Learn One Tool, You Stumble onto New Tools

In 2016, I founded the *Future Directions Forum* (www.jccapfuturedirectionsforum.com). This annual, two-day meeting provides Emerging Academics with professional development training on all elements of research. We discuss tools for mastering such academic tasks as writing publishable scholarship, grant writing, job searching and negotiation, and navigating the peer review system. At the *Forum*, day one exposes attendees to workshops, small-group meetings, and one-on-one consultations covering a variety of tools germane to scholarly work. On day two, attendees learn about the next steps in innovative areas of scholarship about mental health. I mention all this not to promote the event, but because the *Forum* marks the commencement of a story: the origin story of the Shared Universe tool for conceptualizing mentoring relationships and the scholarship resulting from them. My colleagues and I delivered our first *Forum* in 2017. But a little over 10 years ago I drew inspiration for the *Forum* from exposure to a set of invaluable professional development tools.

In this chapter I tell the story of how I discovered the Shared Universe tool. This story conveys important lessons about professional development training. Anyone who learns a professional development tool finds that the tool does not work for everyone the same way. As academics, all of the tools at our disposal require adaptation and improvisation; you need to tailor them to fit your own needs and scholarly work. The process of tailoring these tools to fit your needs reveals insights about your own work. As Anonymous Account 2.1 reveals, these insights often beget greater efficiencies in your work, and perhaps improvements in quality. In fact, tailoring can be a gift that keeps on giving: The process of tailoring professional development tools to your work sometimes reveals new tools.

Anonymous Account 2.1. Writing Schedules	
Post-Doctoral Fellow	Graduate school can feel like an impossible juggling act. You take graduate courses that require hundreds of pages of reading as well as dozens of pages of writing. You teach undergraduate courses. You carry out work in your mentor's lab, and you take the lead on one or more of the lab's research projects. In addition to all of these responsibilities, you must also find time for sleeping, exercising, and maintaining some semblance of a social life. Admittedly, I have been a "binge writer" for most of my academic career. I tend to write for days at a time in order to complete my course papers, reports, manuscripts, and grants. These writing marathons often leave me sleep deprived, overly caffeinated, and exhausted. Several years ago, however, I decided to try a new strategy that involved setting aside at least an hour each day specifically for writing manuscripts. Although I am not a morning person by nature, I decided that times early in the day (i.e., before 8am) would be easier to protect in my schedule and that I would devote this time to any activity that was necessary to complete a manuscript, including reviewing the literature, conducting analyses, or writing. My efforts in this area have seen several starts and stops—there are some days when I just don't feel like writing—but remaining disciplined in this routine has allowed me to maintain research productivity in the face of competing responsibilities, and produce far more scholarly work than I could have using my previous binge writing method.

Writing Time

All my work in the professional development space began with reading Paul Silvia's *How to Write a Lot* (2007). This contemporary classic on writing productivity, now in its second edition (Silvia, 2018), greatly facilitated my developing insight into my own writing. When I find myself writing fewer papers and grant applications than usual, how might I improve? When I find myself in a productive writing period, what am I doing right? I tell Emerging Academics in my laboratory that when my writing productivity is in good shape, I am doing everything Silvia tells me to do. If you have not already, I encourage you to pick up a copy of Silvia's book. Consistent with Silvia's writings on the topic, one of my keys to success in staying productive with my scholarly work is that for the last 10 years, I have set a writing time for myself. My writing time is short, recurring, and devoted solely to writing. It is also specific. I enter each writing time with a small, manageable agenda linked to a specific writing project like a manuscript or a grant application. My writing time consists of the 20-minute train ride to and from work, so 40 minutes round-trip. Forty minutes doesn't sound like much. It shouldn't. It's practical. It gets the job done. And if I follow the rule, "treat writing time like class time," then I rarely skip class. This writing time adds up. As I schedule more and more writing time, I continue to cross items off my agenda until I complete the project linked to my writing time.

I found Silvia's approach so clear, so easy to tailor to my needs, that my first efforts at delivering professional development workshops began with a short, 90-minute workshop on writing productivity: the most current version of which can be found online (De Los Reyes, 2018a; see https://www.apa.org/education/ce/pdp0027). Over time I learned that at 90 minutes, this workshop simply cannot reveal all the tools germane to writing productivity. Thus, I approach delivering this workshop with the primary aim of arousing audience members' curiosity about writing productivity. I seek to motivate them to a sufficient extent that, following the workshop, they take the initiative to change their behavior. In this respect, my workshop on writing productivity has the primary aim of getting members of the audience motivated enough about increasing their writing productivity that they read Silvia (2007, 2018). Sometimes an Emerging Academic's learning environment provides all the motivation they need to change their behavior, as seen in Anonymous Account 2.2.

Anonymous Account 2.2. Writing Schedules	
Doctoral Student	Most times, the day-to-day pressing matters often take priority over the longer-term projects, such as manuscript writing. Finding time to then produce scholarly work—or even setting aside time to interpret research findings—can feel daunting. In some of my busiest seasons as a graduate student, I attempt to do this by carefully crafting my calendar. I work best on manuscripts and research projects when I have at least 90 consecutive minutes dedicated to it –I need time to get settled and focused on my agenda. Before setting weekly meetings, I set aside two, 90-minute blocks a week or one, 3-hour block per week purely for research writing. Often times this block is from 6:30am-8am, and I can complete my work at home before going on campus. Before I began a habit of setting this time aside, manuscript writing continually got pushed to the next week, then the next, then the next—a pattern that was not advantageous for my career. Setting aside dedicated research time—and sticking to it!—makes a world of difference.

Tailoring Silvia's Approach to Fit My Needs: Overtime Writing

A key factor with setting a writing time involves picking the right environment to write. For instance, Silvia (2007) claimed that the writing time he used to write his book occurred on a small computer in the guest bedroom of his house; a computer without an internet connection. No internet equals fewer distractions, and thus a well-protected writing time. Similarly, my daily 40-minute writing time works for me because my writing time is "train time." Trains tend to have relatively poor internet and phone connectivity. Life can't create challenges to my writing time. That 40 minutes is a self-contained space where all I do is write.

Yet, like any approach, train time doesn't always work. Sometimes life creates challenges, and I have to put in "overtime writing" to complete a project. Usually, I turn to overtime writing for projects with a hard deadline. Examples include a grant application, or a manuscript for which a journal editor invited me to revise and resubmit the manuscript for further consideration at that journal. Similar to train time, my overtime writing requires environmental supports. My overtime writing typically occurs at home, so televised media—films in particular—are a perennial temptation. It's not realistic for me to refrain from turning on my television. So, my support system for overtime writing involves keeping the television on, but running a film that I have seen many times. If the television runs a film in which I know what happens at any given point, it ceases to distract me. I am able to tune out that film like ambient noise, kind of like a wave machine. This "ambient film" became one way I tailored Silvia's approach to fit my scholarly process. Anonymous Account 2.3 provides you with an example of how an Emerging Academic tailored Silvia's approach to fit their process.

Anonymous Account 2.3. Writing Schedules

Doctoral Student

During my second semester of graduate school, I was taking a full load of coursework, serving as a teaching assistant for four classes, and defending my Master's thesis. Seemingly urgent yet minute tasks—course assignments, responding to undergraduate students' emails, making cosmetic changes to my thesis—were eating up my days, leaving no time for scholarly writing. Reading *How to Write A Lot* by Paul Silvia, a book recommended to me by a colleague, made me aware of common writing-related fallacies that were holding me back (e.g., the myth that I need a large chunk of time, such as summer break, to get writing done). Following the book's suggestions, I tried scheduling daily blocks of writing time, as well as keeping a log of how many words I wrote every day. It turned out I didn't have the discipline to consistently stick with these. What worked best for me was to establish a location where I *only* do scholarly work. For me, that was my desk in lab. I promised myself I would *not* do class readings or assignments, emails linked to my teaching assistantships, or personal things at my lab desk—those things could wait until I was home. My lab desk was reserved for research only: running analyses, reading relevant literature, and writing or revising manuscripts. As I typically stayed in lab between 9am-5pm on weekdays (except when in class or a meeting), this personal "policy" helped immensely with my productivity, and I managed to publish two manuscripts that semester.

Ambient Films and the Shared Universe Tool

Overtime writing led to my discovery of the Shared Universe tool. After a while, I found my ambient film approach particularly effective when running a fast-paced film. A fast-paced film essentially served as an implicit message: *I should be as busy as the characters on screen.* For a while my ambient film was *Skyfall* (Wilson, Broccoli, & Mendes, 2012), then *Inside Man* (Grazer & Lee, 2006), and then *Spotlight* (Faust, Golin, Rocklin, Sugar, & McCarthy, 2015).

More recently, my ambient film has been *Avengers: Infinity War* (Feige, Russo, & Russo, 2018) but before that, it was the film where I discovered the Shared Universe tool: *Captain America: Civil War* (Feige, Russo, & Russo, 2016). As a brief background, both of these films exist within an interconnected network of films termed the *Marvel Cinematic Universe.* A key element of the Marvel Cinematic Universe is that each film in the universe tells a stand-alone story. However, each film also connects with the other films in the universe, like episodes in a television series. The interconnected nature of these films serves a crucial metaphorical role in this book. Through these films I discovered metaphors that facilitate conceptualizing not only the relationships between Emerging Academics and their mentors, but also how mentoring relationships exist in a larger network of scholars in the academic space.

Back to my ambient film: After running *Captain America: Civil War* (Feige et al., 2016) for what seemed like a hundred times, one particular scene stood out to me and revealed the driving metaphor for the Shared Universe tool we will learn to use. In this scene, a seasoned senior superhero in the Marvel Cinematic Universe of films, Tony Stark (AKA Iron Man), seeks to recruit the services of an emerging superhero—a newly introduced character in the universe—Peter Parker (AKA Spiderman). Take a minute to view the clip: http://bit.ly/ECRToolboxChapter2SharedUniverseClip. It marks a touching point in the film. The scene establishes Stark's mentoring role in relation to Peter. In fact, step back and recall the first time you met one of your mentors. From this perspective, the scene highlights several themes within mentoring relationships in academia. At times Peter displays what Emerging Academics might experience as an imposter syndrome: the unfounded feeling that someone who recently secured a coveted academic position (e.g., admission into a doctoral program or hired as new faculty) cannot meet expectations and will soon reveal to the world an unworthiness of their new position (McCormick & Barnes, 2008). Stark's "why do this" line of questioning of Peter—his prospective mentee—resembles the questions one receives when interviewing for a doctoral program (e.g., *Why did you apply to this graduate program?*). Starks's offer to take his newly found mentee under his wing shares similarities to the upgrades in educational resources and mentoring that accompany an offer of admission to a doctoral program. All of the key elements of mentoring in academia exist in this one scene: a scene that depicts the origins of a mentoring relationship between two comic book characters.

A key bit of context clarifies the utility of this example for our present discussion. In the Marvel Cinematic Universe of films, Iron Man serves a leading role in three stand-alone films (Arad, Feige, & Favreau, 2008; Feige & Favreau, 2010; Feige & Black, 2013), as do some other superheroes in this universe such as Captain America (Feige & Johnston, 2011; Feige, Russo, & Russo, 2014, 2016), and Thor (Feige & Branagh, 2011; Feige & Taylor, 2013; Feige & Waititi, 2017). Further, Iron Man, Captain America, and Thor each play supporting roles in each other's films, as well as central roles in ensemble-cast films like the *Avengers* films (Feige et al., 2018, 2019; Feige & Whedon, 2012, 2015). In this way, these characters each take on an established presence in this shared universe of films. They all function as senior superheroes in the ways that tenured professors function in academia. In contrast, the scene from *Captain America: Civil War* (Feige et al., 2016) described previously—between senior superhero Iron Man and emerging superhero Spiderman—marks the first instance in which the audience has an opportunity to see Spiderman, at least within the Marvel Cinematic Universe of films. In this way, Spiderman begins his tenure in the Marvel Cinematic Universe early on in his development. He is not a senior superhero: at least not yet. Spiderman does not get a leading role in a film: at least not yet. In fact, Spiderman does not even get an "origin story." In that first scene with Iron Man, Spiderman does not get an opportunity to reveal to the audience where he came from. What Spiderman does get is a few minutes—embedded in someone else's film—to give the audience a hint of what he is about. To get you curious to see more. If he sufficiently stirs the audience members' curiosity, and motivates them to want to see more of Spiderman, then Spiderman gets to lead his own films. He gets what other senior superheroes have: the privilege to tell his own stories.

Modeling: The Active Ingredient for Learning How to Apply Our Academic Tools

Within the Marvel Cinematic Universe, the relationship between Spiderman and Iron Man reveals a textbook metaphor for the relationship between an Emerging Academic and their mentor. Although Spiderman does not begin his tenure in the Marvel Cinematic Universe with a suite of his own films, he still gets involved in a larger story. Along the way, he gets a lot of help from his mentor, Iron Man, to begin developing the ability to tell his own stories. That's how every Emerging Academic starts out. That's how all our research programs emerge. We all begin, embedded in our mentor's story. For each of us, our mission is to build a research program that extends from our mentor's research program, and connects to the programs of work built by our mentor's colleagues. This, of course, is easier said than done. This mission includes challenges. Through the tools we discuss in this book, my mission is to help you meet these challenges by giving you a way to build a research program with the resources available to you.

You might ask, *"How do you expect to connect metaphors surrounding films about comic book characters to my academic work?"* I will answer that question with a short story. My mentor in graduate school was Alan Kazdin, now Sterling Professor of Psychology (Emeritus) at Yale University and former President of the American Psychological Association. A little over five years after I completed my doctoral training, I sent Alan a message concerning our collaborative work. While I was on-site at Yale—doctoral students in Clinical Psychology typically spend their last year of training off-site on clinical internship—I published four peer review journal articles under Alan's mentorship (De Los Reyes & Kazdin, 2004, 2005, 2006a, 2006b). In my message to Alan, I noted that his mentoring stylings were so effective, that for each of these articles I could pinpoint the specific places on campus in which he conveyed the respective pieces of advice that led to each article.

For the purpose of this section of the book, one article in particular stands out. The place was the basement of the building where Alan kept the archival data for one of his previous studies. I used these data for the project that eventually became my master's thesis (De Los Reyes & Kazdin, 2006b). As I was working through my thesis, I arrived at a point of frustration with the articles I read. The source of the frustration is not germane to my highlighting this moment in my training. What is germane is that when I conveyed my frustration to Alan, his response was a piece of advice that I still use to this day (loosely paraphrased): *"When I get that frustrated about a topic, I write a review paper about it."*

This moment with my mentor marked the beginning of what to this day is the most highly cited work in my research program (De Los Reyes & Kazdin, 2005). More importantly, this moment demonstrates the power of modeling: a technique for changing or modifying a target's behavior (Kazdin, 2012). With the assistance of tactics like enacting displays of the desired behavior (e.g., "This is how you jump, now you try") or thoughts about that behavior (e.g., Alan's frustration comment), the target of behavior change (me) vicariously learns about the desired behavior from the modeler (Alan). The result should be an increased likelihood that the target begins displaying the desired behavior. Alan thought it would be a great idea for me to write a review paper in the area of research covered by my master's thesis. An effective way to get me to start such a paper is for him to take my current behavior (frustration) and pair it with the desired outcome. He pairs the two together by revealing that when he feels the way I felt at that time, he writes a review paper. Alan writes great review papers (e.g., Kazdin, 1987, 2007). Works for him, so why not give it a shot?

Modeling will be the mechanism—the active ingredient—that underlies how I will guide you to apply the tools described in this book to your own scholarly work. For each of the three questions outlined in Chapter 1, I model examples of how to answer the question. I refer to these examples as Modeling Moments, and in Figure 2.1 I connect each of these moments to the questions outlined in Chapter 1, Figure 1.1. The burning question? In Chapter 4, I show you how I describe my burning question when I discuss my research program. In Chapters 8 and 9, I include Modeling Moments pertinent to responding to commentary from peers evaluating your scholarly work. In Chapters 13, 14, and 15, I present models for how to select the pieces of scholarship you will use to communicate your research program to your colleagues. For Modeling Moments presented in Chapters 13 through 15, I encourage you to focus on the characteristics of the pieces of work and how they thematically connect to one another.

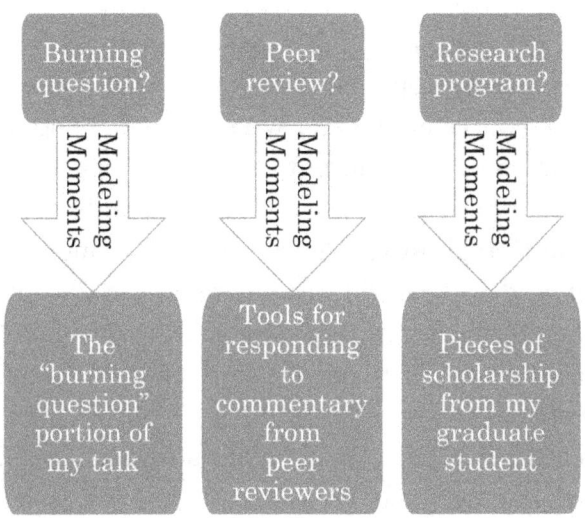

Figure 2.1. **Examples of Modeling Moments for three questions about academia addressed in this book.**

But before we get to the modeling, we have to discuss mentoring: specifically, how you as an Emerging Academic fit within the confines of your mentor's work, and the work of your mentor's colleagues. You may not have the ability to tell your own story just yet, but you have more resources available to you than you think. My advice on how to approach reading the next few chapters: Think big.

CHAPTER 3
A Mentor's Work Exists in a Scholarly Universe

Have you ever heard of rogue planets? I learned about them when preparing this book. Rogue planets develop in a solar system and for whatever circumstance—a large gaseous planet pushes them out, or they collide with a passing star—they exit their solar system of birth and wind up having to go it alone (Laughlin & Adams, 2000; Lissauer, 1987). Some believe that under the right circumstances, rogue planets have the capability of harboring life (Abbot & Switzer, 2011). In the universe of scholarship, rogue planets are lifeless—they cannot function as effective storytelling vehicles. Your scholarship cannot function as a rogue planet. Neither can a mentor's scholarship.

For both mentor and Emerging Academic, scholarly work exists in large, interconnected environments: solar systems, galaxies, and indeed entire universes! An academic leads an interconnected career. Each academic devotes their career to a node of scholarship that projects out to the nodes of scholarship created by other academics who are interested in the same or similar burning questions. Stated another way, the mentor's scholarship develops within a larger *Universe* of scholarship. Over the years, that universe comes to expect certain kinds of scholarship to arise out of a mentor's research program. What this means is that a mentor cannot quickly revise their research program or change course to produce the exact kinds of scholarship that their students might want to produce. A mentor's research program exists within boundary conditions, constraints of its own. In fact, as detailed in Anonymous Account 3.1, Emerging Academics quickly find that their doctoral training exists within the environment their mentor creates for them.

> **Anonymous Account 3.1. First Mentor Meeting**
>
> **Doctoral Student:** The first time I met my research mentor was on interview weekend at the University. I'd previously had a video conference call with my future mentor but had never met them in person. On my first morning on interview weekend, I saw my to-be mentor down the hallway. I looked down at my feet thinking they would not recognize me—at least from that far away and in my formal interview clothes. I heard my name bellowed from the end of the hall as my mentor hurried down the hall with their arms outstretched to greet me in a hug. They told me how excited they were to have me here on campus and that they could not wait to show me around. I felt their inherent excitement and joy in having me on campus and their thrill to show me the research program they had skillfully crafted during their time here—it made me that much more excited to be visiting my top choice university.

All of this means that the mentor's own research program and its underlying theories, methodologies, and findings exert a considerable influence on an Emerging Academic's scholarship. The mentor's research program functions as the Emerging Academic's incubator, as detailed in Anonymous Account 3.2. Incubators function as controlled environments. An incubator serves as the secure base for an Emerging Academic's work. So long as the Emerging Academic puts in the work of learning about their surroundings—so long as they do their part to grow as a scholar and learn about their mentor's research program—the incubator does its part and supports the Emerging Academic's development.

That being said, an Emerging Academic might find this controlled environment stifling. You grow within the confines of what surrounds you. Perhaps the expectation is that you adopt your mentor's theories or the conceptual frames that underlie their work. As you work to produce your first pieces of scholarship, you find that a key component of your research program might involve using a rhetorical device or laboratory paradigm developed by your mentor. You might even begin developing your research program based off of an exciting, recent discovery made by your mentor, and the hope is that you pick up where your mentor left off. All of these possibilities occur frequently and naturally across all of our scholarly universes. The universe within which you reside does not expect you to recreate celestial bodies that already exist. Thus, a mentor's research program assists in focusing an Emerging Academic's attention.

Anonymous Account 3.2. First Mentor Meeting	
Doctoral Student	I met my first research mentor when he interviewed me for an unpaid research assistant position. I was thrilled and intimidated by the prospect of working with a faculty member doing research I felt passionate about, but had little experience in. I was so nervous during the interview that my heart was pounding and I was stumbling over my words. My mentor was patient, warm, and asked me questions that helped me better articulate my interests and motivations for wishing to pursue research in this area. The meeting gradually transformed from an interview into a conversation about how I could contribute to his lab in a way that would also help me develop my skillset. Before meeting him, I hadn't realized the

 importance of having not just a supervisor or an advisor, but a *mentor* who is genuinely invested in your development. I came out of that meeting convinced he would be a good mentor for me. Indeed, he was the one who cultivated my research skills, encouraged me to apply to graduate school, and is still a profound influence in my research career today.

To recap: Your mentor's theories, methodologies, and findings serve as your resources. These resources help fuel your scholarship insofar as they provide you with a secure base for your work. In turn, this secure base facilitates building your research program. Contextualizing mentored scholarship in this way reveals your mission as an Emerging Academic: to create a research program that pivots off of your mentor's work, and at the same time connects your work to the larger universe of scholarship to which your mentor's work connects.

Introducing Ms. Bridget Makol, M.S.

By now, my hypothesis is that you have questions, like:
- *Examples, please?*
- *Last time I checked, universes get pretty big; how much time do you think I have?*
- *How can Emerging Academics build research programs in the ways you describe?*

To begin addressing these questions, I think it's appropriate at this time to introduce you to a colleague of mine: Ms. Bridget Makol (Figure 3.1). You can find a description of Bridget's scholarly record here: http://bit.ly/ECRToolboxChapter3MakolCV. Briefly, as of this writing Bridget is enrolled as a doctoral student in good standing in the Clinical Psychology Doctoral Program at the University of Maryland at College Park. I serve as faculty in this program and as Bridget's primary mentor. Bridget began her doctoral training in August of 2016, and she currently is nearing completion of her fourth year of doctoral training. Before enrolling in our program, she completed a Bachelor of Science (B.S.) in Psychology at the University of Illinois at Urbana-Champaign (2013), and a Master's of Science (M.S.) degree in General Psychology at DePaul University in Chicago (2016). At DePaul, she completed a master's thesis under the direction of Antonio Polo, and following her time at DePaul she published this work under Antonio's supervision (Makol & Polo, 2018).

Figure 3.1. Bridget A Makol, M.S. (left) and Andres De Los Reyes, Ph.D. (right).

These last two elements in Bridget's record—her training at DePaul and her publication based on scholarly work conducted at DePaul—crucially factor into examples presented later in the book. Specifically, how do you leverage the academic tools you will learn in this book to produce a coherent, compelling research program? Examples from Bridget's academic record serve to address this crucial question. By extension, these examples serve as key Modeling Moments that facilitate developing your own research program. In fact, at this stage I am afraid you might think I'm like a magician about to perform an illusion. To be clear: I have no tricks up my sleeve. I am not pulling a fast one on you. I want to be above-ground in my descriptions of Bridget's work, and the utility of this work for illustrating key concepts in the book.

At no point at the beginning of Bridget's master's-level training did she approach me to figure out a topic for her DePaul thesis. She began work on her thesis project under the direct supervision of Polo; I had no design input on the project. I first learned of the project when Bridget presented the findings of the work at a national conference we both attended (Makol, Sajwani, Grocochinski, Reeb, & Polo, 2015). Importantly, before she enrolled in our doctoral program I did provide Bridget with relevant literature to enhance the likelihood of her publishing the thesis. However, I shared none of this work with the intent of shaping Bridget's research program. In fact, in many respects some key elements of Bridget's research program as described in this book will appear as new to her as it will to you. All this being said, the importance of these elements of Bridget's experiences and scholarly record become readily apparent in material covered in Chapters 12 through 16 of this book.

I should highlight some other elements of Bridget's record. Specifically, as of this writing Bridget has published 12 articles in peer review journals. In our discipline articles in peer review journals comprise the building blocks of research programs. Thus, all our examples focus on Bridget's journal articles. Further, as of this writing Bridget has another three manuscripts currently under consideration for publication at a peer review journal. That makes 15 total pieces of scholarship across published and yet-to-be published scholarship. What might surprise you later on is that we will ignore most of this work when describing Bridget's research program.

The Modeling Moments rely on a fraction of the 15 pieces of scholarship from Bridget's record. As alluded to in Anonymous Account 3.3 and discussed at length in Chapter 11, I crafted the academic tools described in this book to fit the scholarly work that Emerging Academics create within mentoring relationships. This work includes thematically connected scholarship produced by an Emerging Academic within what will eventually become their research program. This also includes work that Emerging Academics undertake for the greater good of the mentor's scholarly environment (e.g., laboratory, research team). This "greater good" work often bears little resemblance to the work that comprises an Emerging Academic's research program.

Anonymous Account 3.3. First Mentor Meeting	
Doctoral Student	I met with my mentor for the first time a week before I formally started graduate school. We discussed our expectations for each other, including how often we would meet and what types of projects I would work on. He was receptive to me expressing my interest in specific projects and we were able to negotiate for me to spend some time on projects that specifically excited me and others that benefitted the lab more broadly. He gave me advice about which courses to take and about adjusting to graduate

 school more broadly. My advisor also explicitly told me that I could tell him if I ever feel overwhelmed or stressed, which made me feel supported and that he cared about my well-being. I left that meeting feeling eager to start school and to work with my advisor.

A Sneak Preview of the Next Few Chapters

I wanted to introduce you to Bridget not because I am remarkably proud of her as a scholar and Emerging Academic (although I do not tire of highlighting any of my students' accomplishments). Rather, the academic tools I discuss below are unlikely to make sense without models for applying the tools. In Chapter 4, I describe in granular detail key elements of the Shared Universe tool. Within this conceptual frame, you will learn about galaxies, solar systems, stars, and planets. I will continue to discuss these elements in a metaphorical sense, and then apply the metaphors to the key components of research programs. I will overlay these metaphorical concepts to—in order—the mentor's research program, the Emerging Academic's research program, the ideas that inform the production of scholarship, and the concrete pieces of scholarship that emerge from these ideas. Keep an open mind as you enter Chapter 4. We will learn some new concepts and you may discover links to current or previous mentoring relationships that you may not have perceived before. As the author of Anonymous Account 3.4 would say, you may even experience some moments of serendipity.

Anonymous Account 3.4. First Mentor Meeting

Post-Doctoral Fellow

Before graduate school, I worked in a lab where one of the students was studying serendipity. So, serendipity was on my mind when I first met my advisor. "What can I do for you?" That was how my (soon-to-be) advisor greeted me during our first-ever meeting. "Well, since you asked..." I said. "I read your review paper on this topic I am very interested in, and I am wondering if you have plans to continue that work." The specific topic I was interested in is not important, except to say that it was a topic I really wanted to study. But, I had not been able to find anyone who was working in this area. My advisor turned out to be the one exception. For the rest of the interview, we talked about the research agenda we both hoped to pursue. By the time I walked out of that meeting, I had my heart set on working with this person. It was a perfect fit and a genuinely unique opportunity. I then did my due diligence—I talked to his students and other professors in the department; I researched all of my options, and I hoped that I would receive an offer to work with him. When the offer arrived, I accepted it almost immediately and cancelled my remaining interviews. At the time, it did not even seem like there was a choice to make—given my interests, it was clearly the best option for me, and I was just lucky to have stumbled upon the one person who was eager to support me in the work about which I was so passionate. It felt serendipitous. What I did not realize, was that research fit is not everything. Of course, research fit is huge. But, personal qualities and characteristics—who an advisor is as a person—

are at least as important. I know this because, in addition to being uniquely suited to helping me pursue my interests, my advisor turned out to be incredibly kind, generous, and encouraging throughout my graduate work. Now I realize those qualities were fundamental to my graduate school experience and to my wellbeing. I could have compensated for a less than perfect research fit, but a difficult interpersonal fit would have had a bigger impact and been much harder to problem-solve. When I had first met my advisor, I had been overcome by the research opportunities he presented. In hindsight, I am overcome by how kind, compassionate, and generous he was from our first meeting.

CHAPTER 4
The Shared Universe Tool

Superheroes: So Like Us

I find the concept of a superhero—a being who displays extraordinary qualities that allow them to accomplish unfathomable feats—fascinating. Arguably, an omnipotent superhero makes for a rather bland, predictable story. Thus, a key element of stories about superheroes involves revealing a debilitating weakness harbored by the superhero: a weakness the superhero has to overcome, and often at great personal cost to themselves or those they hold dear. It is no accident that these weaknesses reflect central elements of stories about superheroes. In Randy Olson's *Houston, We Have a Narrative* (2015) we learn that all effective, memorable stories begin with establishing facts (e.g., superhero is awesome), transition to creating a conflict that upends these facts (e.g., superhero also harbors weaknesses), and conclude with events that resolve the tension brought about by the conflict (e.g., superhero battles through weaknesses; saves people, places, and things). And so, Tony Stark (AKA Iron Man) faces an attack that leaves copious amounts of shrapnel embedded near his heart, and he keeps the shrapnel at bay with a protective energy source he installs at the center of his chest (Arad et al., 2008). Wade Wilson (AKA Deadpool) develops a terminal form of cancer, and all that keeps him from death is a genetic mutation that allows him to regenerate healthy tissue, but in the process leaves him physically deformed (Kinberg, Reynolds, Shuler Donner, & Miller, 2016). Bruce Wayne's (AKA Batman) witnessing as a child the traumatic death of his parents is both the source of his motivation to serve the role of vigilante, and also a key weakness in that the mere mention of his parents often leaves him emotionally distracted and vulnerable to attack (Roven, D. Snyder, & Z. Snyder, 2016).

Whenever possible in this book, I highlight for you key aspects of careers in research, in an effort to demystify for you the process of mastering academic tasks. One thing I find irksome about scholarly work is that an academic's successes—the products of our superpowers—all manifest publicly. The scholarship we publish, the grants we receive, the scholarly awards or honors bestowed upon us: Everyone around us knows they exist. This element of academia creates the illusion that seasoned academics harbor some peculiar qualities that as an Emerging Academic, you might not see in yourself. And what perpetuates this myth about seasoned academics is that our failures—the products of our weaknesses—largely manifest privately. The notice I received the other day from a journal editor that they rejected my manuscript for publication. The notice I received last week from a funding agency that they will not fund my grant application. These notices come to me, and thus only I know that these failures exist.

To use a familiar metaphor, academics' successes represent the tiny piece of the iceberg shooting out of the water. These successes rest on a firm foundation of failure underneath the surface. I say "firm foundation" because, as we will discuss later on, a key component of succeeding in research involves learning from and overcoming failure.

What if seasoned academics were more transparent about failure? What if, from time to time, we flipped our icebergs over, and revealed our failures to the next generation of researchers following us? Might increasing transparency about failures translate into Modeling Moments for you and your fellow Emerging Academics? Opportunities for you to engage in vicarious learning; to allow you to model the kinds of adaptive scholarly behaviors necessary to overcome failures? Unfortunately, only under rare circumstances do academics like myself make our failures apparent to others. Beyond publicly broadcasting our experiences with failure, we have few ethical methods for doing this. This reality of academic work informs a practice I follow during my professional development workshops. For example, during my workshops on writing productivity, I pull up reviews of manuscripts I previously submitted for publication. In going over these reviews, I seek to convey to the audience that all academics commonly receive rather harsh critiques about their scholarly work (De Los Reyes, 2018a). Incidentally, we will learn more about navigating the peer review system in Act II of this book (i.e., Chapters 7, 8, and 9).

In this book, I wish to go a bit deeper in revealing failures, in disclosing weaknesses. All throughout my Emerging Academic period, and well into my path from Assistant to Associate Professor, would you like to know what my weakness was, and in all honesty, still is? Story. You read that right: The primary weakness of the author of this book—the shrapnel that perpetually seeks to crawl into one of my top three favorite vital organs—is my difficulty with infusing narrative structure in my work. If it were not for exposure to a set of invaluable professional development tools (Olson, 2015), this weakness would get the better of me more often than not. You see, deep down I am an unapologetic geek for the methodology of my discipline. It's my mac 'n cheese—my academic comfort food. I enjoy writing about methodological tools, often at the expense of cogently describing how these tools help me pursue the burning question that motivates my work. If I had complete control over my scholarly process, my work would likely read a lot differently. And if I had this control, it would be to my detriment because my instincts to neglect story lie in direct contrast with the very reasons why I value academic work. At the core of producing scholarship you find collective action. Disseminating your work facilitates the exchange of ideas with other scholars, and story helps us all communicate plainly to those who might find value in this work. For much of my academic upbringing and beyond, I wrote about my work in a way that made it very hard for my colleagues to understand my research program and ultimately, the value of the products arising from my work. For another example of weaknesses, check out Anonymous Account 4.1.

> **Anonymous Account 4.1. Academic "Weaknesses"**
>
> **Early Career Faculty**
>
> One of my shortcomings that I have struggled with throughout my career is my tendency to be a little scattered when it comes to the projects I work on. I have always enjoyed working on interdisciplinary studies, and my best work has come from collaborations with fun colleagues whose research interests and expertise are unique from mine. At the same time, these interdisciplinary projects often lead me to studying topics that are outside my main area of expertise. As a result, I often encounter what feels like extensive delays while I try to learn a new literature or catch up on a new methodological technique. These delays can turn into real clogs in my research pipeline, and there are times when I miss nearly every deadline or goal that I set for myself. (Perhaps this means another shortcoming is poor time estimation for how long these projects will take...) This issue can become problematic if a collaborator thinks I'm moving too slowly or not making sufficient progress on shared goals. And to compound the problem, I find myself committing to multiple interdisciplinary projects at once, which can lead to a completely overwhelming feeling of taking on too much (and not having sufficient existing knowledge to move forward with the projects in an efficient manner). Before I start working on a new grant proposal or

paper, I find myself needing to read a large body of research, and each time I promise myself that next time I will stick to a topic I've already studied so that I can skip these time-consuming ventures into unfamiliar research territory. I'm currently working with collaborators on a grant proposal that is *completely* outside of my research area, so this issue continues to be an "area for growth" for me.

Accidentally Discovering Story

As with superheroes, whether an academic's weakness makes for a compelling story hinges on their ability to overcome. In my case, overcoming my story weakness came in two phases. In Phase I, I discovered story by accident. It was May 2013. I was working on the research statement one prepares for their tenure dossier. This statement serves as a concise description of your research program and the academic record you built to advance that program. As part of the tenure review process, colleagues both at your home institution and those who affiliate with other institutions (i.e., external evaluators) review this statement along with other crucial documents (e.g., *curriculum vitae* [CV], representative publications). These documents form the basis for determining whether a tenure candidate passes threshold for promotion (Trower, 2012). In fact, tenure review processes function similarly to the faculty hiring processes I describe later in Chapter 10. Thus, the research statement can make or break an academic's chances at promotion. This statement is a key source through which colleagues at your home institution as well as independent, external evaluators decipher your research program and its impact.

For reasons I had yet to fully grasp, the way I described my research program in my statement felt clearer than any academic piece I had written before. Maybe it was the high-stakes context of the writing, but for what felt like the first time I put forth maximal effort to describe my research program as plainly and clearly as I could. The description felt so clear to me that I clung onto it as one would a security blanket. I placed my research statement in the section of my laboratory's website where I describe my work. I used it within autobiographical statements in grant applications. Indeed, a version of this statement served as the opening paragraphs of the first major article I published post-tenure (De Los Reyes et al., 2015). It also formed the foundation of the talk I currently use to describe my research program. Later on in this chapter, we will review the opening minutes of this talk.

Phase II functioned kind of like a combination of Randy Olson discovering the active ingredients of story and my own accidental discovery described in Phase I. In late October 2015 I happened upon a news article describing the then-recently released Olson (2015) text mentioned previously (Shapiro, 2015). The article chronicled Olson's discovery of a parsimonious account of narrative structure, articulated by one of the co-creators of South Park—Trey Parker—in a documentary Olson had viewed about the process through which Parker develops content for episodes of the series. As Olson recalls, Parker delineated a process whereby the first draft of an episode's script includes a series of events listed in succession, separated by "ands"; Parker infuses narrative structure in the episode by replacing some of the "ands" with "buts" and "therefores."

The "ands-only" draft version of a South Park episode reads like most pieces of scholarship many of us consume in our respective disciplines, and disciplines within scientific fields in particular (Olson, 2015): a piece of work consisting of a succession of facts devoid of narrative structure. Such work likely results in unremarkable scholarly products that fail to engage the intended audience. In contrast, research indicates that work housed in a narrative environment engages the audience to a far greater extent, and increases the likelihood that the audience encodes and remembers its key elements (e.g., Hasson, Furman, Clark, Dudai, & Davachi, 2008; Ki, Kelly, & Parra, 2016). Consequently, Olson's (2015) *And-But-Therefore* narrative approach is his attempt at distilling these key elements of story into a scalable format for scholars to implement in their work, with key implications for improving the ability of scholars to disseminate their work to each other and laypeople alike.

That previous paragraph: Did you see what we did there? We read a story! The first two sentences functioned as the "and" portion of the paragraph, an establishment of fact. The "in contrast" sentence functioned as the "but" portion—the introduction of a conflict—and the "consequently" sentence served the role of "therefore"—an attempt to resolve the tension between the "and" and "but" portions of the paragraph. And this is what clicked for me in Phase II of my discovery of story. Through Olson's approach to story, I gained insight as to why my Phase I research statement "felt right" to me. It felt right because it had the components of a narrative. It gave my research program a clear voice, a compelling story. Once I discovered story in my own work, I started practicing story wherever I could. I overlaid Olson's and-but-therefore template on not only my work but on the scholarly work of my colleagues as well. With practice, using story became like blinking. I started using it implicitly. In my writings. In class. When preparing grant applications. In conversations with colleagues on campus and at conferences. You might be saying to yourself: *"I wish I'd learned about Olson (2015) sooner."* Don't say that. Start reading up on story, immediately, and begin learning about story by reading Olson (2015). I began using story nearly five years ago. Do I wish that I had learned this narrative approach to scholarship earlier in my career? Of course. However, even this late in my career, implementing the approach has paid off in scores of ways. For instance, I followed the standard timeline at my home institution for promotion from Assistant to Associate Professor: roughly six years. In contrast, I shaved two years off that timeline on my path to promotion from Associate to Full Professor. Learning to use story played a major role in this accelerated timeline.

An Overview of Our Plan for Applying the Tools of Storytelling to Your Work

We just spent some time learning about my own history with story. I summarized this history to convey three ideas. In one sense, this history serves as an example of how professional development tools can help you overcome some pretty striking weaknesses in your approach to scholarly work. Similarly, our scholarly environments have a way of helping us develop an insight about our weaknesses; a message expertly delivered in Anonymous Account 4.2. More broadly, my history helps illustrate the importance of story for communicating ideas in the academic space generally, and cogently articulating one's research program in particular.

Anonymous Account 4.2. Academic "Weaknesses"	
Early Career Faculty	I am not a perfectionist. I understand that some people who identify with this term ensure everything that they touch is perfect before sending it out and therefore delay and delay before getting things out to the world. I have perhaps the other side of this phenomenon, where things quickly feel "good enough." I have internalized the notion that more papers are better, and that most readers will look at a manuscript's abstract and figures, and that few will read the full text. Furthermore, when evaluating an academic CV, I learned from

mentors in part to look at the length of the publication list. As a result, I think too many of my co-authors and former mentors were left to pick up the pieces of incomplete sentences, tense mismatches, and inconsistencies in terminology. When I really push myself to read a draft just one more time I find these typos and grammatical errors and statements that could use some reworking. I am always glad that I have spent the extra hour reading it over again, but more often than not the temptation to be "done" wins over and I hit "send" or "submit" prematurely. I have had to publish errata for minor errors, and have found more issues in the proofs of my articles than I think is typical. The funny thing is, when I read over my student's or co-author's drafts, I am meticulous. My lab members make jokes about my extreme attention to detail, particularly when it comes to APA style, formatting, word choice, etc. Thus, my weakness is potentially restricted to when I am forced to read and critique my own work.

As an Emerging Academic, how might you leverage story to communicate your research program to key audiences? We will learn the answer to this question in two parts. First, in this chapter we will learn the Shared Universe tool, designed to show you the basic structure of research programs built within mentoring environments. In Chapter 2, we learned that I discovered this tool when watching superhero films from the Marvel Cinematic Universe. To maximize the applicability of this tool to your scholarly work, I describe the tool using metaphors that facilitate learning about key components of scholarly work, and importantly, their connections to each other. Specifically, I describe the Shared Universe tool using celestial bodies: the galaxies and solar systems housed within actual universes. What we learn in this chapter sets the stage for several chapters that follow, including Chapter 5 (finding your mentor) and Chapter 6 (optimizing scholarly work with your mentor), as well as Chapters 7 through 9 (navigating the peer review system). Second, in Chapters 10 through 16, we will learn the Trilogy tool. Once you use the Shared Universe tool to discover the key components of your scholarly work, you will use the Trilogy tool to organize this work into a research program.

Galaxies and Solar Systems

At the opening of Chapter 3, we discussed rogue planets (Lissauer, 1987), and how the research programs of mentors who advise Emerging Academics develop in an interdependent system. The mentor's work exists within a shared universe of scholars who, like the mentor, devote their careers to advancing their own research program. The mentor's research program often addresses topics that highly overlap with the programs of other academics embedded in the same universe. Thus, one can never expect a mentor's research program to expand to be as large as a universe unto itself. Rather, a mentor's research program functions akin to a galaxy embedded in a larger, universe-like system of scholars (Figure 4.1).

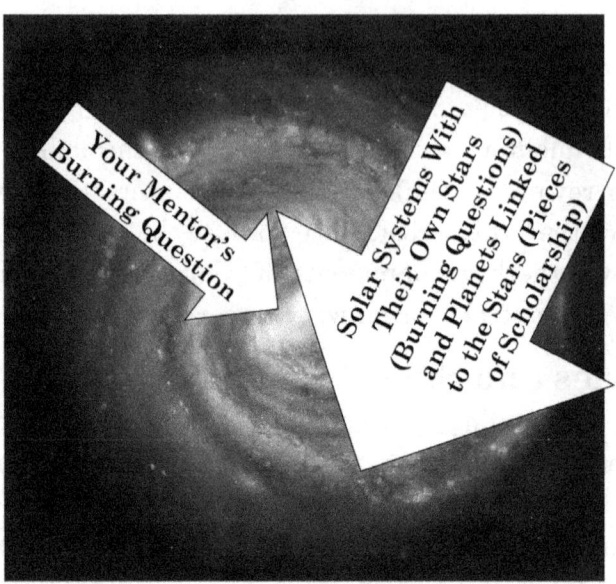

Figure 4.1. **Graphical depiction of your mentor's scholarly galaxy.**

I use a galaxy metaphor to describe the mentor's research program because key celestial bodies embedded within a galaxy also make for useful metaphorical devices to describe interdependent components of a mentor's program. At the very center of the galaxy resides a mentor's burning question. This burning question represents the key topic of curiosity around which the whole of the research program revolves. A mentor's research program develops through individual lines of research. A line of research includes not only its own burning question but also the pieces of work produced based on that question.

Within this galaxy metaphor, *Solar Systems* represent lines of research within a mentor's research program. Each solar system harbors its own star. Each solar system harbors planets that revolve around its star. Importantly, each of these solar systems exist in a symbiotic relationship with the mentor's burning question. That is, the galaxy's burning question projects out to influence all of the individual solar systems—individual lines of research—and the stars and planets that exist in each system. Solar systems are born out of burning questions that spin off from the galaxy's burning question. Within each solar system, the *Star* represents the burning question: the core abstract idea that propels or inspires scholarly work in that system. If the star represents an abstract idea, then the *Planets* in these systems represent the concrete pieces of scholarly work that revolve around the star. As I alluded to in Chapter 3, these solar systems that represent scholarship cannot subsist on a single planet. To thrive, a solar system requires multiple planets. You might ask, "*How many planets must a thriving solar system contain?*" Chapters 10 through 12 provide a concrete answer to this question. For now, let's stay focused on learning more about mentors' galaxies and their constituent solar systems.

An Emerging Academic's Place in Their Mentor's Galaxy

In explaining a mentor's galaxy of scholarship in a metaphorical sense and its constituent solar systems, how does an Emerging Academic's scholarship fit into this metaphor? Put simply: An Emerging Academic's research program is one of those solar systems. Your mission during your formative years as an Emerging Academic involves creating one cohesive solar system of scholarship. This solar system should display some key characteristics. Specifically, your solar system should function in a self-contained space, in that there exists a clear connection between the burning question that drives your thinking (i.e., your star) and the concrete pieces of scholarship that you can argue are great examples of how you go about studying your burning question (i.e., your planets).

There should also exist an interdependence in your solar

system, particularly in reference to other scholarship in your academic universe. That is, your solar system should connect to the burning question at the center of your mentor's galaxy. It should also connect to burning questions at the center of other academics' galaxies, particularly those who reside in the same universe within which your research program and that of your mentor reside. How do you go about accomplishing this task? The broad process manifests in three steps. We will review these steps here, and in Figure 4.2, I graphically depict the result of this three-step process. For the remainder of the book I flesh out these steps, with additional tools designed to facilitate your progression from step to step.

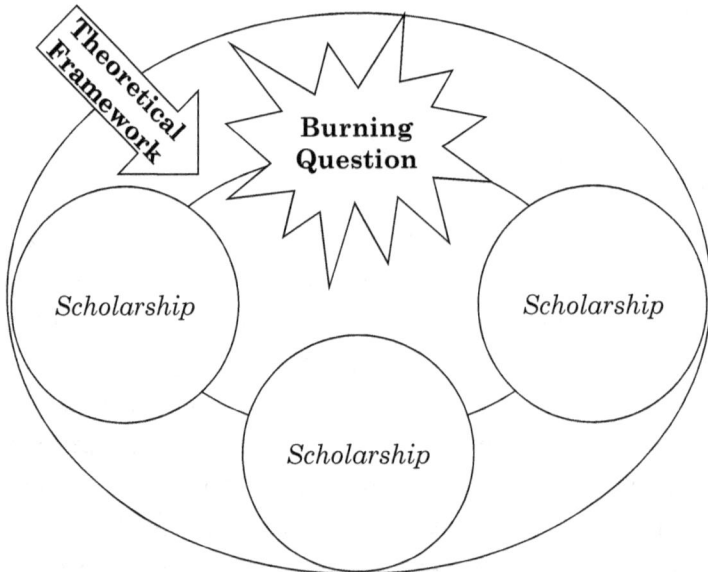

Figure 4.2. **The solar system representing your research program.**

Burning question. Composing your solar system of scholarship begins with identifying your star—your burning question. What question most drives your curiosity? Any of us in the academic space function in a constant state of curiosity. Thus, the purpose of this exercise is not to constrain your thinking, or force you to squish all of your ideas into a box that cannot contain them. Rather, if someone outside of your scholarly universe were to ask what you do, how would you respond? Ideally, that response should begin with a well-thought-out, concise idea phrased in the form of a question or point of curiosity. I will go into this more below in our first Modeling Moment, but here is my burning question: *Why do different people often perceive the same behaviors in different ways?* Short, right? A little vague too, but containing just enough information that if you too share interests in scholarly work about behavior, how people perceive their own behavior, or how people perceive the behaviors of others, you might want to learn more? Mission accomplished. Find your burning question; that's where all this starts. In Chapters 5 and 6 we learn tools for both finding mentors who study burning questions of interest to you, and optimizing your relationship with your mentor. These tools will facilitate developing your own burning question. At this point if your burning question does not immediately come to mind, don't worry; we will tackle this step at several points throughout the book.

Theoretical framework. Once you compose your burning question, your second step should involve leveraging knowledge from your training and work in your mentor's galaxy to provide a cogent answer to your burning question. Stated another way, what is your theoretical framework? Your research program might incorporate the larger theoretical framework that informs your mentor's research program, or that of a colleague of your mentor's. The point here is to get yourself in the space of articulating not just what makes you curious, but also what conceptual frame comes closest to satisfying your curiosity. By articulating an answer to your burning question, you create the *Gravitational Force* (i.e., theoretical framework) that binds your star to other celestial bodies in your solar system. In the Modeling Moment below, try to figure out what my theoretical framework might be.

Scholarship. The first two steps of the solar system process largely exist in an abstract space. The third step involves turning abstract ideas into concrete products. Along these lines, if your solar system includes a star and the gravitational force to bind the system together, then planets represent the celestial bodies that bind to your star. These planets represent pieces of your scholarship that illustrate how you explore your burning question. Specifically, the planets reveal how you as a scholar examine the degree to which your theoretical framework adequately addresses your burning question. As an Emerging Academic you should not anticipate having to form a large solar system. In fact, the approach I lay out for you in Chapters 10 through 16 involves selecting a relatively small number of planets to revolve around your star. You must compose a research program large enough to tell a compelling story about your work, yet small enough to ensure that the forward-facing element of your program (e.g., your job talk) focuses on the most engaging, thought-provoking work you have produced thus far.

Modeling Moment: My Burning Question

During the Modeling Moments presented in Chapters 13, 14, and 15, I reveal examples of how to curate a set of planets that, when combined, make for a structurally sound solar system and thus, a compelling account of your research program. For now, let us focus on a model for articulating your burning question. Below, I include the script I follow at the beginning of my research program talk that articulates my burning question. I also use this as an opportunity to allude to the answer to my question. Following this script, we will debrief and point out patterns in the content that might facilitate your composing a script for your own burning question:

> If you break down our laboratory's work to its basic element it is this: We are very curious about why different people often perceive the same behaviors in different ways. I am trained in Clinical Psychology. Clinical psychologists who work with children and adolescents often encounter this issue when a client visits their office or laboratory, and the clinical psychologist seeks to determine the client's mental health functioning. The clinical psychologist administers a series of mental health surveys or interviews to the client to assess their functioning. The clinical psychologist will also assess the client's functioning by administering similar if not identical measures to significant others in the client's life, usually parents and teachers. Over 50 years of research finds that even when you administer identical measures to all of these informants—with the same items and identical response options—you often receive different responses about the client's functioning, depending on who completes the measures. These discrepancies among informants' reports carry profound implications for mental health service delivery. Depending on the information source, one arrives at fundamentally different conclusions to important clinical and research questions. Who might benefit from mental health services? Among those who ought to receive services, what kinds of services might improve their functioning? In the end, do the services rendered actually improve the functioning of those who receive them? Therefore, the answer to the question—*Why do different informants provide discrepant reports of child and adolescent mental health?*—is an important question to ask. The answer to this question appears deceptively simple: *People lead complex lives.* What do I mean by this? Much of

my research focuses on understanding the discrepancies that often manifest among reports about adolescents who receive evaluations for experiences with social anxiety, or debilitating anxiety that manifests within social interactions with other people, particularly strangers. Adolescents may display social anxiety in a variety of different social situations, and so I may evaluate one adolescent who displays social anxiety within high-stakes performance situations in front of large audiences, like an oral presentation. That same adolescent may function just fine when interacting one-on-one with an adult authority figure like a school counselor. I may evaluate another adolescent who displays the opposite pattern of functioning: Large audiences do not bother them because they do not have to focus their attention on interacting with any one person, but when you shrink the audience down to one person, like that school counselor, that's where their social anxiety manifests. A third adolescent may function quite fine in both of these highly structured scenarios because the rules of social comportment are often quite clear to them. Where they experience social anxiety is in the unstructured situations like parties or other social gatherings, where the rules of social comportment may be quite vague. All three of these adolescents may experience no indications of social anxiety when they interact with a group of friends who they know very well. If I were to place an observer in each of these social situations—a parent or teacher—and ask them to observe these adolescents for a period of time before requesting that they complete measures of the adolescents' social anxiety, should I expect the same responses from each of these informants? I will pitch this question more broadly: *Who among you believes that adolescents behave the exact same way regardless of whether they interact with their parents, teachers, or friends?* That's a silly question, right? At the same time, a great deal of our laboratory's work focuses on reconciling an inconsistency between our understanding of the complexity of mental health functioning and our expectations of the measures we use to assess this functioning. That is, we often assume that those who display mental health concerns do so quite variably across situations, and the informants we task to provide data about these concerns also vary in their capacities for observing these concerns. However, for reasons we will review later on, a key assumption we often hold in mental health services and research is that our confidence in observations about clients—whether their mental health functioning warrants services, or whether our services improve their functioning—should depend, in large part, on whether multiple distinct pieces of data corroborate each other or point to the same conclusions. Thus, our laboratory's work involves testing this broader assumption about data:

- *Should we only focus on identifying when informants' mental health reports corroborate each other or all point to the presence of mental health concerns?*

- *Alternatively, should we also focus on developing approaches for determining when discrepancies among informants' mental health reports reveal meaningful information about how or within which contexts clients experience concerns?*

Modeling Moment: Debrief

After each of the book's Modeling Moments, we will debrief to highlight key components. Let us review issues to consider with the moment we just had. Right at the beginning, I come out with a statement of my burning question and a rationale for its relevance to work in my scholarly universe. That is, I connect my question with mental health services and research more broadly. After all, my scholarship focuses on mental health assessment. The assessments to which I devote my scholarship comprise central pieces of evidence used by my colleagues to make crucial, evidence-based decisions about clients, the services they receive, and the applicability of research to addressing clients' needs (see also De Los Reyes, Augenstein, & Aldao, 2017). In this way, within the first couple of minutes of my talk, the audience knows my burning question and why colleagues in my scholarly universe care about my question.

Following a review of my burning question and its relevance to scholarship in my universe, I immediately jump into a sneak preview of what I believe to be the answer to my burning question (i.e., *People lead complex lives*). This preview includes both articulating the answer and illustrating how the answer plays out in my scholarship. Importantly, later on in the talk I go into far greater detail on this answer and the scholarship informed by it. That being said, at the beginning it's useful to give the audience a heads-up on key portions of the talk to follow. In this way, both the burning question and its answer get a brief introduction right at the outset, along with some ideas as to how you will delve into key issues surrounding them later on in the talk.

My close to the burning question portion of my talk begins with a question (i.e., *Who among you believes that adolescents behave the exact same way regardless of whether they interact with their parents, teachers, or friends?*). I pose this question for two reasons. First, if audience members do not have adolescent children, they at least lived through this developmental period. As such, I suspect that the question resonates with audience members, and at minimum, posing the question tends to create a sense of levity. Second, the question highlights a key issue that guides much of my talk. Specifically, my work involves administering mental health assessments to people who display profound individual differences in how and under what circumstances they display mental health concerns like social anxiety. No two clients experience mental health concerns the exact same way: This idea yields remarkably high consensus among scholars in my universe. Where a lack of consensus exists among scholars, it involves how to interpret clinical information about clients' concerns, particularly when different kinds of clinical information—parent, teacher, and adolescent reports about the adolescent's social anxiety—yield discrepant conclusions regarding such concerns. Thus, at the close of the burning question portion of my talk, I describe the key conflict that my scholarship seeks to resolve, and in doing so I set the stage for the remainder of the talk.

Next Steps

This chapter covered a great deal of ground. We learned about key components of the scholarly universes of mentors and how Emerging Academics fit within these universes. We conceptualized a mentor's work as a galaxy of scholarship embedded in a larger universe of scholars studying topics related to that mentor's research program. We learned that an Emerging Academic's core mission involves developing a solar system of scholarship embedded within their mentor's galaxy, consisting of a star (abstract idea), planets (concrete pieces of scholarly work), and a gravitational force to bind the star and planets (theoretical framework). As a first step toward applying the Shared Universe tool to scholarly work, we reviewed an example from my own work of how I approach explaining to an audience of my colleagues my burning question and the answer to this question. We have two more steps to take. For those of you who have yet to find a mentor, Chapter 5 provides you with the tools you need to accomplish this goal and start the search for your own burning question. For those of you who have already found your mentor, in Chapter 6 we apply the Shared Universe tool to conceptualize your own training, from mapping out your mentor's galaxy to forming your own solar system.

The material following Chapter 6 addresses a key element of academic work germane to leveraging the Shared Universe tool. All the material up until now dealt with how to use this tool to address the first question outlined in Chapter 1: *Where do you fit within academia, and what burning question drives your work?* Interestingly, the Shared Universe tool informs answers to Chapter 1's second question: *On the path to publishing your work, how do you respond to reviews of your work?* I dedicate Act II (i.e., Chapters 7, 8, and 9) to addressing this second question, and be forewarned: Your scholarly universe will get a little more complicated.

In the last part of the book (Chapters 10 through 16), I will discuss some of the challenges an Emerging Academic faces when selecting pieces of scholarship in an effort to compose a coherent, compelling scholarly solar system. In the process, I will build a rationale for learning our second academic tool, that of Trilogy. Then, I will present a series of Modeling Moments inspired by work from my doctoral student, Bridget (see Chapter 3). These moments will illustrate how you might apply the Trilogy tool to curate pieces of scholarship for use in telling others about your research program. I use this material to address Chapter 1's third question: *How do you connect pieces of your work to build a research program?*

CHAPTER 5
Selecting a Mentor

Arguments or conflicts happen among children and their parents, even in warm, supportive family environments. Psychologists know this from decades of developmental science. Children argue with their parents about completing everyday tasks like homework and chores. Adolescents argue with their parents about these and other topics like setting a curfew, getting to wear clothes they like to school, and having fun with friends on the weekend (Smetana & Gaines, 1999). The amount of these conflicts doesn't tend to change much as children grow into adolescents; the intensity of these conflicts, however, does spike considerably (Laursen, Coy, & Collins, 1998).

Think back to your adolescent years. When coupled with all of the significant changes we each undergo on our journeys through adolescence (Paus, Keshavan, & Giedd, 2008; Steinberg, 2005)—how we morph in how we see the world around us and in how we think, feel, and behave—is it any wonder that at some point following at least one of these conflicts, we hit a tipping point? We think or say some pretty negative things about where we live? Here is a common one, perhaps you have a memory of a scene like this from your own life: Picture yourself after a particularly intense exchange with one or both of your parents. You run to your room. You fling yourself onto your bed or chuck yourself into a chair and you say something like, *"I wish I could find a place of my own."* If you find yourself in the process of discovering your mentor, now is your chance to choose a place of your own. Finding a mentor means opting into the environment in which you will receive doctoral training. You have a chance to choose the ideal environment for you to discover your burning question, produce work inspired by this question, and ultimately build a research program.

In Chapter 4 we immersed ourselves in the inner workings of our Shared Universe tool. We now stand on firm footing to conceptualize the mentoring relationship. In fact, the Shared Universe tool informs selecting a mentor. As I describe below, this selection process factors prominently into key decisions Emerging Academics make on the path to doctoral training and building a research program. Selecting a mentor is integral to having positive, productive experiences during doctoral training. As Anonymous Account 5.1 reveals, selecting a mentor is probably the greatest challenge one faces when applying to doctoral programs. It is also the challenge for which we often feel very uncertain about how we get the information we need to make an informed decision.

Anonymous Account 5.1. Applying to Graduate School	
Doctoral Student	My greatest challenge when applying to graduate school was making a coherent and compelling narrative about my prior experiences, and connecting these experiences to my potential mentor's work. I really didn't know what I was doing as an undergraduate student and only finally started to figure out my research interests afterwards. It took some craftsmanship to build a "post-hoc" narrative that connected all the pieces of my CV in a coherent way. Another challenge, further down the application process, was gauging the "personal fit" between myself and my potential mentor. Choosing a mentor in a doctoral program is almost like choosing a marriage partner: not only will I be in an intense working relationship with this person for 4-6 years, but they could also play a huge role in the

rest of my career. Does this mentor's advising style match my needs? Does this mentor cultivate a lab environment that promotes productivity without driving its students mad? Do I *like* this mentor as a person? During interviews I did my best to ask my potential mentors (carefully worded) questions about their advising style, and I asked many questions of current students; the best I could really do was estimate my personal fit with my potential mentors.

For those of you who currently seek a mentor, I wrote this chapter for you. If you already have a mentor, you might be tempted to skip this chapter. I would advise against that. This is because material covered in this chapter will also be of use to you when reading Chapter 6. In Chapter 6, you will learn tools to facilitate building a research program in your mentoring environment. Tools introduced in Chapter 6 stem from content covered in this chapter, and thus those of you already enrolled in a doctoral program and working with a mentor will also benefit from reading this chapter.

Apply to Galaxies, Not Graduate Programs

I hear that each day around lunchtime, the cafeteria housed at the European Organization for Nuclear Research's (CERN) Large Hadron Collider (LHC) tops our planet's list of intellectually stimulating locations. Scholars don't stop thinking and learning, even on a lunch break in between working with the LHC, the world's largest particle accelerator (AKA, an atom smasher). And although the nuts and bolts of what they all do might vary depending on the nature of their training and expertise, these scholars are all in it for the same overarching reasons. They collectively work on the same burning questions. The proof? As of this writing, if you visit the CERN website (https://home.cern/), their home page highlights two burning questions:

- *What is the nature of our universe?*
- *What is it made of?*

The LHC houses a scholarly universe. All of these bright minds, with research programs of their own, each focus on burning questions that, if not identical, overlap to a degree conducive to executing a stimulating array of multidisciplinary, collaborative endeavors. Think of the fields and disciplines that scholars interested in these questions might call home. To name just a few: Astronomy, Biology, Chemistry, Computer Science, Engineering, Mathematics, and Physics.

Now do some perspective taking. What if you, as an Emerging Academic, found that these two LHC-related questions sparked joy, inspiration, and a motivation to devote your career to scholarly work? If you were about to start looking for a mentor, would you really want to limit yourself to mentors from one field of study, let alone a single discipline? What if scholars from several fields and disciplines have the ability to mentor you, to train you to produce knowledge designed to answer the burning questions you find interesting? The answers to these questions reveal a fundamental truth about your search for a mentor. Forget the factors you considered when deciding where to spend your undergraduate years; they're worthless from here on out. Sure, when preparing your applications for doctoral programs, you technically submit an application to a degree-granting program at a university. But your acceptance into that program hinges on whether a specific mentor or mentors who serve as faculty in that program see a strong link between what interests them and what interests you. In this respect, application processes are an illusion. Replace that illusion with this principle: *Apply to galaxies, not graduate programs.*

Two additional factors greatly facilitate following the principle of applying to galaxies, not graduate programs. First, graduate programs typically reside within disciplines like Astrophysics, Chemical Engineering, Social Work, and Sociology. In contrast, a mentor's galaxy resides within a scholarly universe. These universes cut across disciplines and indeed, fields of study. By focusing on scholarly galaxies rather than the specific disciplines to which you formally apply for doctoral training, you greatly expand your options for seeking out the right mentor for you.

Second, even when you leave your mentor's galaxy and begin your career, that galaxy will follow you until the end of your career. You will leave your mentor's galaxy with a set of tools for producing your own scholarly work. You will also inherit a key figure who serves as the centroid of your scholarly network. To this day, I correspond with my doctoral mentor. I asked him for advice when preparing this book. In the years that preceded writing this book, my mentor wrote letters of recommendation for my job applications. When work became difficult and I found myself in a ditch, I solicited his thoughts on how to work my way out of the ditch. I learned the tools of my trade in my mentor's galaxy. My mentor is also my research dad, and that means I also have research siblings. In fact, over the last 10 years, I have lost count over the number of times I called my research big brother Matthew Nock for help on some of the same things for which I solicited my research dad Alan Kazdin's advice. Your mentor's galaxy becomes home. Even when you leave home, on occasion you still call home, right?

Key Factors That Differentiate Mentors: The STAR Framework

Your search for a mentor does not begin and end with identifying a single mentor. In your search for a mentor, you compile a list of potential mentors that you eventually narrow down to a final list of prospective mentors to whom to submit applications. The reasoning behind this process is simple. In a given annual application cycle, mentors select a chosen few applicants to train in their galaxy, usually no more than a handful and many times only one. Further, applicants typically choose one mentor who affiliates with a single doctoral program. Applicants often receive offers of admission into multiple doctoral programs, and an applicant can only accept one offer. For both applicants about mentors and vice versa, one creates lists out of necessity.

You might suspect that you create your mentor lists based exclusively on burning questions of interest to you. Burning questions ought to weigh heavily in your pursuit of a mentor. Yet, whether a mentor's burning question overlaps with your own interests and motivation for doctoral training should represent one of multiple factors to consider. In fact, some other factors that distinguish mentors from each other might become deciding factors. I summarize these factors in Table 5.1. Mentors vary from each other in at least four other ways. I refer to this conceptualization of mentor factors as the STAR framework, and I describe these factors below.

Factor	Description	Range of Factor	
Table 5.1. Summary of Factors Comprising the STAR Framework			
Size	The number of trainees a mentor supervises	Relatively intimate connection between mentor and trainees ⇕ Relatively loose connection between mentor and trainees	
Time	The quantity and quality of time that a mentor spends meeting with their trainees	**Quantity** Mentor spends little amount of time meeting with their trainees ⇕ Mentor spends a great deal of time meeting with their trainees	**Quality** Mentor uses time inefficiently when meeting with their trainees ⇕ Mentor uses time efficiently when meeting with their trainees
Area	The distance between trainees' burning questions and their mentor's burning question	Trainees' burning questions form a tight circle around the mentor's burning question, very little distance between burning questions ⇕ Trainees' burning questions shoot out in all directions from the mentor's burning question, very large distance between burning questions	
Resources	The tangible (e.g., equipment, materials, physical space) and/or intangible (e.g., informal mentoring networks) resources available to a mentor's trainees	**Tangible** Mentor harbors few tangible resources for their trainees ⇕ Mentor harbors plentiful tangible resources for their trainees	**Intangible** Mentor harbors few intangible resources for their trainees ⇕ Mentor harbors plentiful intangible resources for their trainees

Size. When you begin your search for mentors, perhaps the most obvious factor that distinguishes them is the sheer amount of trainees whose work they supervise. You can usually find this information in a mentor's faculty website or the website of their scholarly team. Alternatively, the directory of graduate students for a doctoral program will often list each student's contact information alongside their mentor's name.

The size differences among mentors' galaxies may be

considerable. Some mentors supervise a large number of trainees, doctoral students, and post-doctoral scholars. Conversely, other mentors supervise a small number of doctoral students, and few or no post-doctoral scholars. Often a key characteristic that cuts across the size factor is age. That is, relatively more experienced mentors tend to have larger galaxies than less experienced mentors.

Yet, size is a multifaceted factor. That is, over time a mentor might have grown a large galaxy, but at any given point they supervise relatively few trainees. For example, my doctoral mentor developed an expansive galaxy of previous trainees by the time I began my training. However, at any one time during my training, he supervised no more than three doctoral students. Conversely, you might find a relatively less experienced mentor who, at the time you develop your mentor list, oversees a galaxy on the verge of hitting a growth spurt. Perhaps they are about to develop a new line of research made possible by a recently awarded grant. This relatively less experienced mentor recently reached a point in their galaxy's development that calls for rapid expansion, and by extension an increase in the number of trainees they supervise.

When evaluating a mentor on the size factor, consider your preferences. What kinds of environments do you find conducive to your own learning and development? Think about your prior coursework, or perhaps a laboratory or research team with which you affiliated to gain experience before applying to doctoral programs. Do you tend to thrive in large, bustling environments teeming with scholarly activity, but perhaps a relatively loose connection between you and those who supervise your training (e.g., course instructor or laboratory mentor)? Alternatively, do you prefer more intimate environments: strong connections built with a chosen few around you, and with those supervising you maintaining tight control over your training and development? These questions all really delve around the central consideration of your optimal learning environment. Do you find yourself learning more, or perhaps more efficiently working independently with minimal instructions and loose supervision? Alternatively, do you learn best with detailed instructions and tight supervision? Those who fall into the former environment tend to thrive in larger mentoring environments and the latter in smaller mentoring environments.

Importantly, be mindful to avoid mismatches on the size factor. Indeed, someone who thrives under loose supervision and lots of independence often struggles in an environment typified by tight supervision. The reverse is also true: Even the brightest mind who thrives under tight supervision will find a loosely supervised environment disorienting, disheartening, and perhaps even demoralizing in terms of pursuit of a research career. In this respect, both of these environments produce fantastic scholars who go on to great careers. Thus, when compiling your list of mentors, focus on your perceived learning style, and identify mentors for whom the sizes of their galaxies fit your learning style. As detailed in Anonymous Account 5.2, at the end of your mentor search you might be faced with choosing between mentors who vary considerably on the STAR factors described herein.

Anonymous Account 5.2. Applying to Graduate School

Post-Doctoral Fellow

Applying to graduate school is a daunting endeavor. I felt pulled in several different directions during this process. On the one hand, I had received an offer to work with a productive assistant professor at a strong graduate program whose research was closely aligned with my interests/goals. On the other hand, I had received another offer to work with a more established full professor at an equally strong graduate program whose research was a good, but not great, fit with my interests/goals; in this case, however, the institution was also closely located to my family and friends. Knowing that this decision would shape not only the next 6 years of my life, but my entire career after that, I deliberated on it for probably longer than I should have. I sought guidance from my mentors, family, and friends, but received conflicting advice from each of these sources. In particular, the choice was clear-cut in the minds of my loved ones: I should choose the second option because that would allow me to be closer to them than the first option, which would require me to move 1,200+ miles away to a city they had never heard of. Yet, I had walked away from my interview at the first institution with a strong feeling that it would be the right fit for my career in the long term. I ultimately accepted the offer from the first institution. This proved to be one of the best decisions I have made, both professionally and personally. Although it was difficult to be away from my family and friends, I had the opportunity to conduct research I was passionate about and build a program of research that has set the stage for my future career. I was also lucky enough to meet my fiancé during my time in graduate school.

Time. Another factor that distinguishes mentors is that of time. That is, to what degree does a mentor allocate regular time to meeting with their trainees? One has to go beyond viewing publicly available documents to understand where a mentor falls in terms of time allocation to their trainees. That is, you typically learn about time by corresponding with current and former trainees. You inquire about the amount of time during their training that they currently spend or spent in regular meetings with their mentor. Seeking out this kind of information might be a fairly labor-intensive process. Thus, your first instinct might be to find shortcuts to understanding a mentor's place on the time factor. In particular, as we just considered the size factor, you might think that the size and time factors are redundant with one another. You would be mistaken. Indeed, like the size factor, the time factor is also multifaceted and manifests in at least two distinct ways. The first facet is that of quantity: How much time does the mentor allocate to regular meetings with their trainees? The second facet is that of quality: To what degree does the mentor hold efficient meetings with their trainees?

Viewing the facets of quantity and quality in a four-quadrant space facilitates finding a time allocation that fits your learning preferences. Specifically, someone who prefers independence and loose supervision would likely benefit from a mentor with whom they meet regularly for a short period, yet an efficient one; with each meeting focused on a set of specific agenda items. For example, although my doctoral mentor and I met regularly, we rarely met for longer than 30 minutes. Not only did I receive sufficient advising from my mentor, the nature and scope of our meetings ideally fit my learning style and needs. Indeed, over the course of several years of doctoral training, every meeting I had with him felt like time well spent, without exception. Needless to say, if you value tighter supervision, you might encounter difficulty with a mentor whose time falls into the *low quantity-high efficiency* time quadrant. If you value tighter supervision, seek a mentor who falls into the *high quantity-high efficiency* quadrant. Meetings with mentors who fall into this quadrant typically occur weekly, for at least an hour, with options for additional meeting time during particularly crucial periods (e.g., multiple weekly meetings in the month leading up to a thesis or dissertation defense). As with size, seek mentors who fall into time quadrants that fit your learning style.

Area. You might find information gathering for the last two factors to be the most straightforward, in part, because they focus squarely on the scholarly work produced by trainees in the mentor's galaxy. When determining the area comprising the mentor's galaxy, consult scholarship stemming from the galaxy. Do the mentor's trainees focus on burning questions not unlike the burning question of the galaxy? Alternatively, do trainees' burning questions vary considerably from both the galaxy's burning question and each other? In this respect, the key scholarship on which you focus consists of pieces of work for which the mentor's trainees clearly took the leading role. You might focus specifically on students' dissertations. This strategy might be the most straightforward for determining the mentor's area, in part, because it only takes searching within the archives of the library of the mentor's home university. A university library typically houses in their collections copies of dissertations defended by the university's former doctoral students. That being said, take into account the culture of the scholarly universes in which these mentors reside. If in a mentor's universe students commonly produce scholarly works outside of fulfilling their dissertation requirements, then only focusing on dissertations might yield imprecise estimates of a mentor's area.

Once you have a sense of the scholarship produced in a mentor's galaxy, think of how far out the trainees' burning questions spread, relative to the mentor's burning question. Think of a living room consisting of tables all shaped like cylinders. At one extreme, the area of a mentor's galaxy might resemble a narrow table used to prop up a lamp on one side of a sofa. At the other extreme, a galaxy's area might resemble a broader table in the room like the dining table. A narrow "lamp table" galaxy might appeal to a student who would enjoy the prospect of producing scholarship that tightly aligns with the galaxy's burning question. Alternatively, a student who wants some distance or freedom to focus on a burning question that relates to but does not significantly overlap with the galaxy's burning question might want to train in a more spread out "dining table" galaxy.

Resources. A deep literature search of the scholarship undertaken by trainees in a mentor's galaxy will also allow you to assess the fourth factor in the STAR framework, that of resources. Some of the resources revealed in your searches might be tangible in nature. For example, for mentors within scientific disciplines, focus on sections of students' scholarly work that detail the methods and procedures of the discipline. These sections reveal what tools are at the disposal of the mentor's trainees. Mentors within the social sciences and humanities might advise students whose work details procedures for recruiting study participants and/or evaluating records relevant to historical figures or events. Here too, these pieces of information might reveal the connections or networks cultivated by a mentor's galaxy. These might not be materials per se, but instead resources necessary for gathering the information used to produce scholarly work, such as tools for recruiting study participants or gaining access to highly sought-after historical archives.

As you consider building a list of mentors, think about the kinds of tangible resources you might need to address the burning questions of interest to you. At the same time, do not restrict yourself to considering these tangible resources. Indeed, earlier in this chapter I mentioned my research big brother. My ability to seek advice from my mentor's former trainees proved invaluable at multiple stages in my career. As you assess a mentor's resources, pay close attention to these intangible resources. A mentor's former trainees may become invaluable figures to whom you can reach out with questions on such matters as job searches and producing scholarly work with the mentor. Intangible resources also take the form of academics with whom the mentor has collaborated on scholarly work (e.g., articles and books). Each of these kinds of resources may play key roles throughout your doctoral training and, indeed, your career.

Intersectionality of Factors in the STAR Framework

When I began work on describing the factors comprising the STAR framework, my experiences on the housing market came to mind. My partner and I purchased our first home about five years ago. We worked with a fine real estate agent, and it took us about a year to find a home in what at the time was the very competitive market of Washington, DC. Our agent would often remind us of the factors to consider with each property we visited, namely its:

- Location
- Price
- Size
- Age

Naturally, a property's factors are dependent on one another. One factor's level relates to the levels of the other factors. As such, a push in one direction on one factor—a property might sit in a desirable location—will invariably impact the other factors, such as a relatively increased price tag relative to the price tags of other properties in less desirable locations. In fact, our agent would routinely recite a key pearl of wisdom: *Finding your home will involve compromising on at least one of these factors.* For the home we wound up purchasing, we eventually placed a premium on the location and price factors: We really liked the neighborhood and the property was well within our budget. However, we compromised on the size and age factors. The property was on the smaller side, and we knew all its major elements, such as the kitchen and the master bathroom, needed updating in the near future.

The real estate example nicely illustrates a key element of the STAR framework, that of the intersectionality of the framework's constituent factors. If you gravitate toward a mentor whose galaxy is on the small side, you're likely winning out in terms of receiving high-quantity, high-quality time with the mentor. Yet, that same galaxy might harbor fewer tangible resources relative to those available to students training in larger galaxies. As another example, what if your preferences call for a mentor who built a spread-out galaxy in terms of area? Perhaps that mentor's galaxy includes coverage of a burning question of interest to you, but a student has not carried out scholarship based on that burning question in quite some time. Under these circumstances, the mentor might be willing to guide you on producing scholarship stemming from this question, but they may not have available the tangible resources to carry out the scholarship you seek to conduct. Overall, as you assess mentors on each of the STAR framework factors, definitely focus on their compatibility with your preferences. However, you should consider it normal to find mentors who fit your preferences on some but not all of the factors.

Questions to Consider When Creating Your List of Potential Mentors

At this point, you might be asking yourself, "*I see all of the factors that I must consider when creating my list of mentors, but how do I identify where mentors fall on these factors?*" The reason why you might encounter difficulty with finding information on these factors is that no central repository of information exists that houses all of the information you need. At this point, pretend you are about to embark on a journey into space. You need to cover a great deal of the scholarly galaxies of interest to you, and you need to make a lot of discoveries on your own. In this section I reveal tools for answering three questions that get you closer to creating your first, larger list of potential mentors. I list these questions in the top half of Figure 5.1.

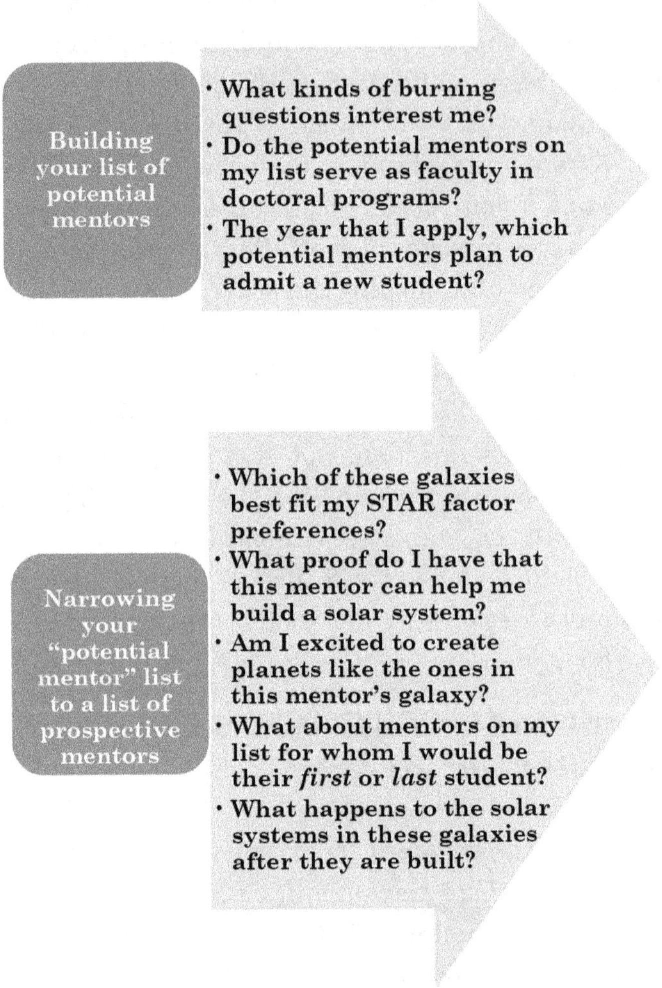

Building your list of potential mentors
- What kinds of burning questions interest me?
- Do the potential mentors on my list serve as faculty in doctoral programs?
- The year that I apply, which potential mentors plan to admit a new student?

Narrowing your "potential mentor" list to a list of prospective mentors
- Which of these galaxies best fit my STAR factor preferences?
- What proof do I have that this mentor can help me build a solar system?
- Am I excited to create planets like the ones in this mentor's galaxy?
- What about mentors on my list for whom I would be their *first* or *last* student?
- What happens to the solar systems in these galaxies after they are built?

Figure 5.1. **Questions to consider when building a list of potential mentors, and narrowing this list down to a list of prospective mentors.**

Burning questions? Begin your journey on the hunt for burning questions: Which ones interest you? What questions can you envision dedicating several years to pursuing, not necessarily throughout your career, but certainly during your years of doctoral training? To answer these kinds of questions, I have found the approach that works best involves making a habit out of reading in the scholarly universe(s) that interest you. For instance, in Psychology there exist scores of journals focused on disseminating scholarly work on topics that traverse the entire discipline (e.g., https://www.apa.org/pubs/journals). If the dissemination of scholarly work in your universe typically takes the form of publishing in journals, pick out a handful of journals that interest you. Focus on work published in the last five years or so. Indeed, this range likely will help you determine the current scope and perhaps future directions of the authors publishing papers in those journals. Further, pick a mix of journals that report primary findings from scholarly work and also journals that disseminate scholarship focused on synthesizing large bodies of work. The *Annual Review* series is a fine example of these latter forms of publication outlets (https://www.annualreviews.org/), and the series includes multiple publications that each touch upon topics that cut across myriad scholarly universes.

Importantly, if you do not have access to a subscription to these journals, you often can view, on freely available websites, tables of contents of their issues, and abstracts or summaries of each of the articles. Obtaining full copies of the articles is also possible without a journal subscription. Often, you might retrieve them through direct requests for a copy of the article sent to the primary or corresponding author of that article (i.e., these articles tend to include this author's email address). You might also contact authors through research communities that house copyright-appropriate versions of their articles (e.g., https://www.researchgate.net/).

Once you identify journals of interest, set up a month-long or four-week cycle that you might reasonably continue as you identify potential mentors. In that first week of your journey, skim the tables of contents from a few issues of these journals, and make note of which articles appeal to you. This should take no more than one or two hours of your time. In the second week, start reading the abstracts of article titles you selected the previous week. You will likely identify a few articles in that second week that you find interesting enough to read in full. In the third week of your cycle, read the articles that passed the abstract stage from the previous week. In the fourth week of the cycle, go back to these articles and take note of their key features, namely (a) the burning questions they addressed; (b) the authors of the articles; and (c) the authors whose work appeared in the reference sections of the articles.

After a couple of these month-long reading cycles, you will likely find yourself reading similar kinds of scholarly work. What likely binds this work together are (a) the burning questions addressed in the work; (b) the authors producing the work; and/or (c) the authors whose work you found in the reference sections. This approach to reading content that interests you will organically generate not only burning questions to pursue further but also leading scholars whose work touches upon these questions. These scholars might very well wind up on your list of potential mentors.

Incidentally, many of you might gravitate toward mentors for whom their scholarly products take the form of books, not journal outlets. For these mentors, follow the same four-week cycle, but focus on publishing houses rather than journals, and on categories of books that interest you. As you discover book titles, focus on the summaries or front/back matter of these books to determine those that you might consider reading in-depth. As you identify a handful to peruse, do not assume you have to read the entire text.

Instead, pick out chapters you find interesting enough to read further. This approach, like the journal approach, will result in you identifying scholars who might wind up on your initial list of potential mentors.

Graduate programs? Armed with your list of potential mentors from your literature search, you continue on your journey. All throughout this chapter you might have noticed my use of the phrase "potential mentor." This is because not all scholars hold affiliations in academic departments or units that offer doctoral programs. A scholar typically cannot serve as your mentor unless you apply to a doctoral program that includes them among their faculty. Therefore, the next question you need to address is whether the potential mentors on your list affiliate with a doctoral program to which you can apply. To answer this question, go back to the scholarly work identified during your search for burning questions. During the last week of your four-week reading cycles, you noted authors whose work you found interesting. Each of those pieces of scholarly work typically include not only the author's name but their institutional affiliation and sometimes the department or unit on campus with which they primarily affiliate. All you have to do now is search online materials for the affiliations of each of the authors on your list, and determine whether they affiliate with a doctoral program to which you can apply.

Taking students? You have one more question to address to develop your list of potential mentors. Now you have to determine which of the scholars on your list plan to take a doctoral student the year you plan to apply. Within the months leading up to the application deadline for doctoral programs, potential mentors typically learn about their ability to take a doctoral student for the following year. That being said, in some disciplines potential mentors might not learn about their ability to admit a new student until the last month or so before the deadline. Thus, sometimes an applicant needs to contact the potential mentor multiple times before learning about an available slot among the mentor's doctoral students.

Given these realities of the application process, my advice is to take a two-stage strategy when learning about the availability of opportunities to study under potential mentors. First, potential mentors often post statements on their primary faculty page in their graduate program that stipulate whether they plan to take a new doctoral student. Second, if the potential mentor does not include such a statement in their online materials, send them an email inquiring about their plans to admit a student for the upcoming application cycle. Keep the email short:

Dear Dr. **[scholar's name]**, I am interested in applying to the doctoral program in **[program name]** at **[university name]**. I am very interested in your work, and I wanted to inquire as to whether you plan to admit a student during this upcoming application cycle? I look forward to hearing from you. Sincerely, **[your name]**

This two-stage approach allows you to acquire this necessary information as efficiently as possible. That being said, you might ask, *"What about first impressions? Shouldn't I try to 'wow' the potential mentor with all that I have learned about their work?"* Keep in mind that potential mentors receive these correspondences from applicants all the time. As such, they are unlikely to remember corresponding with you in this context. If you want to stand out among other applicants, save it for your application materials: Clearly show your interest in burning questions that also interest the mentor. Further, you might learn from questions posed in the next section that some of these mentors will not make your final list of prospective mentors.

Questions to Consider When Narrowing Down Your List to Prospective Mentors

You now have a list of potential mentors who not only affiliate with doctoral programs but also plan to admit students in the application cycle in which you plan to apply. Your list of potential mentors may feel just right to you in terms of the amount of mentors on your list. The norms for that "just right" number may vary considerably by discipline. For example, in my own discipline of Clinical Psychology, prospective students routinely submit anywhere from 10-20 applications to doctoral programs. These ranges have much to do with the fact that not only do mentors affiliated with these programs take few students (i.e., no more than 1-2 students per application cycle), but each doctoral program might receive hundreds of applications in a given year. If you do not plan to apply to programs in highly competitive disciplines, plenty of other factors beyond those of the STAR framework will play a role in you arriving at your final list of prospective mentors. As detailed in Anonymous Account 5.2 and 5.3, these include the presence of geographic restrictions due to family or work obligations, as well as budgetary factors that come with the application process. These budgetary factors include application fees, and for many graduate programs, the costs of travel for in-person interviews. Coupled with these factors, perhaps you feel overwhelmed by the sheer number of mentors on your list.

> **Anonymous Account 5.3. Applying to Graduate School**
>
> **Doctoral Student**
>
> When applying to graduate school, I struggled with balancing my financial resources with my opportunities for interviews. I was fortunate enough to receive more interview offers than I had planned for financially and found myself having to prioritize which interviews to attend. After I was accepted into my first program, I reached out to graduate students, post-doctoral students, and others that I trusted. I consistently was advised to think carefully about which of my remaining schools to interview for, based on my interests and fit, and to politely turn down the others. If I thought a program was a better fit than the one I had already been accepted to, I attended the interview. Otherwise, I contacted the program and explained that I appreciated their invitation but had already been accepted to a program that fit my interests well. Multiple people reminded me that by choosing not to attend an interview, I may be providing someone who was a better fit an opportunity to interview. Most programs were very accepting and understanding of my predicament and generally just wanted to know where I had decided to receive doctoral training.

Regardless of the circumstances, you may encounter uncertainty on how to narrow down your initial list of potential mentors, and thus I devote this section to helping you reduce your uncertainty. Ideally, your final list reflects a number of prospective mentors that reasonably fits your life circumstances such as those described previously (e.g., family or finances). Beyond those circumstances, I highlight five questions that will help you narrow down the final list of prospective mentors to which you plan to apply. I list these questions in the bottom half of Figure 5.1. If your list of potential mentors requires no modification and thus will become the list of prospective mentors to which you will apply, I encourage you to nonetheless consider the questions below when it's time to select your mentor.

STAR preferences? Remember our real estate discussion and determining which factors matter most to you? Now is your time to answer these same questions about the STAR factors. What are your STAR factor preferences? Which STAR factors do you prioritize over others? Where do the mentors on your list fall on these STAR factors? Assuming these mentors vary on the factors, which factors might you be willing to compromise on as you narrow down your list? To facilitate answering these questions, you might consider creating a chart as depicted in Table 5.2. To complete this chart, think about those product comparison charts you see on a website when you consider purchasing one of a set of competing products. Each of the products vary on a set of features. Usually, some products have some features and not others, or have more features than competing products. Here, the mentors and their burning questions are the products, and their STAR factors are the features. As you make your way down the list from mentor to mentor, circle a "+" for those STAR factors for which a mentor matches your preferences. For instance, the mentor's current research team is relatively small, and that fits your preferences on the size factor. Circle a "—" if on that factor the mentor is a mismatch with your preferences. For example, discussions with the mentor's current and former students lead you to determine that the mentor falls into the low quantity-high efficiency quadrant on the time factor, and this is incompatible with your time factor preferences. Completing Table 5.2 allows you to pit mentors' STAR factors against each other in an effort to narrow your list.

Table 5.2. Decision-Making Matrix for Prospective Mentors

Prospective Mentor	Burning Question	Size	Time	Area	Resources
Mentor Name	Brief description of mentor's burning question	+ −	+ −	+ −	+ −
		+ −	+ −	+ −	+ −
		+ −	+ −	+ −	+ −
		+ −	+ −	+ −	+ −

At some point, you may find that some mentors study burning questions that interest you to a significant extent, but few of their STAR factors fit your preferences. Conversely, you might have a mentor on your list whose burning questions do not intrigue you as much as the questions of other mentors, but their STAR factors match your preferences to a significant extent. There is no easy way to reconcile any tensions you observe between burning questions of interest to you and your STAR factor preferences. All I can advise is that you ask yourself two hard questions:

- *If you believe a mentor's galaxy to be incompatible with your STAR factor preferences, how hospitable might that galaxy be to your training?*
- *If you believe a mentor's galaxy to be compatible with your STAR factor preferences but they fall short on your interest in their burning question, do you think you can stay interested enough in the work for the duration of your training?*

With regard to the second question, keep in mind that the burning question you study during your doctoral training does not have to define your career. Your task during doctoral training involves building a research program. If you decide to pursue a research career, you will have the opportunity to take your research program wherever you wish. It will be up to you to continue the work you developed during your training or set it aside to pursue other burning questions. At this point, place a fair degree of weight on each mentor's burning question and the match between their STAR factors and your preferences.

Proof you can build a research program? As you proceed through the remainder of this section, you will notice a pattern to the questions I pose for you to consider. I organized these questions in an order that allows you to winnow down your list of mentors through process of elimination. With the first question, you ruled out mentors whose STAR factors do not align with your STAR preferences. The second question deals with proof of a mentor's ability to facilitate your development of your research program. Answering this question requires you to conduct literature searches of the scholarly work of all of the mentors on your list. Peruse their works and identify those where students under their mentorship took a leading role in the work. If the mentor's scholarship consists primarily of journal articles, focus on those articles where students served as first authors. If the mentor's scholarship consists of books and book chapters, focus on works where students clearly took a leading role in composing the work.

As you identify those pieces of scholarly work for which students took a leading role, focus on both quantity and synergy. Does each student who trains under the mentor publish multiple pieces of scholarly work during their training? Equally important, for any one student's scholarly work, do you notice key themes that cut across the multiple pieces of work? As we discuss later on in the book, to build a research program involves connecting multiple pieces of work into a coherent, compelling story about that work. Thus, the amount of scholarly work a mentor's student produces is one thing, but whether the student has the opportunity to produce pieces of work that build off of each other is quite another. Assuming that the mentor has trained multiple students, you should be able to make a determination of the degree to which their students' scholarly productivity displays both quantity and synergy.

What about the mentors who have yet to train multiple students? Below, I will discuss those mentors in greater detail. For the purposes of this discussion, if you have relatively less experienced mentors on your list, focus on the amount of quantity and synergy in their own first-author work. That is, in the absence of student-led scholarship, a mentor reveals their ability to facilitate the development of your research program by displaying a clear ability to develop their own research program. Do you clearly see a burning question, scholarly work stemming from this question, and a theoretical framework that binds the question and work together? If so, then that relatively less experienced mentor likely has the tools they need to help you build your research program.

Excited about a galaxy's scholarly works? You have a more focused list of mentors who fit your STAR factor preferences and display evidence they can facilitate your building a research program. Now, judge whether you might enjoy the scholarly work you would execute under their mentorship. To facilitate making this judgment, return to the scholarly work you have discovered thus far—both from each of the remaining mentors on your list and their students. Previously, you took notes of the authors of this work, and you assessed the mentor on the resources factor of the STAR framework. Beyond these steps in the process, you have likely spent most of your attention focusing on the content of the scholarly work you have read. Here, focus on the structure of the scholarly work, and in particular on the means by which authors produced the work. For each mentor's galaxy, although you will likely see variation among the pieces of scholarly work in terms of the burning questions that motivated them, any two pieces of work produced by a mentor's galaxy will share some commonalities in their composition. Stated another way, a mentor's galaxy often leverages common structures or sets of procedures for producing scholarly work.

Of course, the scholarly work you produce under a mentor's guidance won't be identical to any one piece of scholarly work their galaxy has already produced. That being said, chances are if you train with a mentor on your prospective mentor list, any work you create will bear some resemblance to prior work produced by their galaxy. Thus, as you go back and review the work you discovered ask yourself, *"Do I see myself enjoying the process of producing this kind of scholarly work?"* Admittedly, this may be a difficult question to address from afar; it would be helpful to learn more about the day-to-day processes of the work from the authors themselves, right? At this point, focus on weeding out those mentors on your list for whom after careful consideration, you honestly do not see yourself producing the scholarly work as described. For the remainder of the mentors on the list, as you wind the list down to your final decision on a mentor, you will likely have opportunities to speak with the mentor and their current and former students. If you do, take these opportunities to learn more about the ins and outs of their work. Use these conversations to determine the fit between what it takes to produce the work and your own preferences in terms of the kinds of work you wish to produce.

Mentors where you would be their first (or last) student? This question deals with special cases of the STAR factor of size. For one or more scholars on your mentor list, you might find that you would be the mentor's very first student. In light of the STAR factors and all of the discussions dealing with mentor experience, you might feel uncertainty about the prospect of mentorship from a newly minted scholar. In this respect, I would advise paying as much attention to your STAR preferences as the experience of the mentor. For instance, do your STAR factor preferences lean heavily toward a mentoring environment on the small, intimate side? Might your learning style call for a mentoring relationship where the mentor spends a great deal of time meeting with you on a regular basis? If so, consider that a mentoring environment where you would be the first student might highly align with your preferences. Further, you might find such an environment to be quite exciting. Indeed, you would start your training at the genesis of your mentor's galaxy. That being said, remember that STAR factors each have trade-offs. In this case, a student mentored in a new galaxy should prefer one that's narrow in area. In this respect, if you wind up keeping a "first student" mentor on your list, make sure that their burning question excites you as well. Chances are your work will highly align with this question.

On the other end of the extreme, you might have a mentor on your list whose galaxy is entering its twilight period; they are on the verge of retirement. You might even wind up being the last student they mentor. A senior mentor at this stage in their career hits all the marks on the STAR framework commensurate with experienced mentors; they tend to:

- Maintain a large galaxy
- Allocate their mentoring time in the *low quantity-high efficiency* quadrant
- Build broad galaxies with a lot of spread among trainees' burning questions
- Harbor a sizeable amount of tangible and intangible resources

If you find that these mentoring characteristics fit your STAR factor preferences, the next step involves determining where else the mentor wishes to take their work before they retire. If you wind up being one of the last, if not the last, student this mentor trains, is the mentor excited to guide and support you as you build your research program? Of course, asking a potential mentor this directly would be the optimal strategy, but the opportunity to do so typically occurs much later in the application process, such as in the interview stage. You might indirectly determine a mentor's motivation for continuing their scholarly work and supporting your research program by looking at patterns in their recent work. Did the mentor recently begin a new line of research? In the past few years, do you see articles or books stemming from new collaborations between the mentor and academics in their scholarly universe? Did the mentor recently publish a piece of work outlining the next few years in a line of research they intend to pursue? In short, for mentors nearing the end of their career, search for signals that they have the interest and motivation to continue their work. These signals (or lack thereof) might tell you whether that mentor has the ability to create a hospitable environment for the development of your research program.

Outcomes of trainees? You have undergone a thorough vetting of your list of mentors across numerous factors. We have yet to address the most crucial factor of them all, that of outcomes. Specifically, during our Emerging Academic period we aspire to attain the professional life that we hope our doctoral training prepares us to lead. Hard work, perseverance, great ideas, thoughtful scholarship: All of these elements play key roles in whether we land a position that meets our aspirations. But throughout the opening chapters of this book I revealed how crucial the mentoring relationship factors into your success.

Before you solidify your final list of prospective mentors, and thus the list of graduate programs to which you will submit applications, the final question you should ask of the scholars on your list of mentors essentially amounts to: *How do the mentor's students turn out?* Naturally, this might be an impossible question to ask for those mentors who have yet to build a long record of training students. However, for a mentor who has trained many students, you have access to publicly available, objective data on their outcomes. These data allow you to determine the likely outcomes of your own training, should you train under the guidance of this mentor. Commence your detective work. Search for the mentor's former students. Figure out where they work and identify their career outcomes. You might break the "outcomes

question" down to a series of questions germane to life after doctoral training:
- Where do the mentor's former students tend to work?
- Do they progress up the career ladder of success?
- Do they pursue research programs like the one I wish to build?
- Would I be happy with their career(s)?

Any mentor will tell you that each of their students differ from one another such that no two are exactly alike. That being said, when you seek answers to the "outcomes question," try not to fall into thinking traps. For example, perhaps you're excited about the prospect of training with a mentor on your list, but you notice that the mentor's students do not appear to attain career outcomes that match your preferences. You might be tempted to think: *But I'm different, I can do better than this mentor's former students.* This may be true. However, it's important to maintain a realistic outlook. The career outcomes of a mentor's former students provide prospective students with a window of what is possible in life post-training. If you encounter a discrepancy between former students' career outcomes and your preferred outcome, that discrepancy is a real phenomenon that you must accept and not explain away or ignore.

Next Steps

I must acknowledge that, because disciplines vary widely in terms of the nature and scope of application processes for their doctoral programs, it is beyond the scope of this book to provide much specificity in terms of applying to these programs. In this chapter, we focused our attention on the process by which you will arrive at a final list of prospective mentors. For information on the specifics of applying to doctoral programs, you might consider consulting discipline-specific guides to the application process (e.g., Prinstein & Patterson, 2013).

My hope is that the questions posed to you in this chapter facilitate the creation of a final list of prospective mentors to which to apply for doctoral training. In Chapter 6, we will acquire tools for optimizing your relationship with the scholar who will eventually become your mentor. However, many of you will follow circuitous paths to finding this mentor. Some of you may receive more than one offer of admission, and you will encounter the good fortune of having multiple mentoring options. Under these circumstances, use your answers to this chapter's questions to make a final selection of your mentor.

One commonly traveled yet circuitous path involves applying to doctoral programs, only to find yourself without an offer of acceptance into any program. For various reasons, many Emerging Academics enter the application process multiple times before finding the mentor and doctoral program that's right for them. For those of you who find yourselves in these circumstances, I close this chapter with a moving, inspiring narrative. In Chapter 4 we learned about scholars overcoming challenges. The Emerging Academic who provided Anonymous Account 5.4 overcame their fair share of challenges. This Emerging Academic is my hero.

Anonymous Account 5.4. Applying to Graduate School

Doctoral Student

I had to overcome a nontraditional path to applying for Ph.D. programs in my area of study. Several years earlier, I was in the advanced stages of a Ph.D. program in another area of study, funded by a federal training grant. Then, the unthinkable happened. My physical health suddenly deteriorated, and I had to take a medical leave of absence. This experience caused me to rethink my personal and professional values and goals. I made the excruciating decision to withdraw from my program. I moved back to where my family and friends lived to surround myself with a supportive environment. I also obtained a research position where I could explore my interests in the area I would ultimately apply to for graduate school, and learn advanced quantitative methods. Two years later, I was itching to return to graduate school and advance towards my goal of being an independent principal investigator with a programmatic line of research. Despite my passion, I was afraid. I was afraid to move because I felt settled, supported, and healthy. I also did not want to ask my partner to uproot his life. As such, I applied to two Ph.D. programs at local universities. Neither program was a great fit; they did not have mentors that I was excited to work with, but I was trying to do things differently this time around. I panicked about how to address my leaving graduate school and shifting my research focus because I felt deep shame for "quitting" the first time around. Looking back, this shame and self-consciousness manifested in my personal statement. I was rejected from both programs, one of which I was certain was a "safety" school. Initially, I was devastated and was convinced that my career was over. Many conversations with mentors, colleagues, and my partner allowed me to reframe these rejections as blessings in disguise; I would not have been challenged or satisfied in those programs. I came up with a new plan. I would reapply the following year to programs that were exciting and with mentors who inspired me, as well as significantly expand the range of locations to areas where my partner felt comfortable living. I also asked three professors I knew from my current position to write recommendation letters, and retained only one letter from my previous program. Finally, I reframed my personal statement to portray more autonomy and agency in my choices. The differences in the application process were remarkable. I applied to 15 programs across the U.S., and was admitted to 12—most of them being top-tier programs at Research 1 Universities, with my would-be mentors as leaders in the field. I also received the top university fellowships for 8 of the programs to which I was admitted. During my interviews, there was little focus on my medical leave of absence and shift in research focus; people were interested in what I was currently doing and my professional goals. My prior experience, which I thought was my Achilles heel, suddenly felt like one of my greatest assets as I could have in-depth conversations about publishing, advanced statistics, and complex research designs. Many professors remarked that my professional maturity, publication record in top journals, and interviewing skills made me stand out from my peers. I learned many lessons from this process: listen to your mentors, focus on fit, apply broadly, be brave, and always persist.

CHAPTER 6
Optimizing Your Relationship with Your Mentor

In the final year of my doctoral studies, I had the privilege of fulfilling degree requirements for clinical internship training at the Institute for Juvenile Research at the University of Illinois at Chicago. A key component of my training involved supervision by a research mentor. Laurie Wakschlag agreed to serve as my mentor during that year. Laurie now serves as Professor and Director of the Institute for Innovations in Developmental Sciences at Northwestern University. Working with Laurie proved instrumental in my landing my first job. In fact, during my first job interviews, half of the research I discussed during my job talk focused on my work with Laurie (De Los Reyes, Henry, Tolan, & Wakschlag, 2009). And like any great mentor, all these years later Laurie's mentorship is the gift that keeps on giving.

Quite vividly, I still remember my first meeting with Laurie. This meeting served as inspiration for this portion of the book. Like many introductory meetings with mentors, she asked me what I would like to focus on in terms of research for the coming year. That was a fun part of the conversation and it signaled the beginning of a productive year. In addition, Laurie took a portion of the meeting in a distinct (and insightful) direction. She asked me to describe two of my previous mentors. In hindsight she asked me to describe how they fell on some of the STAR factors I described in Chapter 5. Before my internship, I had the pleasure of working with two mentors who varied widely between each other on the size, time, and area factors. After describing these mentors, I still recall the first thing Laurie said in reaction to my description, loosely paraphrasing: *"I fall somewhere in the middle."* Her reaction made perfect sense to me: Laurie conceptualized her place in my training relative to my other mentors. In the process, Laurie conveniently set my expectations for the coming year. In fact, on several of the STAR factors, she foreshadowed my expectations for my own approach to mentoring. I see my own mentoring as falling "somewhere in the middle" between Laurie and one of my other mentors.

This brief story serves to highlight a key theme that will cut across this chapter, that of setting expectations. I wrote this chapter for those of you in the midst of training. You might be currently working toward your doctoral degree. You might find yourself in a post-doctoral training period, paired with a mentor. In any of these mentoring scenarios, the Shared Universe tool facilitates both conceptualizing your place in your mentor's galaxy and understanding how this galaxy functions. In turn, setting reasonable expectations about working with your mentor allows you to make informed decisions about your scholarly work, make the most of your mentoring environment, and optimally leverage what that environment has to offer.

Map Out Your Galaxy: Me and My Mentor's Galaxy (MMMG) Worksheet

In Chapter 5, I advanced a plan for those of you still searching for a mentor. Some of you might have followed that plan and returned to this book in the midst of your doctoral training. Some of you might have started reading this book following the start of your doctoral training or perhaps during your post-doctoral training. I wrote this section of the chapter to be of value to you regardless of your current training stage. This includes those of you who followed the Chapter 5 plan to find your mentor. Granted, if Chapter 5 informed your mentor search, you invariably evaluated your mentor's galaxy. That being said, your evaluations following the start of your training might diverge compared to the evaluations you made during your mentor search. The burning questions you find interesting might have changed. New information or recent changes in your mentoring environment might shift how you perceive the STAR factors and where your environment falls on those factors. Conversely, for those of you who find yourselves conceptualizing your mentor's galaxy for the first time, performing an honest, sober evaluation of your mentoring environment will allow you to determine the kinds of scholarly work you might be able to undertake during your training.

To facilitate making current evaluations of your mentoring environment, Figure 6.1 depicts a worksheet you might complete to assess the galaxy on all of the key factors germane to developing your own burning question. We will review each of these factors below and how they specifically relate to your interests and training, with the long-term goal of facilitating the development of your research program. I refer to the document in Figure 6.1 as the *Me and My Mentor's Galaxy* (MMMG) worksheet, and below I describe each of its elements. One suggestion: If you have not already, let your mentor know that you are reading this book. Share with them some of what you learned from the opening chapters of the book, in particular the Shared Universe tool and its conceptualization of mentorship. Walk them through Tables 5.1 and 5.2. With this shared knowledge, you can request that your mentor complete this worksheet with you, perhaps at one of your individual meetings. Completing the MMMG worksheet with your mentor will likely result in a more accurate set of information than if you completed the worksheet on your own. In fact, the shared completion of the worksheet might also facilitate discussion of optimizing the fit between your mentoring environment and your training needs.

Burning Question Describe the burning question driving the mentor's work: _____

- _____
- _____
- _____

STAR factors Assess where the mentor falls on each of the STAR framework's factors: _____

- Size: _____
- Time: _____
- Area: _____
- Resources: _____

Research Program Identify the research program closest to the scholarship that most excites you, and describe the program's: _____

- Burning question: _____
- Work Example #1: _____
- Work Example #2: _____
- Work Example #3: _____
- Theoretical framework: _____

Figure 6.1. **Me and My Mentor's Galaxy (MMMG) Worksheet.**

Mentor's burning question and their STAR factors. Begin completing the worksheet by describing your mentor's burning question and where they fall on the STAR factors. Notice that I do not frame this evaluation in terms of your preferences on the STAR factors. In Chapter 5, focusing your attention on STAR factor preferences facilitated the key aims laid out in the chapter, namely finding a mentor. You've already found that mentor. Now, place your focus on the mentor's STAR factors as they exist right now. Jointly completing this worksheet with your mentor is kind of like a standardized version of my "mentor discussion" with Laurie that I described at the opening of this chapter.

Ideally, working together with your mentor to map out the galaxy as it exists now facilitates two subsequent discussions. First, conceptualizing the galaxy on these elements opens the door to discussing what you want to do during your time in this galaxy. Second, if you see a mismatch between your preferences and the mentor's STAR factors and/or burning question, completing the worksheet facilitates discussing ways to tailor your training opportunities to meet your needs. For instance, one tailoring strategy might involve identifying an additional "co-mentor" whose galaxy augments your training. This co-mentor fills gaps in your training that, if left unaddressed, could pose long-term problems to the relationship with your primary mentor. Below, we elaborate upon this and other special cases of mentoring. For now, let's focus on completing the last portion of the MMMG worksheet, namely the portion dealing with research programs created in your mentor's galaxy.

Research programs in the galaxy. At various points in this book, I note important elements of mentored scholarship, those of guidance and discretion. Producing scholarship with your mentor involves collaborating with them to build your own research program. This research program comes alive at the guidance and discretion of your mentor. To make informed decisions about building your own research program, you leverage your mentor's experience with scholarly work. They know how to produce work stemming from their burning question. More broadly, they have experience turning questions into scholarly products. If they are the expert in building research programs, then you are the expert in what work you personally find interesting. To facilitate building your research program, you have to clearly communicate to your mentor the kinds of scholarly work that motivate you. What better way to make this decision-making concrete than highlighting research programs that already exist in your mentor's galaxy.

Using the bottom portion of the MMMG worksheet, identify a research program already present in the galaxy. Ideally, this research program reflects the scholarly work in the galaxy that most closely approximates the kinds of scholarly work you aspire to produce within your own research program. The research program you identify might stem from work conducted by your mentor's former doctoral students or post-doctoral fellows. If you work with a relatively less experienced mentor, the research program you choose might reflect a body of work previously carried out by your mentor. As another possibility, consider a circumstance where you cannot identify a research program of interest to you within your mentor's galaxy. This might be the appropriate time to point this observation out to your mentor, which might spark a discussion that leads you to identifying a research program outside of your galaxy. This realization is by no means a bad thing in and of itself. In fact, an exercise like this might come as a welcome surprise to your mentor, as a new opportunity to branch out and spread their galaxy to new places. Alternatively, what might transpire is a compromise of sorts that results in discussing the kinds of research programs that might be feasibly developed in your mentoring environment. Whichever of these routes gets you to the point where you identify a research program, the next step involves mapping it out. Describe the research program's burning question. Next, identify some of the research program's pieces of scholarship—three will suffice—to make concrete the work produced within the research program. Finally, describe the research program's theoretical framework: the concepts that bind together the program's burning question and pieces of scholarly work.

What outcomes might you expect from completing the research program portion of the MMMG worksheet? In essence, you make concrete to your mentor the kind of research program you aspire to develop. Learning about your aspirations allows your mentor to begin an honest conversation with you about what their galaxy can and cannot offer you. You might also find that the mere act of identifying a component of an existing research program results in new ideas for scholarship. For instance, the theoretical framework you identify might lead your mentor to think about a burning question that someone in your mentoring environment has yet to pursue. A piece of scholarly work you highlight might inspire both of you to ponder how you might expand upon the knowledge produced by the scholarship represented by that work. All of these discussions about the mentor's galaxy not only set expectations for your training, but may also yield ideas that inform the development of your own research program.

The Future of Your Research Program

At this point, I should make something clear. When developing the MMMG worksheet, I proceeded with a fair degree of trepidation. I did not want the worksheet to give off the wrong impression about research programs. If you find yourself at the beginning of your training and indeed even near the end of your training, it is completely normal to not have your research program planned out. As I will make clear in Chapter 15, Emerging Academics work for years before composing their research program. That is not the purpose of the worksheet. This worksheet helps with planning ahead, learning about your galaxy, and communicating your training needs to your mentor. For now, focus on creating an environment conducive to producing a research program, or features that will facilitate:

- Identifying a burning question that motivates you to produce scholarly work;
- Finding a theoretical framework to bind your burning question and scholarly work;
- Immersing yourself in tools used in your mentor's galaxy to produce scholarly work; and
- Pursuing scholarly work that your mentor's resources allow you to create.

Special Cases of Mentorship

In the process of completing the MMMG worksheet, you might have discovered that you find yourself in a rather complex mentoring environment. In this section, I outline three of the more common of these special cases of mentorship.

What if you need more than one galaxy? At roughly around their third year of doctoral training, each of the doctoral students who have trained in my galaxy have submitted a predoctoral training grant application to a federal funding agency. A key element of each of these applications involves identifying the mentor(s) who will guide the student through the grant period, should the student receive grant funding for their proposed work. Needless to say, in each of my student's applications, I was listed as a mentor. However, germane to the discussion about special cases of mentorship, each of the applications submitted by my students has included a co-mentor. You might ask, *"Are you saying that for each of your students, your mentoring simply has not been good enough for them?"* In a word: Yes! Indeed, three elements factor into the fundability of these applications, namely the training goals of the application, its level of innovation, and its feasibility. Specifically, these applications involve a student proposing an innovative study that cannot feasibly be accomplished unless the student also receives funding to augment their training. In the case of my galaxy, students typically propose studies for which they seek to learn a new research modality, set of statistical techniques, or in fact an entire scholarly literature for which I have no demonstrated expertise. By necessity, for these applications to demonstrate feasibility, I must guide my students toward identifying additional scholars who might serve as co-mentors to fill in gaps in my expertise. In this way, the student hits all the elements noted previously: They get to submit an innovative application with discernable training goals, and a mentorship team with the expertise to execute both the training plan and proposed study.

I mention this aspect of my galaxy to normalize one of three special cases of mentorship. You might find after completing the MMMG worksheet that your mentoring environment, as supportive as it may be, meets some but not all of your training needs. Now is the time to make these training gaps clear to your mentor. The means by which you might work with your mentor to fill these gaps may vary depending on the mentoring environment. As with my own example, some funding mechanisms facilitate a student's plan to fuse their primary mentor's galaxy with that of a secondary or co-mentor. Beyond the obvious financial advantages, these funding mechanisms serve to formalize a mentoring plan that traverses mentoring environments.

Yet, branching your training out to another mentor might

manifest in far more informal ways. Sometimes a viable co-mentor exists at your current institution and as such you might not need to formalize a co-mentoring plan. Other times a prospective co-mentor already exists in your primary mentor's network of colleagues, and identifying such a co-mentor might be as easy as perusing your mentor's CV. Colleagues who appear as co-authors on your mentor's scholarly work already have an established relationship with your mentor. As such, there exists evidence that your mentor enjoys working with these colleagues. If you might enjoy receiving mentorship from such a colleague, your mentor might relish at the prospect of bridging your training needs across mentors, and of connecting you with a colleague with whom they already enjoy working. In sum, if you find yourself needing more than one mentor, make your needs clear to your mentor, and work with your mentor to identify a viable co-mentor to support your training.

What if you currently reside in an inhospitable galaxy? For some of you, a combination of previous experiences with your mentor and completing the MMMG worksheet might confirm a daunting concern about your relationship with your mentor. Evidence of these concerns might manifest in several ways. For some of you, perhaps you find that your interests and training needs are so incompatible with your mentor that adding an additional mentor will fail to address your concerns. In raising concerns to your mentor that might be addressed with an additional mentor, some of you might find your mentor to be unwilling to include an additional mentor into your training. Or worse, what if your mentor was even unwilling to work with you on completing the MMMG worksheet? These and other experiences might signal a common yet disturbing reality for many Emerging Academics: Your galaxy appears inhospitable to your training needs and thus to your quest toward building a research program.

At this point, you might ask yourself, *"Why did I only learn now about the inhospitable nature of this galaxy; what did I miss in my mentor search?"* The truth is, you might not have missed much in terms of information that comes available to you during the application process. If you did your homework on your prospective mentors, you largely formed your impressions of these mentors based on publicly available information, like the mentor's CV, their publication record, and outcomes of their former students. You also relied on your own interests and goals, and when possible collected information during the interview process, based on such sources as meetings with the mentor and current or former students. Each of these data sources has their strengths and limitations. Publicly available information might be objective data. Yet, the experience of working one-on-one with a mentor includes a set of subjective experiences. Perhaps you've discovered a "personality clash" in your interactions with your mentor that create challenges with working together. Keep in mind of course that personality clashes are not in and of themselves "deal breakers" for mentoring relationships. Some relationships work just fine even after they run into difficult times.

As another example, when selecting a mentor, having access to "inside information" from the mentor's students might reveal useful insights regarding their day-to-day experiences with the mentor. Alternatively, the mentor's students might be unwilling to disclose information to a prospective student about some of the more inhospitable aspects of working with the mentor. In particular, they might fear that the mentor could trace "negative reviews" back to them. Thus, some aspects of the mentoring relationship might come as a surprise or even shock to you once you begin working with your mentor.

I raise all of these possibilities to provide you with some solace if you discover yourself in this particular mentoring environment.

Sometimes you can only learn about truly inhospitable mentoring environments by spending time in them. Unfortunately, no optimal strategy exists to address concerns with an inhospitable mentoring environment. The strategy that works best for your situation depends on the support structures available to you. You might confide in a faculty member in your home unit or department to discuss your situation and solicit advice. Do you suspect that current or former students of your mentor shared similarly negative experiences? If so, might they be able to advise you on next steps? In the end, students in these scenarios often face making one of two disparate and equally difficult choices.

First, you might choose to stick with it and finish your doctoral work with your current mentor. If you lean toward making this decision, confide in your mentor's former students and seek advice on how to make the situation work as best you can. Further, you might find a significant amount of support with sticking with your mentor comes from fellow doctoral students in your program. In this respect, don't underestimate the power of seeking out their advice and support. Other students in your program may encounter similar mentor-related issues, and these realizations often facilitate troubleshooting strategies for adapting to challenging mentoring relationships.

Second, if you decide to leave the mentor but continue your doctoral training, a key element in this process involves identifying a new mentor. Doctoral programs typically require a student to have an identified mentor in order to complete their training. Thus, in these scenarios make sure to identify a faculty member who might serve as your new mentor before formally severing ties with your current mentor. An important consideration with this second option is that, in all likelihood, the new mentor will differ from your current mentor in terms of their burning question, the research programs trainees produce with them, and where the mentor falls on the STAR factors. Given this, it is imperative that you repeat with your new mentor the processes outlined in this chapter: (a) explain to them what you have learned so far with the Shared Universe tool; (b) ask that they work with you to complete the MMMG worksheet; and (c) use this time to clearly articulate your training needs and goals.

What if you realize you do not wish to pursue a research career? At some point during your training, you may reach a crossroads that reflects something other than a loss of confidence in your mentoring environment. Specifically, you may find yourself in a supportive mentoring environment, but for whatever reason no longer wish to pursue a research career. If you find yourself in this situation, this too is a common yet special case of mentorship. Further, you may feel that it's a poor use of your time to focus on building a research program. I disagree with this sentiment.

Think about all this from the perspective of a future employer. Perhaps you now see yourself considering a career in a space distinct from academia, such as industry, policy, or the non-profit sector. Regardless of your revised career pursuits, an employer will want to learn about the work you completed during your doctoral training. As you build your research program you will acquire myriad tools that translate to career paths across various employment sectors. If you follow the approach laid out in this book, you will pick up invaluable storytelling tools. What better way to describe yourself than to tell a compelling story of your area of expertise: your research program. In sum, stick to building your research program. At minimum, you will attain tools for communicating your interests and expertise. And once you learn these tools, you will find yourself in a strong position to describe yourself if you choose a path other than academia.

Next Steps

This marks the close of Act I of this book. We learned tools to help you address the first question outlined in Chapter 1: *Where do you fit within academia, and what burning question drives your work?* You now have a conceptual map of your place in your mentor's galaxy, along with your key training aim. In Act I, we learned that your key training aim is to build a research program informed by your mentor's work. Research programs consist of a burning question, pieces of scholarly work, and a theoretical framework that binds the question to the work. Now, you must learn tools for publishing scholarly work, the primary focus of Act II.

As with the close of Chapter 5, here again I must acknowledge that disciplines vary widely in the preparation of scholarly work for publication. Act II deals with key issues germane to publishing, and so we will focus our attention on issues regarding publishing that cut across disciplines. Training within your discipline will provide you with many of the tools you need to prepare scholarship specific to your discipline. You might take coursework in research design. You might attain didactic experiences within your mentoring environment that facilitate producing scholarly work within your discipline. Consequently, it is beyond the scope of this book to provide specificity in terms of how to prepare scholarly work.

In fact, a key rationale for writing this book was to facilitate Emerging Academics' mastery of core academic tasks that not only cut across disciplines but also receive little in the way of instruction within formal training contexts like the classroom. I used about a third of the chapters of this book to facilitate your mastery of the first question outlined in Chapter 1. In doing so, I set the stage for you to begin your journey along the path of preparing scholarly work under the supervision of your mentor. Needless to say, your mentor is far better equipped than I to guide you in preparing scholarly work that fits within the confines of your mentoring environment. Following our coverage of the first question outlined in Chapter 1, I hope this book proves invaluable to you when addressing the second question outlined in the chapter: *On the path to publishing your work, how do you respond to reviews of your work?* You need to address this question to move from preparing scholarship to publishing scholarship. I dedicate Act II (i.e., Chapters 7, 8, and 9) to facilitating your mastery of the peer review system that academia uses to determine which pieces of scholarly work ought to be published or disseminated.

If you have yet to prepare scholarly work that you wish to submit for publication, it may nonetheless be instructive for you now to at least read Chapter 7. When you have reached the point of submitting your work for publication, come back to the book and study Chapters 8 and 9. If you have work in front of you that you either wish to submit for publication soon or have had trouble publishing after several attempts, the next three chapters will empower you with the tools needed to respond to reviews of your work on the path to publishing it.

As I make clear in the next three chapters, the peer review system seems daunting and difficult to navigate. Yet, it does have a discernable structure and can be demystified. Demystifying the peer review system involves breaking it down into its basic components. With its components broken down, you can acquire the tools needed to address each component, fight your way through the system, and publish your work. We have arrived at the point in our journey where we encounter an opposing force, and we acquire the tools for fighting back.

ACT II:
YOUR COMBAT TOOLS

CHAPTER 7
Basic Training for Peer Review

I ended Chapter 4 by stating that your journey to learning the Shared Universe tool does not end with identifying your place in academia and the burning question that drives your work. You must also leverage this tool to answer questions about publishing your work. This chapter and Chapters 8 and 9 all focus on addressing the question: *On the path to publishing your work, how do you respond to reviews of your work?* How does this question relate to your mentor's galaxy, the larger universe in which it resides, and the research program you seek to build?

Your scholarly universe contains many galaxies, including your mentor's galaxy. Many of these galaxies touch upon areas of scholarship that directly relate to the scholarly topics addressed in your work and that of your mentor. Up until now, I've discussed how these galaxies contain your mentor's colleagues. One can break these colleagues down into two broad groups. The first group contains *Collaborators*: colleagues with whom your mentor shares previous scholarship and/or ongoing scholarly pursuits. Collaborators may include former mentors as well as colleagues your mentor acquired during or following their training.

The second group contains *Evaluators*: colleagues with whom your mentor has yet to collaborate but nonetheless harbor the necessary expertise to understand and interpret your mentor's work. It's this second group of colleagues to which we will devote our attention in this chapter and the two that follow. Why? Because their tireless efforts evaluating your mentor's work and the rest of the colleagues in your scholarly universe help to ensure the universe's sustainability and functionality. You might ask, "*Why can't collaborators serve as my mentor's evaluators?"* Your scholarly universe cannot afford to rely on your mentor's collaborators to evaluate your mentor's work; we call that a conflict of interest. Indeed, collaborators often become as much close friends as they are colleagues, and don't you want your friends to succeed? If a colleague harbors a vested interest in your mentor's success, then that kicks them out of the group of colleagues who might evaluate your mentor's work.

I cannot overstate the importance of evaluators to your mentor's scholarly universe. Your mentor and all of the colleagues with whom they share a scholarly universe make a tacit pact with one another to leverage the expertise of scholars in the universe to ensure quality control of the scholarship produced in that universe. Quality control requires that evaluators have the opportunity to voice any potential concerns with the scholarship their colleagues produce. Each evaluator must harbor an independent voice free of conflicts of interest. Thus, your scholarly universe relies on this second group of colleagues—these evaluators—to ensure that your mentor and all other colleagues in the universe produce scholarship of the highest quality. Scholarly universes cannot assume that all work produced will be of sufficient quality, and fit for dissemination. Thus, scholarly universes require systems for ensuring quality control.

The Peer Review System: Quality Control for Your Scholarly Universe

Quality control requires an infrastructure. We cannot expect academics to produce scholarship, place it in a public space that allows for posted commentary (e.g., website), and assume that all scholars would use posted comments to improve their work. Such a scenario would lack both safeguards and accountability. Indeed, how would your scholarly universe handle academics who prove unwilling or unable to use commentary to improve their work? Thus, in scholarship, quality control takes the form of an evaluative system known as *Peer Review* (Johnson & Hermanowicz, 2017).

Whenever your mentor seeks to publish a piece of scholarly work, they submit that work to undergo evaluative processes encapsulated in the peer review system. These evaluative processes begin with your mentor identifying a publication outlet tasked with disseminating scholarly knowledge, typically an academic journal or book publisher. They submit this work for consideration at that specific publication outlet.

To assist in making publication decisions, the publication outlet consults with a team of expert evaluators. For each piece of scholarly work that your mentor submits, these evaluators assist the publication outlet in determining whether they ought to publish that submitted work. Typically, an established figure in your mentor's specific discipline, field, or scholarly universe—an *Editor*—leads the evaluation of the submitted work. Along with their own evaluation, the editor solicits or invites two or more additional evaluators—journals often refer to these evaluators as *Editorial Consultants*—to review the submitted work. The editorial consultants independently evaluate the submitted work, and submit their evaluations of the strengths and weaknesses of the work. These evaluations most often take the form of narrative commentary about the work, including concrete suggestions for how your mentor might improve their work. These evaluations also often include a summary judgment about the quality of the work and whether it passes the threshold for dissemination or publication. Although many publication outlets also prompt editorial consultants to make quantitative ratings about the quality of the work, the key decision-making processes regarding the work rely on qualitative summary judgments. A summary judgment may take the form of a range of options that include:

- Rejecting your mentor's work for publication;
- Inviting your mentor to revise and resubmit the work for further consideration; and
- Recommending your mentor's work be accepted for publication.

> **Anonymous Account 7.1. Experiencing Rejection**
>
> **Early Career Faculty**
>
> Many students beginning competitive Ph.D. programs are accustomed to acceptance—at least when it comes to their scholarship. Despite setbacks and adversities we might have faced in other domains (social, familial, personal), we managed to achieve enough academic success to gain acceptance into a doctoral program. This was certainly the case for me: When I started graduate school, I prided myself on my ability to succeed, at least scholastically, consistently and at a high level. My self-perception as "successful" had come to fuel my self-worth. It didn't take long to learn how challenging this would make manuscript rejections (or any type of academic failure, for that matter). In my first two years of graduate school, my manuscript rejections outpaced my acceptances by five to one. That ratio scared me. *What happened?* I remember thinking. *I used to be good at this stuff. Maybe I'm not cut out for this after all.* In this sense, the biggest challenge I faced related to peer review was not structural but psychological. Essentially, I had to re-evaluate what "success" looked like and how to achieve it—and what success meant (and didn't) for my worth as a person. Hearing about others' experiences, seeing successful academics' "failure CVs" (seriously, Google it!), and talking to faculty

mentors I admire were all instrumental in changing my perspective. I'm now quite proud of my ratio of paper acceptances-to-rejections (still around four to one!) and hope to instill similar pride in my graduate students; more rejections means more effort, learning, and growth, *and* better science, at the end of the day. But it took me a long time, and a lot more effortful self-compassion than I was once comfortable with, to get to this place.

With regard to these summary judgments, please keep two points in mind. First, Anonymous Account 7.1 reveals a grim reality about peer review: Authors in the academic space quickly become used to receiving notices of rejection about their work. In research, notices of rejection greatly outpace notices of acceptance. This ratio of rejections to acceptances often feels quite distinct from experiences with rejection one sees in other lines of work, or perhaps during earlier stages of education and training (e.g., exams and term papers from undergraduate coursework). Second, among the summary judgments I just described, note that the options include something called *Revise and Resubmit* (R&R). As I describe in greater detail below, you mentor commonly receives these kinds of summary judgments about their submitted work. In fact, refer back to the scholarly works you listed in your MMMG worksheet (Figure 6.1). These works most likely went through this peer review process, and benefited from several rounds of R&R invitations before you had a chance to read the finished product.

If your scholarly universe contains evaluators of your mentor's scholarship, it logically follows that these and other colleagues will also evaluate your scholarship. Thus, your development as an Emerging Academic requires you to master tools for effectively navigating the peer review system. And when I use a term like "navigating," that means that peer review includes several components that you have to understand and master. On the path to disseminating your scholarship, these components serve as both structural barriers and structural supports, which I outline in Table 7.1. You can view these components as representing the unfair and fair segments of your scholarly universe, respectively. In fact, you might find peer review's structural barriers to be remarkably unfair. Thankfully, peer review's structural supports often result in demonstrable improvements to your scholarly work. Thus, learning about these components of the peer review system serve to increase the likelihood of your reaping the benefits of this system, and at the same time limiting your exposure to its more seedy elements.

Table 7.1. The Peer Review System's Structural Barriers and Structural Supports

Structural Barriers	Structural Supports
—Inter-rater (un)reliability —Rater biases	—Multiple scholarly outlets —Listings of editors and editorial consultants —Standardized submission, review, and publication processes —Revise and resubmit process —The system rewards persistence

Structural Barriers in Peer Review: The Unfair Segments of Your Universe

The origins of our modern system of peer review trace back several centuries (Spier, 2002). Currently, scholars implement various forms of peer review, and each exists for a common purpose:

to serve as quality control for the dissemination of scholarship (Lipworth, Kerridge, Carter, & Little, 2011). Make no mistake, the quality control one sees in peer review bears little resemblance to quality control in other industries, like manufacturing. For example, one definition of quality control focuses on "freedom from deficiencies": a system that creates products devoid of the kinds of errors that result in consumers being unable to use the product efficiently, safely, and/or to their satisfaction (Juran & Godfrey, 1999). In this respect, the need to revise products coming off of a manufacturing line of, for instance, automobiles or coffee makers, may revolve around detecting tangible elements of these products that, if not corrected, result in deficiencies or even dangers with consumer use. Further, in manufacturing, a failure to attend to quality control translates to objectively poor outcomes. Poor quality control for a model of a mobile phone translates to such measurable outcomes as poor phone sales or the emergence of consumer injuries resulting from phone use (e.g., phones that catch fire; Samsung, 2017).

When applied to scholarship, much of the quality control in the peer review system lies in the eye of the beholder. Stated another way, evaluators do not have an "answer key" to see if a comment they make on a piece of scholarly work objectively results in improvements in the quality of that work. As detailed below, this lack of an objective index to identify comments that result in improved quality translates to inefficiencies in the system. For right now, let's review an extreme example. Evaluators can and do make factually inaccurate comments on scholarship they review. For instance, an evaluator might comment that authors on a manuscript used a statistical technique incorrectly, when in fact the authors appropriately applied the technique. Under this circumstance, if the editor greatly values the evaluator's judgment on the issue, they may inadvertently count the erroneous comment against the author when making a summary judgment on the work. When editors fail to identify errors in the review process and ultimately reject a piece of scholarship for publication, often the only course of action available to the author is to submit their work for publication at another outlet. Consequently, structural barriers present in the peer review system result in authors having to leverage innovative tools to ensure quality control in reviews of their work. In essence, formal quality control systems exist for evaluating scholarly work, like the presence of expert evaluators to review the work. Yet, these formal systems are insufficient for ensuring quality control of the evaluations themselves. Emerging Academics need to implement informal quality control systems to protect themselves against structural barriers present in the system. I restrict my discussion to two structural barriers in peer review that characterize key components of poor-quality evaluations of scholarly work. In Chapters 8 and 9, I detail specific tools you might leverage to reduce your exposure to poor-quality evaluations of your work.

Inter-rater (un)reliability. Part of the difficulty with leveraging peer review as a quality control system lies in the reality that reviewing is, by construction, a subjective process. Two or more evaluators independently review the same scholarly work and subsequently submit commentary to the editor that reflects their subjective evaluations of the work (De Los Reyes, 2017; Marsh, Jayasinghe, & Bond, 2008). Editors receive these subjective evaluations, interpret them, and make decisions regarding the publication of the scholarship under consideration. Editors make these decisions under uncertain conditions. Indeed, as with the evaluators who editors invite to review scholarly work, editors do not possess an answer key to determine if they made the "right" decision about publishing this work. This is because no "gold standard" method exists for determining whether one subjective evaluation of a submitted piece of scholarly work is objectively "right" or "more valid" than another subjective evaluation of that same work. As a result, one hopes that different evaluators of the same scholarly work will often reach the same conclusion about that work. Indeed, if two evaluators of the same scholarly work tend to reach the same conclusions, then evaluators' judgments become interchangeable with one another. Scenarios in which evaluators' judgments corroborate one another might reduce some—but not all—of the issues stemming from the subjective nature of the judgments. To empirically address these issues, one might turn to scholars in the area of *Psychometrics*. As a sub-discipline of Psychology, scholars in Psychometrics seek to understand and in some cases improve measurements of mental processes and related domains (Borsboom, 2005). In Psychometrics, examining the degree to which two or more evaluators converge on their reviews of the same scholarly work falls within tests of *Inter-Rater Reliability* (Nunnally & Bernstein, 1994).

Unfortunately, tests of inter-rater reliability reveal the most widespread problem with peer review: the ubiquitous occurrence of remarkably poor levels of such reliability (see also De Los Reyes & Wang, 2012). Two evaluators can review the same scholarly work and arrive at not only different recommendations for how to improve the work, but also fundamentally different conclusions as to whether the work ought to be published (Cicchetti, 1991). For instance, one evaluator might find your paper's Introduction to be very clear and well-written, whereas another evaluator might find your paper's Introduction to be the most confusing piece of scholarship they ever read. As another example, one evaluator might comment favorably on the approach you took to your scholarship, whereas another evaluator might suggest a complete redesign of this same approach before the scholarship you produced becomes suitable for publication. For both of these kinds of examples, authors of submitted work commonly find that one but not both evaluators recommend rejection of their work.

The kinds of evaluator discrepancies I just described can and do happen, and they happen often (see Smith, 2006). Further, no scholarly universe is immune to low inter-rater reliability. That is, unreliable evaluations occur when evaluating manuscripts submitted to publishers in myriad scholarly disciplines (Bornmann, 2008). They even occur within high-stakes decisions with millions of dollars on the line, such as reviews of research funding applications (De Los Reyes & Wang, 2012; Pier et al., 2018).

Low inter-rater reliability has important implications for an Emerging Academic's approach to navigating the peer review system. Recall any other context in which you received feedback about your work, from mentors on your thesis to course instructors on a term paper. Your mentors and instructors likely taught you to maintain a fully responsive stance, heed an evaluator's feedback, and make revisions to your work until you have fully addressed the evaluator's concerns. Indeed, scholars might criticize authors who fail to fully revise scholarship that has been rejected for publication at one outlet before submitting the work for consideration elsewhere (see Ioannidis, Tatsioni, & Karassa, 2010). Yet, when it comes to strategically navigating the peer review system, where is the logic in that? If peer review suffers from poor inter-rater reliability, why should an author be fully responsive to an evaluator's commentary in one review context before taking that revised work and resubmitting to a completely different review context? By "completely different" I mean two things. First, if your work encounters rejection at one publication outlet, and you decide to submit your work for publication at another outlet, you have no guarantee that the same evaluators who rejected your work at the first outlet will also evaluate your work at the second outlet.

Second, as I mentioned in Chapter 4, academics' failures all occur privately. If we get a rejection notice from a publisher, no one else knows unless we broadcast the news. This also means that the previous round of commentary that informed the rejection of a piece of scholarly work at one publication outlet remains confidential when that work undergoes evaluation at another outlet. Does that mean that you should always ignore commentary stemming from a rejection of your work and just submit your work as-is somewhere else, hoping you hit the lottery of favorable reviews? Of course not. If you see a great piece of advice embedded in commentary that led to a rejection of your work for publication, take the commentary to heart and improve the quality of your work. But choose wisely in terms of what you revise.

Think about this: Any two evaluators of your work will likely submit discrepant evaluations of that work. What happens when you add evaluators to the mix on a future submission of that work somewhere else? Most likely, you are looking at more unreliability. If this is the case, you have no assurances that any one revision you make to your work in response to evaluations of your first submission will result in a different outcome on a future submission. Let's walk through an example. Reviewer 1 on your first submission of a manuscript downright detested your tables and figures and found them remarkably unclear. Let's assume the editor rejected your manuscript for publication. Before you submit the manuscript to another publication outlet, you plan to fix all of the tables and figures along the lines of Reviewer 1's suggestions. On the next submission of this work to another publication outlet, will all of the reviewers appreciate your revised tables and figures? Who knows! An entirely new set of reviewers may even make recommendations that involve revising all of the tables and figures back to the way they were (i.e., in your first submission).

In sum, the poor inter-rater reliability present in the peer review system begets scores of inefficiencies in the production of scholarship. The negative effects of these inefficiencies increase exponentially for Emerging Academics. You do not have a lot of time on your hands to begin with; only a few short years to train and build the scholarly record to get a job and keep it. In addition, you run the risk of encountering poor-quality, unreliable evaluations of your work that slow down the process of producing scholarship. By now, I hope you and I have built an understanding. If I show you a barrier to succeeding in research, I will also provide you with a ton of advice on how to smash that barrier to pieces. I promise to do that in Chapters 8 and 9. For now, I have to drop one more bit of depressing news. I admit that low reliability in peer review reflects poorly on academia as a whole and creates significant structural barriers to overcome. One more structural barrier makes navigating the peer review system all the more challenging.

Rater biases. In this section, I use the term "bias" with a great deal of trepidation. I get it: "Bias" is a loaded term across many facets of contemporary society. At the same time, in Psychometrics bias reflects a systematic process that profoundly impacts the veracity of data one obtains from a rater or source of measurement. One can distinguish bias from reliability indices like inter-rater reliability (see Nunnally & Bernstein, 1994). Let's say Reviewer 1's decision to reject your paper for publication disagrees with Reviewer 2's decision to accept your paper for publication. If the reason for the disagreement lies in Reviewer 1 always rejecting papers for publication regardless of the quality of the work, psychometricians would see that as a constant error within the "family" of sources of unreliability. Constant error affects all observations equally (i.e., all papers evaluated by Reviewer 1 get a recommendation of rejection for publication). Thus, constant error reduces measurement reliability. Indeed, in this example,

Reviewer 2's evaluations would suffer from constant error only insofar as they have the opposite tendency as that of Reviewer 1, namely that they recommend acceptance of every paper they evaluate. (As an aside, who wants to tuck Reviewer 2 in their pocket and take them to every publication outlet to which they submit their work? Yes, please!)

Let's continue with the example of Reviewer 1's reject judgment and Reviewer 2's accept judgment. What if Reviewer 1 does not always reject, but tends to make rejection judgments based on characteristics that do not directly reflect the quality of the evaluated work? These judgments might focus on characteristics that, at best, circumstantially relate to the work's quality. Examples might include the institutional affiliation of the author, whether the author studies a scholarly topic of interest to Reviewer 1, and whether the author examines controversial scholarly topics. These examples all reflect sources of rater bias. Whereas constant error directly impacts measurement reliability or precision in measurement, *Bias* directly impacts measurement validity or accuracy in measurement (Nunnally & Bernstein, 1994). By "accuracy" I mean that, because Reviewer 1's judgments systematically reflect characteristics of the evaluated work other than its quality, Reviewer 1 makes judgments that do not facilitate quality control. If the goal of soliciting Reviewer 1's judgment of the work was to obtain an index for the purpose of quality control, Reviewer 1's judgment would have failed miserably in this respect.

Unfortunately, as with low inter-rater reliability, scholars across disciplines have long decried the peer review system for not only the presence of biases but their intractable nature (De Vries, Marschall, & Stein, 2009; Lipworth et al., 2011; Resch, Ernst, & Garrow, 2000; Smith, 2006). However, rater biases introduce new structural barriers apart from those stemming from low inter-rater reliability. Not only might rater biases slow down the process of scholarship, the systemic nature of these biases means that their negative impacts might "follow" an author from publication outlet to publication outlet. What if the source of rater bias contaminates the reviews of many evaluators, such that an author encounters this bias across multiple submissions of the same scholarly product to different publication outlets? Anonymous Account 7.2 provides a common example, namely with regard to the publication of null findings. Thus, in Chapter 9, I describe tools for reducing your risk of encountering not only unreliable evaluations but also biased ones.

Anonymous Account 7.2. Experiencing Rejection	
Doctoral Student	When attempting to publish my master's thesis—a carefully designed methodological study with null results—I was very aware that many publication outlets might not find the null results interesting or novel enough to publish. I carefully worked on the results section, including some innovative Bayesian analyses in hopes of convincing the reader that these null results were truly meaningful and had practical applications. However, after my first submission, Reviewer 2 (…it's always reviewer 2…) provided feedback that the design was "an unclear mess" and that this manuscript was "clearly a fishing expedition." This was brutal feedback for someone who had attempted to closely design an experimental study for their thesis project—it certainly was not a "fishing expedition." While I was tempted to ruminate over these comments, I instead focused on how I had presented the article that would have contributed to this comment. Understanding what would have made me, as a reviewer, make a similar comment helped me reframe the manuscript entirely to yield better results at another publication outlet. For instance, I had reported on several measures that were conducted

that did not yield significant results—most of these measures were secondary measures not directly pertaining to the aims of the study. I removed these measures from the paper as they were not primary to the research question, did not add significant content to the paper, and may have appeared to be "hooks" with which to conduct my fishing. I also tried to be explicit in my introduction for what initiated the design of this project and what larger questions guided the project's conceptualization. While I will continue to make jokes about my "fishing expedition" of a master's thesis, I don't think the intent of the reviewer was malicious. By situating myself in the reviewer's shoes, it helped me reformulate my conceptualization to reach a larger audience, and to have greater success in its publication.

Structural Supports in Peer Review: The Fair Segments of Your Universe

Authors who fall victim to low inter-rater reliability and/or rater biases often have the same recourse available to them if they receive a rejection notice from a publication outlet: Submit your work to another publication outlet. Emerging Academics might find these components of peer review disheartening, and in fact, infuriating. At the same time, I argue that when you as an author capitalize on the saving graces of the peer review system—its structural supports—you can instill balance in the system. Embedded in the peer review system one finds several structural supports that represent the fair aspects of the system.

Multiple scholarly outlets. When I tell an Emerging Academic my strategy for preparing manuscripts for submission to scholarly journals, they often look at me incredulously. As I write the manuscript, I ponder my "Plan A" journal. I have daydreams about Plan A. Of opening the pages in a future issue of a journal and seeing my paper in that issue. However, I also ponder my "Plans B, C, D, and E" journals. Sounds morose, right? Not to me! I have a sound rationale for this strategy. If low inter-rater reliability and rater biases lurk around every corner of my scholarly universe, do you think it makes sense for me to have just a "Plan A" journal? At least if I set the expectation that rejections are the norm within the peer review system, then the rejections don't hurt as much. Further, every time I use this strategy, when I get to the "Plan E" journal on the list, I say to myself, *"You know, it would be awesome for this paper to appear in that journal!"* The presence of multiple venues for publishing your work: This part of the peer review system is fair.

Listings of editors and editorial consultants. If you follow the "Plan A through E" approach to selecting publication outlets, you might ask, *"How do I identify the outlets that find value in my work?"* In Chapter 8 I provide you with a deeper dive into the answer to this question. In keeping with the focus on structural supports, part of the answer to this question lies in two interrelated components of peer review. As of this writing, I serve as editor of *Journal of Clinical Child and Adolescent Psychology (JCCAP*; De Los Reyes, 2017), a peer review journal published by Taylor and Francis Group, LLC. As a multi-disciplinary publishing group, Taylor and Francis publishes over 2,600 journals and releases over 5,000 new book titles per year (https://taylorandfrancis.com/about/). And so, one of these interrelated components lies within how many options scholars have available to them to publish their work.

The second of these components concerns the information publication outlets make available to prospective authors. To return to *JCCAP*, when I began my term as editor, one of my first tasks involved inviting scholars to serve as evaluators of submissions to the journal (i.e., editorial consultants) as well as associate editors to assist me in handling the editorial roles for manuscript submissions. Taylor and Francis keeps a current listing of *JCCAP*'s editorial board on its website (https://www.tandfonline.com/toc/hcap20/current). This listing of scholars who serve evaluative roles at *JCCAP* is a crucial resource for authors. Indeed, this list allows scholars to answer the question: *Does JCCAP seek the input of scholars who have the expertise to provide fair evaluations of my work?* You may not have certainty that any one scholar on an editorial board will evaluate your work (although more on this in Chapter 8). At the same time, the range of content expertise of scholars on an editorial board provides authors with information about the kinds of work valued at the publication outlet. Publication outlets making public their list of editors and editorial consultants: This part of the peer review system is fair.

Standardized submission, review, and publication processes. Once a scholar selects a publication outlet to submit their work, the outlet includes standardized processes prospective authors follow to prepare their work for submission. For instance, *JCCAP* includes requirements for both length (e.g., page count limits) and specific content the manuscript ought to include: https://www.tandfonline.com/action/authorSubmission?journalCode=hcap20&page=instructions. All prospective authors must follow these requirements for their work to undergo peer review at the journal. Further, each submission undergoes an initial evaluation by the editor for suitability for peer review at the journal. Although a number of submissions receive a desk rejection or triage notice based on this initial review, prospective contributors whose submissions move past this initial review stage all receive a full evaluation of their work. This review involves one editor to lead the review who selects evaluators from either the list of the journal's editorial consultants, or when needed, consultation from ad-hoc evaluators not on the list. Lastly, each year as editor of *JCCAP* I must submit publicly available information on journal operations from the previous year, including the number of submissions, number of articles published, and the overall rejection rate for submissions to the journal: https://www.apa.org/pubs/journals/statistics. The use of standardized submission, review, and publication processes applicable to all prospective contributors to a publication outlet: This part of the peer review system is fair.

Revise and resubmit process. The structural barriers described previously tend to have direct implications for the first submission of a piece of scholarly work for publication at an outlet. That is, unreliable and/or biased reviews typically have their greatest impact on an editor's decision to reject the first version of a manuscript they evaluate. However, as mentioned earlier in the chapter, the published version of a piece of scholarly work often undergoes multiple rounds of revision and evaluation—multiple R&R's—before an editor eventually accepts that work for publication. This is where the peer review system shines. Specifically, the editor who believes a manuscript they evaluated should not be rejected for publication but at the same time thinks it "needs some work" will invite the author of that manuscript to revise and resubmit it for further consideration. As mentioned previously, in peer review the shorthand for revise and resubmit is R&R. An R&R invite might take one of many forms. Some R&R's reflect an editor's requests for minor, stylistic changes to the manuscript's content. Other R&R's involve an editor's request for a full-on "page one rewrite" or complete overhaul of the manuscript's content. For these latter invites, an editor might highly value the premise or aims of the work. Yet, the manuscript's content requires significant restructuring to get it into publishable form.

The most talented academics in your scholarly universe routinely receive R&R invites for their submitted work. In fact, if you sit down with a senior colleague in your universe and ask them about their experiences with peer review, I guarantee you that their stories will include a mix of R&R journeys. You might find journeys that range from, *"I was surprised to see that paper fly through the review process,"* to, *"I went through five R&R rounds before the editor gave up and accepted that paper."* I also suggest that you ask them this question:

- *"Have you ever submitted a manuscript, revised it as per reviewer commentary, and upon acceptance, felt that your first submission was better than the accepted one?"*

A successful senior colleague will belt out a laugh and emphatically say, *"No way!"* For myself, as of this writing, I am about 100 peer review articles into my career. For every one of these articles, I can confidently say that the peer review system did its job. The published version of each of these papers is of higher quality than the first version I submitted for publication. The R&R process: This part of the peer review system is fair.

The system rewards persistence. I want you to focus on a statement from the last section: *"I went through five R&R rounds before the editor gave up and accepted that paper."* All of the structural barriers and supports in peer review share one thing in common: They take hard work and persistence to either overcome or leverage to your benefit. Refer back to Anonymous Account 7.1: All successful academics possess an inbox replete with notices of rejection. An academic's rejection notices far outweigh their acceptance notices. This is the business academics choose: They fail a lot. In fact, academics succeed only after they fail.

Think about failure as the steps you follow during an exercise where failing means falling down, like riding a bicycle. Scholars fall off their bikes often, so to speak. In academia, you fail when you fall down and stay on the ground. Of course, like bike riding, you can also fail if you get up without learning why you fell. Without learning why you fell off your bike, it doesn't take long before you wind up back on the ground. Producing scholarly work means falling down and learning why you fell. Armed with new ideas on how to succeed the next time, you get back up. By the way, you should probably get used to the process of falling down and learning from failure. The process repeats itself, sometimes multiple times for each piece of scholarly work you submit through the peer review system. For each piece of work, you keep on falling down and getting back up until you succeed. Until your work becomes good enough to publish.

Your battles with peer review pit you against the system, and not the editor and evaluators. The most powerful tools in these battles are not the material weapons you see on traditional battlefields. The two most potent weapons you wield in your battles with the peer review system exist inside all of us in various degrees and kinds. They are our wills and intellects. Your willingness to continue the battle factors prominently in these scenarios, because battles with the peer review system are those of attrition. If you prepare high-quality work, submit your work for evaluation by your colleagues, and you thoughtfully and successfully address your colleagues' concerns, you further improve the quality of your work. And you continue making these improvements until the peer review system relents and you receive your notice of acceptance. In relenting, the system acknowledges that it provided you with a vehicle for disseminating high-quality work to those in your scholarly universe. The system rewards persistence: This part of the peer review system is the fairest of them all.

Next Steps

As with Chapter 4, in this chapter I covered a great deal of content. We learned about the peer review system and its use in evaluating scholarly work. Chapter 4 laid the foundation for Chapters 5 and 6. Similarly, in this chapter I laid the foundation for Chapters 8 and 9. Specifically, in describing the peer review system's structural barriers and structural supports, you might ask, "*What tools might I use to overcome the barriers and capitalize on the supports?*" I think about these barriers and supports as reflecting the unfair and the fair aspects of the peer review system, respectively. In Chapter 8, I describe specific tools for capitalizing on the fair aspects of the peer review system. In Chapter 9, I describe tools to assist you in avoiding the unfair aspects of the system. One element of the next two chapters provides us with an optimistic outlook on successfully navigating the peer review system: We acquire four times as many tools in Chapter 8 as we acquire in Chapter 9.

CHAPTER 8

Peer Review Tools When the System Treats You Fairly

I closed Chapter 7 with the idea that publishing scholarly work resembles a battle of attrition. A traditional battle requires both physical and mental prowess. In academia, you find yourself in private battles with the peer review system. You wage these battles with the system, not with those who evaluate your work. In fact, as Anonymous Account 8.1 details, many times evaluators seek to help. They may provide you with constructive commentary that promotes thinking about new ways to approach your scholarly work.

Anonymous Account 8.1. Constructive Feedback	
Post-Doctoral Fellow	It can be difficult not to take the feedback you receive during the peer review process personally. You have undoubtedly spent hours upon hours conducting the study, analyzing the data, writing the manuscript, and waiting (im)patiently for months to hear back from the journal you submitted it to. When you receive critical responses from reviewers, especially when those lead to a rejection, it can make you feel frustrated and disheartened. I have received two valuable pieces of advice that have helped me to navigate this process. First, after you initially read reviews of your work, set them aside for a day or two and then come back to them when you have fresh eyes and a clear head. Second, be sure to celebrate the successful completion of each stage of this process, from the initial submission of your manuscript to its

eventual acceptance; this helps you remain motivated despite the long delay of gratification that is associated with academic research. When I have received an invitation for a revise and resubmit or even a rejection, I have always found that the reviewers have raised issues that I had not previously considered and helped to improve the overall quality of the manuscript. For example, in my most recent manuscript, one of the reviewers highlighted the need to test whether the association between my independent and dependent variables was indeed linear—one of the central, but sometimes overlooked, assumptions of regression models. Although there was theory to support the notion that it could be nonlinear, I was not able to find any other studies that had tested this idea. Indeed, my analyses revealed that there was a nonlinear association between my independent and dependent variables, and this reviewer's feedback helped to improve the contribution of my study to the extant literature.

Academic battles take place in the mental space, but these battles require more than bright minds. These battles require strategic, tenacious minds. Scholars successfully win their battles with the peer review system with will, intellect, and importantly, strategy. In Chapter 7, we completed basic training in the peer review system, and I armed you with knowledge about key components of this system. Yet, recall the second question listed in Chapter 1: *On the path to publishing your work, how do you respond to reviews of your work?* In Chapter 7 we learned about the path. What we need to learn now is the "how" part of the question. We need to acquire tools for succeeding in battle.

Modeling Moments

If Chapter 7 consisted of basic training on peer review, consider this chapter and the chapter that follows "life after boot camp." The U.S. Marine Corps refers to post-boot camp training as the School of Infantry (MarineParents.com, 2019). In this chapter I reveal combat-ready tools for "fair fights." In Chapter 9, I reveal combat-ready tools for "unfair fights." Your training begins with a set of Modeling Moments focused on providing you with tools for navigating the peer review system when the system works the way it's supposed to. In Table 8.1, I provide a summary description of each tool. For each tool, the table also includes a brief description of materials I use to model implementation of the tool in academic work. When possible, I include links to online materials that serve as models for your own scholarly pursuits. This chapter's figures include excerpts of the complete materials accessible via these links, and you can access these and all of the book's downloadable files here: http://bit.ly/ECRToolboxAllDownloads.

Table 8.1. Peer Review Tools to Use When Your Scholarly Universe Treats You Fairly

Tool	Description	Modeling Moment Material	Online Access to Material
Choose publication outlets wisely	Carefully research the publication outlets that you believe may provide you with a fair evaluation of your work	Main website for *Journal of Psychopathology and Behavioral Assessment*	https://link.springer.com/journal/10862
Recommend evaluators for your work	Identify specific evaluators—including contact information—who you believe can provide a fair evaluation of your work	Template for cover letter requesting evaluators for your submitted work	http://bit.ly/ECRToolboxChapter8CoverLetterInitialTemplate

Accept how you react to reviews of your work	Maintain a mindful stance about the natural emotional reactions we have when we first receive evaluations of our work	Example of a decision letter for a previous manuscript submission from my laboratory	http://bit.ly/ECRToolboxChapter8DecisionLetterReaction
Pause after receiving reviews of your work	Peek at the letter or email communicating the decision about the evaluation of your work, and then wait a few days to begin the revision process	Copy of the manuscript and decision letter for the manuscript submission that forms the basis of Modeling Moments below	http://bit.ly/ECRToolboxChapter8SubmissionInitialJOBA http://bit.ly/ECRToolboxChapter8DecisionLetterInitialJOBA
Begin with your cover letter	Begin the process of revising your manuscript with a thoroughly itemized cover letter that outlines your revisions to the manuscript	Template for cover letter outlining changes on revised manuscript	http://bit.ly/ECRToolboxChapter8CoverLetterRevisionTemplate
Plan a revision schedule	Make a deal to address one comment on your itemized cover letter daily	Example of itemized cover letter	http://bit.ly/ECRToolboxChapter8CoverLetterRevisionJOBA
Empathize with your evaluators	Your cover letter should include a "word-for-word" quote of each evaluator comment, as well as the location in the manuscript	Example of itemized cover letter and revised manuscript linked to this letter	http://bit.ly/ECRToolboxChapter8CoverLetterRevisionJOBA

	where you addressed each comment (e.g., line and/or page number)		http://bit.ly/ECRToolboxChapter8SubmissionRevisionJOBA
Make all possible revisions	Address every comment evaluators ask you to address	Example of itemized cover letter	http://bit.ly/ECRToolboxChapter8CoverLetterRevisionJOBA
Seek advice on handling tricky comments	If you encounter uncertainty with how to address an evaluator comment, solicit advice from colleagues and/or the editor	—	—
Develop a keen eye for detail	Carefully proofread your revised manuscript and cover letter, many times!	Example of material from a previous editorial decision letter	—
Approach peer review as a battle of attrition	Throughout the process, tell the editor you are pleased to make any further revisions	Example of conclusion of cover letter	http://bit.ly/ECRToolboxChapter8EndofCoverLetterRevision
Give your time to the peer review system	Pay back the system that sought out evaluators to review your own work; serve as an evaluator yourself	Example of an email offering your services to peer review publication outlets	—

137

Choose publication outlets wisely. Recall in Chapter 7 my approach to selecting journals, the "Plan A through E" approach. How do I get to the point of picking any one of these journals? To illustrate the publication selection process, I review the considerations for selecting the publication outlet to which we submitted the manuscript profiled in several of the Modeling Moments in this chapter (Glenn et al., 2019). The outlet: *Journal of Psychopathology and Behavioral Assessment*. Several factors weighed heavily in our decision to submit to this outlet. Prior success was an obvious factor: Between 2012 and 2018, my laboratory published six other articles in this outlet, so we knew that, at this journal, we could receive a fair evaluation of our work. But underlying that previous success was the key question in any evaluation of submitted work: *Who might the editor select to evaluate the submission?* Take a look at the first row of Table 8.1; you will find a link to the journal's editorial board. There, we found a number of scholars who might provide a fair review of the manuscript. The first part of our decision-making process was now set. We had one more thing to do to ensure a fair evaluation of the work.

Recommend evaluators for your work. Perhaps making the right call on our first decision-making point—selecting the publication outlet—would have been enough for us to receive the fair evaluation of our work that we expected. But why take any chances? If you see fair, expert scholars on the editorial board of a publication outlet to which you plan to submit, can't you also make a request to the editor to have those scholars review your work? In short, yes you can! In fact, recently for some journals I have been required to list possible reviewers within the submission portals in order to submit the manuscript.

As an Emerging Academic, you should take this part of the process seriously. Indeed, editors might not know the evaluators who have the expertise to provide fair reviews of your work, particularly if your area of expertise reflects an emerging body of literature about which the editor might have little background. Further, if you do not suggest evaluators, then you may put yourself at a disadvantage compared to more senior authors. Senior authors have established research programs, and that means editors likely know which scholars might provide fair evaluations of their work. For many submissions from my laboratory, Emerging Academics receiving training under my supervision serve the role of lead author. Thus, whether or not a journal requires us to recommend reviewers, submissions from my laboratory always include a cover letter that lists possible reviewers. The second row of Table 8.1 provides you with a link to the template of this cover letter. Near the end of the letter (see Figure 8.1), you will see how we identify scholars with the expertise to evaluate our work. We make these selections based on a combination of expertise and reputation. We identify scholars based on not only what they know, but also their stature within scholarship. Importantly, we choose carefully based on what the "word on the street" is in terms of scholars who provide fair evaluations of their colleagues' work. Over time, you learn who might be fair and who might be unfair. Any scholarly universe harbors both fair and unfair evaluators.

In our experience it has been quite difficult to identify reviewers knowledgeable in the specific area on which this manuscript is based, that being **DESCRIPTION OF CONTENT AREA**. Thus, we are happy to provide names of reviewers who are knowledgeable in the manuscript's primary area of focus: **NAME OF REVIEWER** (REVIEWER EMAIL), **NAME OF REVIEWER** (REVIEWER EMAIL), and **NAME OF REVIEWER** (REVIEWER EMAIL).

Figure 8.1. Excerpt of cover letter involving selection of evaluators for a manuscript submission.

If you find yourself at a stage in your career in which you encounter uncertainty as to who might provide fair evaluations of your work, then ask your senior colleagues. Ask your mentor. Ask your mentor's collaborators. Start making lists of the "fair evaluators" who come up in those conversations. For each of your submissions, include in your cover letter no more than 2-4 of those evaluators. As you build up submissions and publish more of your work, rotate those evaluators on your cover letters. That is, evaluators vary as to how much time they have available to review your work versus producing their own work. Thus, evaluators may decline to review your paper not because they do not find your work interesting or valuable, but because they simply do not have time. Among fair evaluators on your list, spread them out across manuscript submissions. Spreading out evaluator recommendations increases the likelihood that evaluators you suggest in your cover letter say "yes" to editors' invitations to review your work.

Accept how you react to reviews of your work. Have you ever participated in an event where you had to initiate an action and wait a short while to see the outcome? Playing darts at a local bar or restaurant. Poker with your friends. Placing a wager at a roulette table, purchasing a lottery ticket, or playing pinball at an arcade. Think about how you felt immediately preceding learning the outcome of your efforts. Did you notice your heart racing or some other feeling of intense anticipation? Now, think about a time you felt the game did not work out quite how you expected; how did you react? Did you remain calm? Did you find yourself remarkably poised and ready for the next round? If so, you have a gift. For the rest of us, our reactions might include a combination of teeth grinding, fist clenching, and inappropriate utterances that hopefully no one in our immediate vicinity heard.

Your reaction to a decision letter about your manuscript

includes the same kinds of thoughts, feelings, and behaviors that people display at roulette or poker tables. You might notice a sharp increase in your heart rate as you open your browser and the email containing the letter sits in your inbox. As you read the letter, although you react in some of the same ways one reacts at a poker table, your reaction is quite a bit more intense. Indeed, with a decision letter you waited not minutes for the outcome, but weeks or months. All of the ways in which we react to the news from a decision letter often come devoid of rationality. Indeed, even when an editor transmits a letter that includes an R&R invite, it's still difficult to absorb because an R&R invite translates to more work until you see a letter of acceptance.

Perhaps a worse outcome: What if you find that commentary within the R&R invite not only requires a lot of work to address, but also some of the commentary comes off as unnecessarily harsh? You might benefit from an example of these kinds of comments. Take a gander at some of the highlighted comments of the decision letter linked to the third row of Table 8.1. These comments came from an R&R decision letter on a manuscript that my co-authors and I submitted to *Journal of Youth and Adolescence*. A revised version of this manuscript eventually graced the pages of this same journal (De Los Reyes, Goodman, Kliewer, Reid-Quiñones, 2010). Yet, you might think it had not stood a chance at publication based on comments from Reviewer 2 (see Figure 8.2). Not only did their commentary affirm various "reviewer memes" (e.g., http://bit.ly/ECRToolboxChapter8ReviewerMeme), Reviewer 2 literally told our team that the Introduction section of our manuscript "absolutely misses the boat." Reviewer 2 even admitted to the editor that they did not read the whole manuscript. How might you react to receiving an evaluation like this? I showed you this extreme example to highlight the need to remain mindful of your emotional reactions to receiving commentary from evaluators

First, although the study does address important issues and addresses relevant literature, the study fails to engage literature relating to the adolescent period. In this regard, the manuscript absolutely misses the boat. A look at its references reveals no focus at all on Effects. Given these, it is really difficult to be convinced that the proposed manuscript is making an important, original contribution since the authors themselves have not bothered to examine relevant literature.

Second, although the literature review is interesting, it is quite lacking not just in the substantive content relating to the research areas (see above) but also in terms of what a literature review is supposed to do. It is supposed to give readers a sense of the field, address key variables that will be studied, and then lead to testable hypotheses. The current paper does not do that. In addition to the content issues reported above, there would need to be research presented relating to the group that is studied (high risk neighborhoods). In short, the literature review should be closely tied to the hypotheses, data/methods. The current paper simply does not do that.

Given the above issues, I have not read the rest. But, I could not help to take a peek at the discussion. The discussion fails to engage relevant literature.

Figure 8.2. **Excerpts of evaluator commentary from a previous manuscript submission.**

Pause after receiving reviews of your work. When you find yourself frustrated by editorial decisions about your work or commentary from evaluators, consider this a normal reaction to not only the effort you put into producing scholarly work, but the time you spent waiting for evaluations about that work. As the title of the previous section stipulates, accept your emotional reactions to these evaluations. At the same time, give yourself some space between reacting to the news and taking action following the news. Indeed, how cool, calm, and collected do you expect to find yourself in the period following receipt of criticism about your scholarly work?

Here is what I do following receipt of an editorial decision, and I suggest you do the same: Peek at the decision, and let it sit. That is, you waited all this time to receive word about a decision on your manuscript submission. Alleviate the suspense and just skim down to the place where the editor communicates their decision about your submission. Regardless of the outcome, just let the message rest in your inbox before preparing your next steps. When you are ready to proceed, the fourth row of Table 8.1 provides you with the manuscript and decision letter that serves as the foundation for the Modeling Moments below. Incidentally, Anonymous Account 8.2 notes that "peek and let it sit" is a tool that many others use.

Anonymous Account 8.2. Constructive Feedback	
Doctoral Student	One of the best pieces of advice for success in academia that I have received is to "give yourself a day (or two) to mourn" when a paper is rejected. This has been especially important for me when I receive unnecessarily unkind comments from reviewers. Although my initial reaction is typically a mix of anger, frustration, and sadness, I try to remind myself that a rude comment from a reviewer, or a rejection in general, is not a reflection of my own abilities or my future success in academia. I allow myself to be disappointed for a day or so and, once that passes, I re-read the reviewer comments and often notice all of the useful and constructive feedback that I have received. Once I am feeling less upset about my rejection, I often notice that the useful feedback outnumbers and outweighs the hurtful comments. This makes me feel hopeful about the prospects of publication once I improve my paper and go through the peer review process again.

Begin with your cover letter. Implementing the "peek and let it sit" tool involves waiting a few days to react to the editor's decision on your submission, and withholding action. If you used this tool, by now you returned to the decision letter to begin working on the revision to the manuscript. For those decisions where you receive an R&R invite, I designed the next few tools for battling through the revision process on the path to acceptance. As you "suit up" for battle, don't add anything to that manuscript just yet. Remember, this is one battle of attrition among many. Each of these battles are dictated, in part, by your will or motivation to push on despite adversity. Equally important is your ability to strategize your approach to combat. On the battlefield, the general who leads their troops into battle without a firm grasp of the terrain is a general begging to lose their troops. So, a general enters battle with a "military map" that includes precise information about such aspects of the battlefield as enemy bases and other areas of strategic value (United States Marine Corps, 2015). On the peer review battlefield, your map is the cover letter that accompanies the revised manuscript that you send back to the editor.

On the fifth row of Table 8.1, I included a template my laboratory uses to prepare cover letters for R&R invites. Recall that the cover letter for a first submission focuses on providing the editor with the names of evaluators who might provide a fair review of your work. In contrast, the cover letter for an R&R submission focuses on how you revised your manuscript in response to the previous round of commentary provided by the editor and evaluators. As you begin the revision process of your manuscript, use the cover letter to create a "to-do list" of changes you have to make to satisfy concerns raised in the previous round of commentary (see Figure 8.3). Ascribe a number to each comment made by the editor and each of the evaluators, even if they themselves did not use numbers to itemize their responses. As we learn with the next tool on the list in Table 8.1, itemizing comments facilitates creating a plan for addressing them in a timely, efficient manner. Further, sometimes two evaluators actually raise the same critique. When this happens, you might be able to tackle two critiques with one response. Thus, numbering the comments in your R&R cover letters allows you to reference your response to a previously identified critique (e.g., see Reviewer 2, Comment #4). Additionally, sometimes evaluators provide discrepant comments that you cannot address in the same revised manuscript (more on this in Chapter 9). Numbering comments in the cover letter facilitates pointing out to the editor these discrepant comments.

Dear Dr. **XXXX**:

    Thank you for the positive feedback regarding our manuscript, "TITLE". We are very pleased that you have invited this manuscript for revision and resubmission to the *JOURNAL* for review. We are also very grateful for your helpful suggestions and those of the reviewers. Indeed, the comments allowed us to carefully rethink SOME STUFF, OTHER STUFF, and STILL OTHER STUFF. **Specifically, we have…. Further, we have….** We have highlighted in yellow all of the text revisions. Permit us to describe our revisions and their scope:

Editorial Commentary	**Reviewer 1**	**Reviewer 2**
1. COMMENT:	1. COMMENT:	1. COMMENT:
a. RESPONSE:	a. RESPONSE:	a. RESPONSE:

Figure 8.3. **Cover letter template for manuscripts invited for revision and resubmission.**

On the R&R cover letter template, you will see color-coded lines for comments—word-for-word quotations of concerns raised by an evaluator—and for responses you make to each comment. Responses consist of a summary of how you addressed the specific concerns raised by the comment to which it is linked. As a first step in preparing for your R&R battle, map out the battlefield terrain, and fill in the template with all of the comments you must address before submitting your revised manuscript back to the editor for further evaluation.

Plan a revision schedule. In Chapter 2, I provided you with a brief origin story of my start in the professional development space (De Los Reyes, 2018a). Recall that the key source of inspiration for this work came from reading Silvia's (2007, 2018) *How to Write a Lot*, and constructing my own writing time. I use this built-in, daily writing space to get much of my scholarly work crossed off my agenda. This approach works wonders for R&R invites.

An illustrative example may be helpful. Let's say it's near the end of the summer, and right before the beginning of the fall semester at my home institution, the University of Maryland at College Park. Immediately preceding the first day of classes (this typically falls near the end of August), I receive a long-awaited decision letter for one of my manuscripts. Following receipt of the letter, my inner monologue might flow accordingly:

- *It's an R&R invite, awesome!*
- *Wait, my class starts tomorrow, did I have to get this letter now, seriously?*
- *The submission system said that the reviews have been complete since the end of July!*
- *Why did the editor take so long to make a decision?*
- *Now I have to do this R&R, plus teach, hold weekly meetings with students, serve on committees, create that presentation for the conference in November, and oh yeah, no pressure, but that grant has to go out at the beginning of October!*

In any event, I get the decision letter, and yes, the timing sucks but at least it's an R&R. I wait a few days and on August 31st, I draft out my cover letter comments. Armed with my writing time, I make a deal with myself: *Address one itemized comment on my cover letter per day of writing time.* Do the math. If September 1st falls on a Monday, by happy hour on Friday of that same week I've vanquished five comments. What if in total, the R&R invite involves addressing 30 comments across the editor and evaluators? I'm done in six weeks. In my discipline, most of these R&R invites provide me with 60-90 days to resubmit the manuscript for further review. In particular, you receive a timeline like this if the editor decides that the manuscript needs considerable work; what an editor deems as an R&R invite with suggestions for "major revisions." Typically, having to address 30 comments puts your manuscript in the "major revisions club." Thus, even facing considerable work for an R&R invite, using an "address one comment per day" rule allows sufficient time for: (a) completing a revised manuscript draft and cover letter; (b) re-reading and editing the manuscript and letter; and (c) when applicable, requesting commentary from co-authors on the R&R manuscript. In short, the combination of preparing your cover letter as a "to-do list" and developing a daily regimen for addressing R&R commentary sets the stage for a streamlined, time-efficient revision of your work.

Empathize with your evaluators. We have yet to address the issue of payment. That is, all throughout the evaluation process of your work, several colleagues in your scholarly universe spent precious hours of their time reading your work, thinking about its place in the universe, and determining whether it rises to the quality necessary to disseminate it in published form. When do you plan to compensate them for their time and efforts? The answer is: You won't. In submitting your work for evaluation, you essentially receive *pro bono* advice from your colleagues on how to improve the quality of your scholarly work.

You optimize the value of advice from evaluators insofar as you empathize with them. That is, you know that your evaluators provide you advice on your work at no cost. Your job at the R&R stage is to make it easy for your evaluators to serve in their advisory roles. Look at the two links located in the seventh row of Table 8.1. For each evaluator comment, the cover letter includes information on the page number in the manuscript containing the revision that addressed that comment (see Figure 8.4). Further, near the end of the opening paragraph of the cover letter, on page 1, you will find this statement: *"We have highlighted in yellow all of the text revisions."* The revised manuscript also includes highlighted text to indicate exactly which portions of the manuscript underwent revisions to address evaluators' concerns with the previous submission. In sum, if you incorporate these practices into your R&R process, you will increase (a) transparency in the review process; (b) certainty among those involved that you take the review process seriously; and (c) convenience for the editor and evaluators in detecting revisions designed to address the previous round of commentary.

On p. 3, the authors note that "In the transition from childhood to adolescence, youth increasingly spend time outside of the home (Ingersoll, 1989)." They follow this point with the assertion that "In line with this transition, a key target for assessing and treating adolescent social anxiety involves maladaptive reactions to interacting with unfamiliar peers (Beidel, Rao, Scharfstein, Wong & Alfano, 2010)." It would be helpful if they went a bit further to demonstrate that the increased time children/adolescents spend outside the home is spent with others who are not already friends. As a parent and observer in 2018 (read: not an expert on adolescence or emerging adulthood, and not in 1989), I have noted a major trend for families to handle after-school hours for children by arranging activities with known acquaintances as opposed to allowing/encouraging their children to simply "go play" with others at some playground, park, etc., where they are likely to engage unfamiliar peers. I offer this suggestion mainly to encourage the authors to bolster what appears to be one of the authors' major bases for the current study's design of focusing on social anxiety experienced with unfamiliar peers.

a. RESPONSE: Page 3. We provide additional support for the ideas noted by Reviewer 2:
    i. "In fact, entire bodies of work on adolescent development focus on how this transition among adolescents to more time spent outside of the home (i.e., relative to younger children) often results in parents having relatively little knowledge of adolescents' whereabouts, activities, and peer associations (i.e., parental monitoring; for reviews, see Racz & McMahon, 2011; Smetana, 2008)."

Figure 8.4. **Example of cover letter response to evaluator commentary.**

Make all possible revisions. As I began describing cover letters for R&R submissions, you might have asked, *"Don't you have to remind the editor which scholars can provide fair evaluations of your work?"* No you do not. Recall from Chapter 7 that one of the peer review system's key structural barriers is that of relatively low inter-rater reliability. Further, one cannot count on commentary from one evaluation at one publication outlet "setting up" a revised manuscript for success at another outlet. Indeed, publication outlets each have their own editor, and thus the specific evaluators editors choose likely differ across these outlets. The R&R process represents the rare exception to these peer review practices. As such, the R&R process provides a key structural support to the peer review system. Specifically, when evaluating a particular manuscript for publication, editors tend to use the same evaluators from the start of the review process to its end. What this means is that an R&R manuscript benefits from stability in identification of evaluators. If the evaluators remain constant, the inter-rater reliability from submission to submission of the revised manuscript should increase as a result.

If evaluators remain constant during the R&R process of your manuscript, your toolbox must include tools for keeping your evaluators happy. From submission to submission, you want these evaluators at each point in their commentary to say something like, *"I appreciate that the authors were responsive to my concerns."* When evaluators make comments like this, it signals to the editor that you remain committed to improving the quality of your work; you're helping the peer review system perform its key function. In fact, at their core the template and example cover letters referenced in Table 8.1 exhibit a commitment to full transparency in the review process. Through your cover letter you communicate to the evaluators that (a) you read their comments and (b) you took concrete steps to address their comments. In fact, with only rare exception you should revise your manuscript such that the finished product directly addresses each and every comment you received on the previously submitted version.

Your cover letter typically serves to direct the editor and evaluators to descriptions of revisions you made to the manuscript. Sometimes you encounter circumstances in which you find yourself unable to address one or more of an evaluator's comments. Perhaps your manuscript reports findings of empirical work, and the evaluator suggests a new statistical test or additional experiments that for whatever reason you cannot perform. Perhaps an evaluator fundamentally disagrees with the conceptual frame of your work, or otherwise an element of your work that you might be unwilling to revise. Here, your cover letter serves one additional, crucial function: to argue why, after carefully considering a particular comment made by an evaluator, you cannot revise the manuscript in line with that comment.

The cover letter linked to the eighth row of Table 8.1 includes a few examples of how to strike a compromise between an evaluator's comment and your inability to address the comment. By "compromise" I mean that the manuscript to which the cover letter refers reported findings from empirical work stemming from a larger study. In this manuscript, we were unable to change key elements of the larger study. These elements were "baked into" the manuscript. We could not revise these elements *post-hoc*. Yet, one of the evaluators highlighted these elements as important limitations of our work. Thus, the best we could do is acknowledge these limitations where appropriate; in this case the Discussion section of the manuscript.

If you find yourself having to take this compromise approach when addressing commentary, one more strategic element warrants comment. Specifically, evaluators value being listened to and validated for the comments they make. Perhaps the best you can do is acknowledge in the revised manuscript that a comment an evaluator made reflects a limitation of your work. If so, one way to make the evaluator value your work even more involves describing how future work examining the topics covered in your manuscript might address or avoid this limitation. In this way, not only have you attended to the evaluator's concern, you go a step further: You highlight ways to improve the quality of future work in your area of scholarship.

One caveat with this discussion has to do with the discretion editors have in selecting evaluators for future R&R submissions of a manuscript. That is, within the R&R process for a particular manuscript, editors do not make a binding agreement with authors to select the same evaluators throughout the process. Sometimes editors look for "second opinions" on revised manuscripts depending on commentary from the previous round of reviews. Perhaps the evaluators on the first submission compose very discrepant reviews, and the editor looks outside the original set of evaluators for additional input. Other times, an editor solicits commentary from the same evaluators on the previous submission but one or more of them decline to evaluate the revised submission. In any event, be wary of exceptions to the general rules that editors follow when soliciting reviews on revised versions of R&R manuscripts.

Seek advice on handling tricky comments. Building on previously discussed tools, let us suppose that you find yourself very close to addressing all of the commentary from the editor and evaluators. However, you have a "straggler" comment about which you feel uncertain. Perhaps you have yet to devise a plan for addressing the comment. Perhaps you know you cannot address the comment to the evaluator's satisfaction. Importantly, you suspect that a suboptimal response to the comment might constitute a "deal breaker," such that the evaluator might not ultimately recommend acceptance of your work for publication.

With these circumstances, nothing keeps you from soliciting the advice of others.

For example, you might have a colleague who is not involved in the manuscript but nonetheless might provide some useful advice for how to address the comment. Perhaps the comment falls in their area of expertise. Call them up and solicit their advice. As another example, perhaps after reading the reviews you cannot tell whether one of the comments constitutes a "deal breaker" in the review process. Importantly, the editor decides whether an inability to address a comment constitutes a deal breaker with your manuscript ultimately receiving a notice of acceptance. Commit an adage to memory:

- *Editors accept manuscripts they like.*

If the editor wants to publish your manuscript, they will not let a straggler comment keep them from accepting a high-quality version of it. Thus, contact the editor if you want to know if a comment you cannot successfully address is a deal-breaker comment or alternatively if there is leeway in how you respond to the comment. Lay out your concerns with the comment and the approach you intend to take. Then, ask the editor directly whether you outlined a sound response to the comment. The editor should be able to give you a straight answer. Depending on their response, you know whether to proceed with the revision or to take your business elsewhere.

Develop a keen eye for detail. As part of a group of Emerging Academics reading this book, I suspect that you and fellow readers are keen on advancing your research careers. Thus, please do not take offense at the advice I am about to convey. I cannot stress the importance of submitting work for publication that you have already scrubbed clean of grammatical and typographical errors. You know this already. Yet, I am using this as an opportunity to convey to you how editors and evaluators perceive manuscripts that contain these errors. Put simply, when a manuscript contains grammatical and/or typographical errors, people draw negative inferences about the scholarly work underlying the manuscript. Here is the key thought that runs through my mind when I see a submission that contains these errors: *If the manuscript is sloppy, how can the work that went into it be anything but sloppy?*

For a manuscript reporting empirical work, a sloppy submission signals to editors and evaluators that the authors carried out a poor-quality study. For a paper reporting a narrative review or quantitative review of a scholarly literature, a sloppy submission may signal that the authors' literature search omitted key bodies of work or statistical models that ignored "best practices" in quantitatively synthesizing data coded from studies. In my editorial work, I often include a short paragraph in decision letters for manuscript rejections, for which the rejected work contains these kinds of errors. To avoid comments like these, read and re-read (and re-read) your work before you submit it and cross it off your to-do list:

Finally, although not representing the biggest concern with the manuscript, but certainly a concern reviewers and I encountered, was the number of errors (e.g., references not cited in text, measures noted in tables that were not included in tables, general typographical errors) observed throughout the manuscript. Of course, these issues are clearly addressable in a revision. However, the amount of these present throughout the manuscript undoubtedly raises cause for concern.

Approach peer review as a battle of attrition. During his training for what would become his career-defining victory as a middleweight boxer—against the future Hall of Fame boxer

Thomas "Hitman" Hearns—Marvelous Marvin Hagler wore a red hat with one word across the front in all capital letters: WAR (Rota, 2003). Hagler's training prepared him well for war. Hagler's match with Hearns would become a short—roughly eight minutes in length—but intense affair that some call one of the greatest matches in the history of the sport. Years later during an interview (Rota, 2003), Hagler recalls a thought he had during the match. This thought illustrates an invaluable peer review tool:

> After he hit me with the right hand, I think that was his best shot, and I knew for myself that, [in] order for you to knock me out you better hit me with that ring post because I ain't goin' nowhere.

Conquering the peer review system involves continually reminding the editor that, like Hagler, you too "ain't goin' nowhere." Follow the link on the eleventh row of Table 8.1. That link takes you to the end of one of my cover letters (see Figure 8.5). I end all of my letters with this line: *"Needless to say, we would be quite pleased to make any further revisions."*

> Thank you for the encouragement, support, and feedback that you and the reviewers have provided. Whether the manuscript is ultimately accepted or not, the comments helped us clarify key issues, and allowed us to better convey the study's findings and their contributions to adolescent development. Thank you for considering the manuscript further. We look forward to hearing from you. Needless to say, we would be quite pleased to make any further revisions.

Figure 8.5. **Example of conclusion to cover letter for response to evaluator commentary.**

Whether you find yourself preparing the first revision of a manuscript or the tenth, end the cover letter the same way for both. At all points in the review process, send a strong signal to the editor that you are eager to make any additional revisions they or the evaluators see fit to implement. If an editor knows you plan to persist until the end of the line, they tend to give you the benefit of the doubt. That is, if you are willing to stick it out and revise whatever the editor and evaluators deem necessary, then surely you seek what every other person involved seeks: a finished product of the highest possible quality. If you approach peer review as a battle of attrition, then at some point the system relents, and the editor accepts your work for publication.

Give your time to the peer review system. Evaluators review your work on the path from first submission, through the multiple R&R's, and up to the formal acceptance of your work for publication. They receive these invites to evaluate your work because they are successful academics who editors believe provide fair evaluations of their colleagues' work. If you too encounter success with publishing, at some point editors will begin soliciting your advice about publishing your colleagues' scholarly work. Accepting these invitations will definitely leave you with less time for your own scholarly work. Yet, consider two thoughts. First, your scholarly universe ceases to spin on if you and your colleagues only tend to your own work. Recall in Chapter 7 that academics in your scholarly universe made a tacit agreement to ensure the quality control of work produced in that universe. By construction, the agreement means dedicating time to pursuing your own scholarly work, and also time to serving the greater good and evaluating your colleagues' work.

Second, serving the peer review system improves your own work. In evaluating your colleagues' work, you see great examples of scholarship as well as unacceptably poor examples of scholarship and all examples in between. You learn from other colleagues' approaches to effectively conveying ideas. You also learn about effective as well as ineffective approaches to responding to commentary from evaluators. In the end, the more exposure you receive to the "evaluator side" of the peer review system, the easier it becomes to navigate the system when you subject your own work to peer review. In fact, once you begin publishing your work, nothing keeps you from returning to publication outlets where you have encountered success (or any other outlet within your scholarly universe) and offering your services as an evaluator. Along these lines, here is text for a message to send to an editor:

> Dear Dr. **[editor's name]**, I understand that you are the current editor of **[publication name]**. I wanted to inquire as to the possibility of serving as an ad-hoc reviewer for **[publication name]**. My expertise is in **[describe expertise]**. In case it is helpful, I have attached a current CV to this message. I look forward to hearing from you, and to serving **[publication name]** in any way that you see fit. Sincerely, **[your name]**

Next Steps

We acquired tools for effectively navigating the peer review system when the system functions as it should. These 12 tools prepare you for much of what you will encounter as you navigate the peer review system. However, recall that in Chapter 7 we learned that the peer review system often functions inefficiently and, dare I say, unfairly. Your navigations through the peer review system will undoubtedly take you into choppy, dangerous waters. You need to also acquire tools for getting your work through untoward conditions. Thus, Chapter 9 reveals tools for conquering these exact conditions.

CHAPTER 9

Peer Review Tools When the System Treats You Unfairly

Chapter 8 provided you with combat-ready tools for succeeding in peer review battles that occur on an even playing field, when the system functions as it should. On occasion, you might require tools for fighting your way through peer review battles replete with mudslinging, hits below the belt, and overall destructive behavior. Other times, the peer review system places you in a battle where no one means any harm, but you just find yourself in an unfair set of circumstances. This chapter provides you with combat-ready tools for just these kinds of battles. As Anonymous Account 9.1 reveals in vivid detail, conquering the peer review system requires tools for battling fair and unfair circumstances alike.

> **Anonymous Account 9.1. Harsh Feedback**
>
> **Early Career Faculty**
>
> An Assistant Professor in my department left academia altogether after a promising graduate career, top-notch postdoctoral training, and a great start on the tenure track. The reason: all of the negative feedback. I imagine that in part this is the experience many have when 18 to 22-year-old college students judge your attire, voice, and personal choices. However, it was peer review that was considered the most brutal. Negative reviews can cause one to question their career path, and perhaps even their own knowledge and competence. I actually find revise and resubmit (R&R) invitations in which the editors indicate that they aren't certain you will be able to

address the concerns sufficiently to be the most difficult. In one of my earliest first-author papers, I was thrilled to receive an R&R from a top journal in the field. One reviewer suggested an alternative analytic strategy, and this approach led to a change in the p-values that would be considered statistically significant. Some of the original group differences diminished to a trend-level finding, and when I resubmitted the journal rejected it. I learned at that point that sometimes the work is far from over when the paper is submitted the first time. I have spent far more time on revisions than I have on the original paper draft that was submitted, and that is an important lesson for students to learn too. Revisions may result in rejections, and revisions may be substantial. I still find myself discouraged by long peer reviews, even if they are largely manageable changes. I close the email, sleep on it, and then start drafting a "to do" list the next day (or week). Usually there was a reason you wanted people to know about the work and thus it is almost always worth seeing through to find it a home.

Modeling Moments

As in Chapter 8, training in this chapter consists of a set of Modeling Moments, only now we focus on tools for navigating the peer review system when the system throws unfair obstacles your way. In Table 9.1, I provide a summary description of each tool. Table 9.1 also includes a brief description of materials I use to model implementation of the tool in academic work, as well as links to online materials for you to repurpose for your own scholarly pursuits. This chapter's figures include excerpts of the complete materials accessible via these links, and you can access these and all of the book's downloadable files here: http://bit.ly/ECRToolboxAllDownloads.

Table 9.1. Peer Review Tools to Use When Your Scholarly Universe Treats You Unfairly

Tool	Description	Modeling Moment Material	Online Access to Material
Point out discrepant comments to the editor	Highlight for the editor discrepant comments from reviewers	Example of how I address discrepant commentary in a cover letter outlining revisions for a recently evaluated manuscript	—
Alert the editor to harsh reviews	If you find an evaluator to be unnecessarily caustic in tone, alert the editor	Example of correspondence I sent an editor and the follow-up cover letter responding to evaluator commentary	http://bit.ly/ECRToolboxChapter9HarshReviewerEmail http://bit.ly/ECRToolboxChapter9HarshReviewerCoverLetter
Avoid biased evaluators	If you identify an evaluator who may harbor biases against you or your scholarly work, respectfully request that they not serve as an evaluator for your manuscript	Template for cover letter requesting "not evaluators" for your submitted work	http://bit.ly/ECRToolboxChapter9CoverLetterNotReviewers

Point out discrepant comments to the editor. In Chapter 7, we learned a great deal about the inner workings of low inter-rater reliability and its ubiquitous presence in peer review. In Chapter 8, we learned that a key element of the R&R process—continuity in the specific evaluators who, from submission to submission, evaluate the "R&R manuscript"—infuses a greater degree of inter-rater reliability than one typically observes in peer review. Nonetheless, R&R's are not completely immune to unreliability. For example, unreliability emerges in an R&R process when two evaluators independently make widely discrepant comments about the same element of the submitted work.

As an example, consider a review of a manuscript reporting findings from an experiment. Reviewer 1 suggests that the authors revise their plan for statistical analyses and recommends a new set of statistical tests. In contrast, Reviewer 2 suggests revisions to the analytic plan but recommends a completely different set of statistical tests than those recommended by Reviewer 1. As an example of how these discrepant comments manifest in the theoretical space, both Reviewers 1 and 2 recommend that you revise the conceptual frame of your work. However, each reviewer advocates for completely distinct "schools of thought" for revising your conceptual frame. In both of these contexts, the author revising the manuscript cannot reconcile the two evaluators' comments via revisions to the manuscript text. At best, revising the manuscript involves addressing one evaluator's comment and not the other.

For these scenarios, the cover letter becomes your key tool for accomplishing two goals. To start, use the cover letter to make clear that this discrepancy in evaluator feedback exists. The editor must know that the two comments result in fundamentally different kinds of revisions. As such, the revised manuscript cannot include material that satisfies both comments. Next, in the cover letter you must diplomatically address the discrepancy. That is, state that you carefully considered both options, but then revised the manuscript in line with one comment and not the other. The text of such a response might look like this, but whichever approach you take, focus on maintaining a respectful stance that validates both of the evaluator's comments:

> Reviewer 1 suggested that I revise the manuscript in line with **[insert description of comment]**. In contrast, Reviewer 2 suggested that I revise the manuscript in line with **[insert description of comment]**. After much thought, I decided to **[insert which comment you decided to address and how you addressed it]**.

Incidentally, another option involves arguing to keep the material highlighted by the reviewers in the manuscript "as is." The previous example deals with choosing to make revisions in line with one of the reviewer's comments, but the same rules apply: You must make a strong argument in the cover letter for why you choose to retain this portion of the manuscript as you intended, despite comments from the reviewers.

Alert the editor to harsh reviews. The last two tools we learn in this chapter deal with battling through, for lack of a better term, "mean reviews." In the second row of Table 9.1, I include two links. These links take you to material relevant to the first set of reviews on a manuscript submission that we eventually published in *Journal of Youth and Adolescence* (De Los Reyes et al., 2010; see also third row of Table 8.1). Recall from our discussion in Chapter 8 that with this set of reviews, Reviewer 2 admitted to the editor that they did not read our entire manuscript, and made several comments that my co-authors and I found to be unconstructive and unnecessarily harsh. Several aspects of Reviewer 2's commentary gave us pause, namely with respect to their tone. Honestly, our team felt pessimistic that we could receive a fair review from an evaluator who used such a tone to communicate their feedback about our work. Importantly, although one would hope reviews like these are low base-rate events, they do happen across many scholarly galaxies. For another example, see the narrative in Anonymous Account 9.2.

Anonymous Account 9.2. Harsh Feedback	
Early Career Faculty	"I fear they have combined apples and oranges (and maybe even bananas and pears)…" This colorful comment was one of many dispersed throughout pages of a harsh review. Researchers often dampen the blow of one harsh review by taking solace in the others—critiques of one persnickety reviewer (likely Reviewer #2) can be drowned out by constructive criticism of other, surely more level-headed reviewers. This was not the case here. All reviewers and the Editor agreed with Dr. Fruit. Here's the Editor's summary comment: "I do wish to point out that their comments pertain to critical aspects of your study, including your theoretical framing, hypothesis development, elements of your study design, data analysis, and the interpretation of the results." Now *that* is a sentence worth rereading. A more direct approach could have been: "every part of your paper sucks." My gut reaction was to abandon ship. The paper felt unsalvageable. But here's the thing. Reviewers are humans, and humans have opinions, and those opinions differ from one another. For this manuscript, four humans converged on the opinion that my paper was a pile of rotting fruit, but this is not to say that these four opinions are generalizable to all the opinions of other humans who might read this paper. So how do you bounce back? My lab has a 48-hour rule with every rejection or revise-resubmit. After we receive the decision letter, we wait 48

hours before typing a word. We have a built-in buffer to dampen our immediate emotional reactions. The power of two days is striking. When the clock strikes 48, we are ready to rock. We use the criticism (and/or rejection) as fuel. Harsh criticisms, though biting, are a gift—they are free advice! (Ask any lawyer how they feel about giving free advice.) It is our responsibility to extract the nuggets of wisdom to improve the quality of the manuscript. Of course we *feel* like the critiques are personal. Academics are deeply tied to their work. And maybe the reviews are personal. But if you respond to them as if they are attacks on your character and ability as a scientist, you are dead in the water. Academia is replete with rejection. Ask any successful researcher to share their ratio of wins to losses. My bet is on ratios hovering around batting averages in baseball. Take your work seriously, not yourself seriously.

With our paper under review at *Journal of Youth and Adolescence* (De Los Reyes et al., 2010), we followed a two-step process to implement a tool for battling what felt to us like an unfair evaluation of our manuscript. First, we sent a correspondence to the editor (see Figure 9.1). We suspected that, because editors handle so many manuscripts at any one time, this editor might not have looked as closely at Reviewer 2's tone as we did. Thus, the correspondence focused on communicating to the editor our keen interest for revising and resubmitting the manuscript for further consideration, but we also sought to highlight the reviewer's tone. To be clear, our intent with raising these concerns was not to remove Reviewer 2 from the process—far from it. With the peer review system as unreliable as it is, the last thing our team wanted to do was have the editor bring another reviewer into the mix. At least with Reviewer 2, we knew what we were getting.

> With regard to the reviewers, we are eager to address their helpful comments. For the most part, we were pleased with the constructive commentary. We believe that by addressing the commentary the result will be a far stronger manuscript than the version initially submitted for consideration.
>
> However, we were quite surprised to see the overall tone of Reviewer 2's commentary. Indeed, much of the commentary was quite incendiary (e.g., "In this regard, the manuscript absolutely misses the boat.") and by the reviewer's own admission, they did not carefully read the manuscript (e.g., "Given the above issues, I have not read the rest."). Finally, Reviewer 2 even went so far as to advocate for a particular editorial decision within their commentary to us (e.g., "The manuscript would need to start the review process from scratch given the severe limitations of the current version."). Needless to say, each of us was quite taken aback and in some respects offended by Reviewer 2's commentary.
>
> In any event, we simply wanted to raise to you our concerns with the manner in which some of the commentary was conveyed to us. We welcome any thoughts that you might have on these issues and thank you very much for your kind and prompt attention to this manuscript. Take care.

Figure 9.1. **Example of email correspondence noting concerns about the fairness of evaluator commentary.**

Soon after sending the correspondence to the editor, the editor asked us if we wished to start the review process over again with a new set of reviewers. We declined this offer. Indeed, we had already received an R&R invite from this editor. Instead, raising these issues with Reviewer 2's tone allowed us to maximize the effectiveness of the second step of our tool.

The second step of our tool reminds me of a memorable line that I encountered near the beginning of President Barack Obama's first term. I read an article detailing the outcome of a public argument between the filmmakers Clint Eastwood and Spike Lee. I cannot recall the origins of the argument. What I can recall was how Lee reacted to a comment Eastwood directed at him. At one point in this public argument, Eastwood stated, "*a guy like him should shut his face*" (Adler, 2008). When a reporter sought a response from Lee, this is what the reporter got: "*I'm going to take the Obama high road.*" Lee refrained from directly responding to Eastwood's disparaging comment. That's the second step of this tool.

If you follow the second link on the second row of Table 9.1, you land on our cover letter in response to the reviews that prompted our email to the editor (see Figure 9.2). Does it not exude the "Obama high road?" Michelle Obama would be proud: When Reviewer 2 goes low, we go high! The second step of this tool involves leading the editor to take Reviewer 2's comments with a grain of salt. To execute this step, refrain from "fighting fire with fire." That's taking the easy way out. It may even hurt your chances at acceptance. If you submit a cover letter that seeks to punch back at Reviewer 2 as hard as they punched at you, the editor sees you in just as negative a light as they likely see Reviewer 2. Instead, taking a diplomatic stance with the revision instills a course correction to the review process. By taking an open stance on revising your work and responding constructively to destructive comments, you greatly improve the likelihood that the editor accepts a revised version of your manuscript for publication.

Reviewer 2

1. We thank Reviewer 2 for noting that our manuscript "has important strengths, not the least of which are its use of strong measures and longitudinal data".

Pages 2-3. We thank Reviewer 2 for pointing us toward articles in the adolescent development literature that speak to issues of informant discrepancies. Indeed, much of the informant discrepancies work conducted in the last 20 years has been done specifically within examinations of parent-adolescent discrepancies in reports of each other's behaviors, as empirical papers cited in past reviews of the literature attest (Achenbach et al., 1987, *Psychological Bulletin*; De Los Reyes & Kazdin, 2005, *Psychological Bulletin*). In light of these comments, rather than cite reviews on the broad topic of informant discrepancies research in child and adolescent assessments, we sought to focus more specifically on citing primary developmental and clinical research studies on informant discrepancies as observed in assessments of adolescents and their families. In so doing, we highlight that the phenomena of informant discrepancies is readily present in the assessment literatures dedicated to the measurement of adolescent behavior, in much the same way as informant discrepancies are observed across the psychological sciences. As Thomas Achenbach (2006) noted in a recent review, the observation of informant discrepancies represents one of the most robust observations in assessments of children, adolescents, and adults.

Figure 9.2. **Example of constructive reply to comments provided by an unnecessarily harsh evaluator.**

Avoid biased evaluators. Tools for responding to harsh reviews greatly facilitate addressing a particular kind of unfair, destructive commentary. It's a tool for battling through unfair commentary on a single piece of scholarly work, and in the context of an editor's R&R invite for that work. The source of destructive commentary might simply stem from transient circumstances. Evaluators are human, they make mistakes, and sometimes an evaluator having a "bad day" accurately reflects the source of these mistakes. Other times, you receive unfair commentary, not because an evaluator had a bad day, but because that evaluator has it in for you. Perhaps that evaluator sees your work as competing against their work, because you each provide accounts about the same scholarly phenomenon that disagree with one another. Perhaps you and the evaluator come from different scholarly galaxies in the same universe, and the commentary reflects struggles between the galaxies that trace back decades. The source of this commentary might even reflect petty factors: Maybe the evaluator just doesn't like you.

The sources of these kinds of commentary do not reflect the quality of your work. Further, when an evaluator's comments stem from one or more of these sources, you should assume that how this evaluator reviews your work would remain stable across multiple submissions of your work. Thus, rater biases best characterize the sources of such commentary. These biases do not go away. Further, they may even go so far as to reflect an evaluator's hope that you go away. Thus, when an evaluator's comments reflect rater biases against you or your scholarly work, your main recourse lies in requesting to the editor who handles your submission to refrain from inviting that evaluator to review your work. You might ask, "*How is making a 'not-evaluator' request possible, aren't reviews anonymous?*" Yes; in fact, under the grand majority of circumstances, the peer review system follows a masked format where the evaluators remain anonymous. Only under rare circumstances do evaluators voluntarily disclose their identity to the authors about whose work they review. Yet, evaluators reveal their identities in ways other than voluntary disclosure. Sometimes they leave fingerprints.

Leveraging this tool involves two steps. First, you must make an educated guess as to the identity of these evaluators. By "educated guess" I mean that the masked nature of these reviews means you make decisions about evaluators' identities under conditions of uncertainty. Further, you don't make these guesses in a court of law; they do not require "proof beyond a reasonable doubt." Rather, these guesses arise from observations you make about reviews you receive, and these observations raise suspicions about whether you can receive a fair review from a specific evaluator. An evaluator leaves fingerprints in many different ways. Some evaluators provide "cite me" commentary: Your work's main fault lies in them not seeing their name enough in your work. Other evaluators provide "I hate your framework, use mine" commentary: They come from a school of thought that differs from yours. In the sciences, still other evaluators provide "I hate your method, use mine" commentary: Key elements of your study design differ from their approach. Each of these fingerprints allow you to narrow down your search, and in some cases, you might identify a not-evaluator with pinpoint accuracy.

The second step in using this tool involves how you request that an editor keep this evaluator from reviewing your work. You must approach this request diplomatically. As I note throughout this book, my success in academia has never been a solo effort. To paraphrase a line from a Beatles song (Lennon & McCartney, 1967): *I get by with a lot of help from my colleagues.* One colleague—they will remain anonymous due to the sensitive nature of the material—proved instrumental in the development of this step of this tool. Early on in my path from Assistant to Associate Professor, I identified one of these evaluators in reviews of my work. After receiving a few reviews of my work, I became certain that this evaluator was involved. I concluded that if this evaluator were involved in all reviews of my work, I would get nothing published. Nothing published would equal no tenure. I resolved myself to ensuring that this evaluator failed in their efforts to get rid of me.

I cannot overstate how important my anonymous colleague was to my career; they literally saved me from a negative end to this difficult battle. I had to open this discussion by telling the colleague who I thought the evaluator was. This colleague validated my assessment of this situation for me: Not only did this colleague tell me this occurs often, but that they too had had one of these evaluators. In doing so, this colleague laid out the active ingredients of the second step in using this tool. The third row of Table 9.1 provides a link to an example cover letter that illustrates use of the tool. To knock a potentially biased evaluator out of the review process for your work, here is what you do in your submission cover letter (see Figure 9.3):

- Identify the evaluator by name;
- Respectfully request that they not serve as a reviewer of the submitted manuscript;
- Tell the editor that you and this evaluator harbor philosophical differences in the approaches you take to topics covered in the submitted manuscript; and
- Place the blame on both sides; state that you yourself may lack objectivity.

Due to scholarly conflicts of interest, I respectfully request that Drs. **XXXX (XXXX)** and **XXXX (XXXX)** not serve as reviewers on this manuscript. The philosophical differences between Drs. **XXXX** and **XXXX** and I prevent any one of us from providing objective evaluations of each other's work. In fact, as a general rule I decline to review any manuscript submitted for publication in which I suspect that either Drs. **XXXX** or **XXXX** are authors on the manuscript.

I am aware that identifying reviewers with a conflict of interest may increase the difficulty in identifying suitable reviewers. Thus, I am happy to provide names of reviewers who are knowledgeable of the manuscript's primary area of focus and can provide a fair evaluation of the work: **XXXX (XXXX)**, **XXXX (XXXX)**, **XXXX (XXXX)**, and **XXXX (XXXX)**.

***Figure 9.3.* Excerpt of cover letter requesting that specific evaluators not be invited to review a manuscript.**

Two elements of this tool warrant comment. The component highlighting philosophical differences highlights to the editor that the concerns raised will not go away. Essentially, you and the evaluator harbor irreconcilable differences in how you each approach the work. The fairest decision here involves honoring your request to divorce this evaluator from the process of reviewing your work. The last element of this tool also factors prominently in the decision-making process. Specifically, your request reveals to the editor your judgment that this evaluator lacks objectivity. What this likely means is that you have such a strong reaction to this evaluator, you too would lack objectivity if you served as a reviewer of the evaluator's work. All of this means that you should acknowledge your own issues with objectivity when making this request.

One final caveat with this tool warrants comment: Use it sparingly. That is, when I use this tool, I typically identify no more than two not-evaluators. The more of these not-evaluators you request in your cover letter, the more the editor may find you to be defensive in reaction to evaluations of your work. To counteract the possibility of the editor perceiving you as defensive, I recommend that you identify several evaluators who might provide fair evaluations of your work (see second row of Table 8.1), in addition to any not-evaluators who you identify.

Persist and Proceed

We spent the last three chapters acquiring tools for navigating the peer review system. In time, your efforts in successfully navigating this system will pay off in multiple pieces of scholarship. Some of these pieces of scholarship may align with your burning question, and some may not. Regardless of the focus of each of these pieces of scholarly work, I promise you that your battles within the peer review system make you a better scholar. I close Act II of the book with some words of motivation, adapted from a set of remarks that I use to end my workshop on peer review (http://bit.ly/ECRToolboxChapter9PersistandProceed; De Los Reyes, 2018b):

Over the years, I have found that the best professional development resources do two things. First, they provide you with tools to apply to your work. Second, they spark a fire inside you; they motivate you to do more. In Act II, we acquired many tools germane to peer review. I want us to conclude Act II with some fire. I begin by citing an excerpt from a poem I greatly enjoy. The following lines appear at the end of the poem *Ulysses* by Tennyson (1833):

> We are not now that strength which in old days
> Moved earth and heaven, that which we are, we are;
> One equal temper of heroic hearts,
> Made weak by time and fate, but strong in will
> To strive, to seek, to find, and not to yield.

In Act II, we learned more about the peer review system and its use in evaluating scholarly work. Academics created this system centuries ago, and the system is as imperfect as those tasked to sustain it. But the system itself reflects the very nature of the scholarship it's tasked to serve. Producing scholarship is hard, full of obstacles, slow, not pretty, and not perfect. It is easy to view the peer review system as a barrier to getting your work out for others to see, to use, to improve the world around them, and to inspire the people who inhabit it. But here is the thing: The best parts of this system also strengthen our scholarship. Each time a scholar subjects their work to evaluation by their peers, the process of revising and finalizing their work hardens their resolve and sharpens their thinking, and both the authors of scholarly work and the peers who review this work become better scholars because of it.

So, when peer review gets to you, remember that you are part of a universe, a universe of scholars, and each scholar goes through the same things you do. And peer review? It is only a system. It doesn't have aspirations, spirit, dreams, drive, grit, or tenacity. You do. This system can never be stronger than you, it can never get the best of you. So long as you persist. So long as you proceed. Books like this exist to give you and other Emerging Academics the tools to become great scholars. For some of you, this book may even help to rekindle that fire inside you that drew you to academia in the first place. In return, all I ask is that when you finish reading this book and return to your work, you push harder than you did before you opened this book. Persist, and proceed. I devote the remainder of this book to describing the tools you need to select, integrate, and synthesize separate pieces of your scholarly record into a research program—a compelling story about your work.

ACT III:
YOUR RESEARCH PROGRAM

CHAPTER 10
Basic Training for the Job Talk

Chapters 10 through 16 detail the inner workings of the Trilogy tool. We first learned about this tool back in Chapter 1 (see Table 1.1). For the remainder of the book, we will focus on how the Trilogy tool applies to delivering academic job talks. Granted, as detailed in Anonymous Accounts 10.1 and 10.2, job applications and indeed job interviews contain many components. More broadly, as you build a scholarly record, the research program that arises from that record originates from a considerable body of material, and surely much more than can be described in a single job talk. That being said, we focus on job talks because this one component of the application allows us to learn about the principles of research programs, all in one self-contained space. These principles generalize to other means for disseminating scholarly work, including conference presentations and scholarly manuscripts. Indeed, during an academic job talk, the speaker seeks the singular objective of describing their research program: a coherent, compelling story about their work. This objective necessitates connecting multiple pieces of work to tell a story that effectively communicates your research program. As a practical matter, these talks weigh heavily in selecting candidates for faculty positions, and they play an integral role in launching a scholar's career. Thus, although we primarily focus on applying the Trilogy tool to job talks, the principles underlying this tool apply to multiple contexts for communicating your research program to your colleagues.

Anonymous Account 10.1. The Job Market

Early Career Faculty

The first time (or sometimes second, or third...) on the job market can be very challenging. It might feel like there are a lot of unspoken rules about how to prepare materials and snag that dream job. Now that I'm on the other side of this process, I can assure you that there's no one right way to organize your materials or prepare for the job market. (Although I think the advice to "start preparing materials earlier than you think you need to" is a good recommendation for everyone.) People may give you well-intentioned advice about steps you absolutely must take (or avoid), but the truth is that there's a lot of randomness and luck involved in the process. There's no shortage of barriers that can make the job market feel overwhelming and unpredictable, and maybe even a little hopeless. Given these challenges, I recommend finding ways to give yourself "the illusion of control." There are some things you can manage: You can create sparkling materials that highlight what you would bring to the department and why they should consider you for the position. Not sure about how to write a cover letter? Now is the time to use your network (peers, mentors, professors in your department) to get feedback from lots of people—both people in your research area as well as others who may have a different research focus. It's likely that at least one member of the search committee will not be familiar with your specific discipline, so your goal is to simplify your materials just enough so that an educated non-expert hears about your work and thinks, "how cool!" For general advice, the Chronicle and Inside Higher Ed websites have helpful materials. For specific questions, I relied heavily on supportive mentors and friends who had already gone through the process. I've found that this network can provide a great sounding board for your pitch because they know you, your work, and your potential for a productive career. These people can weigh in on questions you might have. "How long was your teaching statement?" "Did you provide any personal details, like why you want to live in that particular town, in your cover letter?" You may find some consensus about the nagging questions you are struggling with. Or, you'll find that everyone has a different opinion, which likely means that the applicant pool will also have lots of variability.

Anonymous Account 10.2. The Job Market

Early Career Faculty

I had not planned to go on the job market when I ultimately did. I was starting year 2 of a 3-year postdoctoral fellowship and had a partner who was not able to move until the end of his own postgrad training. That coupled with an infant meant that I was unable to leave my location for nearly 2 years from the date the job ad came out for what I saw to be a "dream job." I immediately felt excited and sick to my stomach, not knowing how I could pass up the chance to apply to this position but also worrying about what would happen if I did get the offer. I convinced myself that just applying to this one job would not likely result in an offer, and that perhaps I would be able to defer the start date if I was selected. I did get an interview, and during the interview, I was asked whether my preference would be to start a position in the fall or defer my start date. I froze, after I had gotten advice from online resources that departments want you to start right away and not defer. I deflected, saying that I would love to follow through the work I started on my postdoc but understand that there may be an

 immediate need. Thankfully, after I returned I spoke with my postdoc mentor, who had connections within the dream job department. He found out that the department and college saw a deferral as a good thing, and when I ultimately received the job offer and entered negotiations, I could more confidently request a delayed start date.

During a successful job talk, the speaker cogently explains their research program, and does so based on a subset of their scholarly work. As detailed below, a key element of a successful job talk involves the speaker organizing and integrating multiple pieces of scholarly work to tell the most compelling story possible. As you might suspect, the Trilogy tool I describe in this book carries with it some key assumptions about academic job talks. In the past, you might have seen great academic talks that violate the assumptions I describe below. On that point, I agree that not all great academic talks are created equal. That being said, the context in which speakers give academic job talks dictate that, on average, the assumptions I make with the Trilogy tool will result in a talk that allows you to deliver a compelling account of your research program.

The Context Surrounding the Academic Job Talk

Four elements of the context in which speakers give academic job talks facilitate composing your own job talk. I summarize these elements in Figure 10.1. First, your job talk happens after a careful applicant screening. The search committee weeded out applicants who did not meet threshold on key screening criteria: not enough pieces of published scholarship, low-quality scholarship, weak letters of recommendation, programs of scholarship that lacked synergy with other faculty in the department, or applicants for whom the initial phone or videoconference interview did not pan out as well as the search committee had hoped. If a search committee chair gives you a call to let you know that you made it to their "short list" and they would like to invite you for an on-campus interview, you passed their screening criteria.

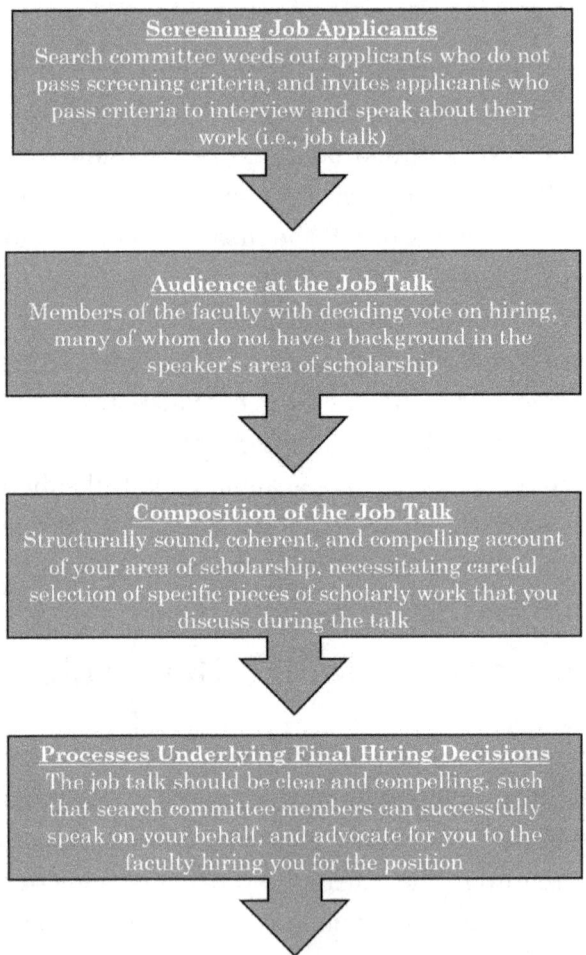

Figure 10.1. **Elements of the context surrounding the academic job talk.**

Passing the screening criteria comprises a very important step in the process. Once you begin composing your job talk, assume that you do not have to emphasize any of the screening criteria. The search committee already knows you are productive enough to join the faculty. They enjoyed reading your letters of recommendation. As a group, they even found your research program interesting. They want to learn more about you. All of these things are true for you, and they are also true for the other candidates interviewing for this faculty position. As you compose your academic job talk, take comfort in knowing that on the screening criteria, you and the rest of the candidates are on similar footing. What this also means is that showing how productive you are in terms of the amount of scholarly work on your record or where you publish your work—high-impact journals on your CV, prestigious companies who published your last book—is a fool's errand. The other candidates have that too. You have to leverage alternative means to outperform other candidates.

Second, the audience receiving your job talk is like the bar scene in *Star Wars* (Kurtz & Lucas, 1977): many scholars, from many different areas of expertise, many of whom have zero background in your area of scholarship. For a diverse audience, you communicate your research program by carefully structuring how you describe your work. To reiterate: Forget about impressing them with productivity; that's not enough. In fact, the "wow with productivity" approach can backfire. I have been on faculty in a Psychology department for about 12 years. You know which talks I find irksome? The talks with the "one-slide studies." If you affiliate with a department in any area of science or engineering, you likely have seen at least one of these talks. A speaker opens their talk with a summary about what they do, and then they begin reeling off a series of studies, each encapsulated in a single slide. Each slide includes a figure or table intended to depict the take-home message of the work. These talks are like scavenger hunts. Look at this study over here, and that one over there, and this one was under a rock in the left-hand corner of the backyard, wow! Not wow. No structure, no story, and within 15 minutes the speaker better hope that everyone in the audience was on a caffeine drip right before the talk. As we get into the academic tools, I will elaborate on what I mean by "structure," but suffice to say that your ability to logically walk the audience down the path of your scholarship is the great equalizer. With the right kind of structure, you can get anyone in the audience, regardless of their background, to understand your academic job talk, and by extension your research program.

Third, composing a structurally sound academic job talk necessitates careful attention, even curation, of the pieces of scholarship you plan to use to describe your research program. What this means is that in the context of the academic job talk, you should focus on how the pieces of scholarship intersect with each other, not the total amount of scholarship you describe during your talk. Indeed, after your interview, the search committee will meet, make decisions on which candidates pass threshold for joining the faculty, and then make decisions on priority or ranking. That is, among those who pass threshold, to whom should we make the offer first to join our faculty? If the structure of your talk translates into a compelling story about your scholarship, then that streamlines the rest of the search committee's discussion about—and advocacy for—hiring you for the faculty position.

A fourth element of the context surrounding academic job talks involves understanding what happens after the talk. To facilitate understanding the post-talk process, pretend the search committee members are about to audition for a film role. They have to learn key lines in a film script that you wrote. However, when they are in the audition room, they aren't auditioning for themselves. They are auditioning on your behalf. In all likelihood, your job talk (i.e., your film script) was the first time they saw a way to articulate your research program to other scholars. After your talk, they have to explain your work clearly to the other faculty, and advocate for hiring you. All they will have to prep for advocating on your behalf are your application materials, and crucially, the key lines they took from your job talk. If your talk clearly articulates your research program and convinces the search committee to advocate for hiring you, they will formulate a plan for achieving that aim. And if you want the search committee to execute a successful plan, then make it easy for them. Your talk should tell a coherent story so that scholars who do not know your work as well as you do have the means to advocate for hiring you.

The Basic Structure of an Academic Job Talk

By now, you might have a sense of what I mean by the "basic structure" of the academic job talk, but in the spirit of demystifying the process, let's take a bit to flesh it out. Kelly Brownell was a professor of mine when I was in graduate school at Yale University; he has since moved on to assume the role of Professor and Director of the World Food Policy Center at Duke University. He was the one who first told me a tried and true adage of public speaking; three straightforward steps: (1) tell them what you are going to say; (2) say it; and (3) summarize what you already said. The academic job talk has an only slightly more complex structure, which I graphically depict in Figure 10.2.

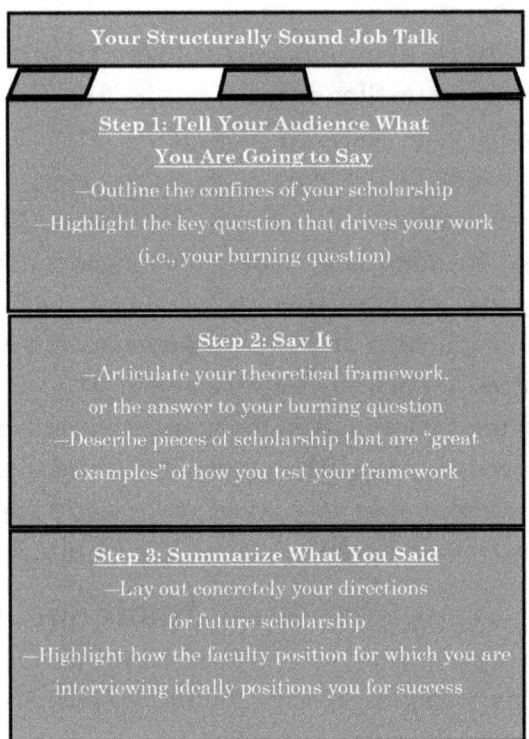

Figure 10.2. **The structure of the academic job talk.**

You begin a well-structured job talk by outlining for the audience the confines of your scholarship. You define key concepts. You make clear what your research program focuses on and what it doesn't. Crucially, you highlight for the audience the burning question we learned about in Chapter 4: the one question that drives your curiosity and motivates your scholarship. This process allows you to logically advance to the next stage of your talk; explaining the theoretical framework that binds your scholarship. We learned about this concept in Chapter 4 as well: Your theoretical framework reflects what you think is the answer to your burning question.

After articulating your theoretical framework, you then

describe for the audience several pieces of scholarly work that you believe are great examples of how you explore key elements of your theoretical framework and by extension, your burning question. As I describe in Chapter 12, we set a concrete value on the number of "great example" pieces of scholarship: three. You read that right: The Trilogy tool I describe in this book requires just three pieces of scholarship to compose a compelling job talk. If your academic record consists of 20 pieces of scholarship, congratulations! Use this book to identify the three pieces that will go into your talk, and the 17 you will ignore as you describe your research program.

Every well-structured academic job talk concludes with a summary of the work discussed during the "say it" portion of the talk, but with a purpose. At the conclusion of your talk, you should make clear to the audience that your academic pursuits are not over. Your "great example" pieces of scholarship mark the beginning of how you will pursue your burning question. You have more work to carry out, more stories to tell. Lay out concretely for your audience where you plan to take your scholarship. Ideally, make clear why the faculty position for which you are interviewing would provide you with an ideal environment to take your scholarship to new heights.

Incidentally, you may have found this discussion of the academic job talk context overwhelming or even frightening. I encourage you to please read on. I am here to demystify academia for you, not scare you away. I hope the next few chapters calm you down, empower you with tools to succeed, and leave you in a safe space to pursue your work. On the topic of "safe spaces," we learn in Chapter 12 that the origin of the Trilogy tool stems from a pretty unlikely source. However, before we get to the Trilogy tool we have one more thing to do. In Chapter 11, I advance to you the rationale for learning the Trilogy tool in the first place.

CHAPTER 11
Selecting Scholarship for the Job Talk

In Chapter 4, we learned about the Shared Universe tool. I designed this tool to function as a conceptual frame for scholarly work produced under the supervision of your mentor. In turn, this frame serves as a foundation on which to map out the path toward your research program. Within this frame, the Emerging Academic's research program resides within the research program of their mentor, and at the same time connects to colleagues whose research programs relate to that of the mentor. Further, this frame conceptualizes the mentor's research program as a galaxy that surrounds a burning question. The mentor's galaxy exists in a scholarly universe of colleagues whose burning questions relate to the mentor's research program. Within the mentor's galaxy, Emerging Academics produce research programs that stem from the burning question that drives the mentor's work. Each of these research programs includes a: (a) burning question that drives the scholarship for that particular program; (b) set of scholarly works stemming from the burning question; and (c) theoretical framework that binds together the burning question and scholarly works. In sum, this conceptualization of mentored scholarship facilitates creating the key components of research programs built within mentoring environments.

At the end of Chapter 4, we encountered our first Modeling Moment. This moment focused on illustrating how to engage an audience at the outset of a talk, particularly with a compelling account of your burning question. The remainder of the book's Modeling Moments focus on how to compose the rest of your talk. Specifically, the Modeling Moments focus on the processes underlying the selection of pieces of scholarship that best represent your approach to studying your burning question. Along these lines, in this chapter I present the rationale for learning the second of our two academic tools, that of Trilogy. This tool facilitates accomplishing some of the aims detailed in Anonymous Account 11.1. The Trilogy tool helps you establish a flow to your talk. It allows you to communicate your research program to audience members of varying backgrounds, in particular those whose areas of expertise differ from your own.

Anonymous Account 11.1. The Job Talk

Early Career Faculty

Academia is a strange path, in that you're continually tasked with hurdles you never get trained to jump. The job talk is one of those hurdles. I found myself frustrated by the conflict between past, grad school expectancies—"Produce as much quality work as you can! Collaborate with lots of people! Expand your skills and interests!"—to the primary task in a job talk: "Distill your research to one, *maybe* two main ideas with important implications for the field, in order to appear simultaneously laser-focused, friendly, and highly fundable." My first mistake was spending more time dwelling on the intra-system contradictions than on actually preparing my talk. This felt cathartic for the first five minutes, but became very unhelpful very fast after that. Ultimately, I attribute the talk I eventually created to three main sources of guidance:

- I attended as many talks as I could as a graduate student, whether or not they related to my area of study, and paid attention to faculty members' responses to each one. Which talks went over well and not well? Which ones did I find exciting and why? Paying attention to these kinds of questions

helped me identify characteristics of talks more and less likely to 'land' well.
- I ran job talk outlines by mentors *other* than my primary faculty advisor. Getting feedback on the flow—and the extent to which I focused on the goals of my research program versus specific studies versus future directions—was incredibly instructive.
- Once I put a talk together, I practiced. A lot, for as many people as would listen. This included folks who were highly familiar with my work *and* for colleagues with Ph.D.'s in totally different disciplines. This practice helped me make sure my talk made sense—and was interesting!—to audiences with varied disciplinary backgrounds. I had the talk pretty much memorized by the time I was actually giving it. (This proved to be very helpful, because technology setups differed across campuses, and I didn't always have access to my notes!)

I designed the Trilogy tool to fit your lived experiences as an Emerging Academic and the circumstances surrounding your scholarly work. In fact, the Trilogy tool and Shared Universe tool complement each other. Each tool addresses challenges with applying the other tool. Indeed, how might an Emerging Academic compose a research program if they cannot conceptualize the circumstances that surround creating scholarly work with a mentor? There is a reason why we learned about shared universes before learning about trilogies.

Now you know that your scholarly work exists in an interconnected mentoring environment, and your task is to build a research program within this environment. You battled your way through the peer review system several times. You now find yourself at a point where you have produced several pieces of scholarly work. What remains unclear is the journey toward fusing your work into a research program that not only makes sense to you but also to other people. I designed the Trilogy tool to demystify this point in your journey. Here lies the challenge: As an Emerging Academic, you have but a few years to produce scholarship of any kind, let alone scholarship that you can organize into a compelling research program. Further, because your work occurs within the context of a mentoring relationship with a relatively more experienced academic, you might encounter challenges with composing a coherent research program.

Normally, Emerging Academics' experiences with scholarship involve producing work at the discretion of mentors who themselves have research programs. The mentoring relationship often constrains an Emerging Academic's work toward a narrow topic area within the confines of their mentor's research program. However, the opposite might occur. For example, some Emerging Academics might train with mentors who find themselves in a transition period of their scholarship. These mentors might seek to expand their work to new frontiers, but these frontiers remain uncertain. In this environment, an Emerging Academic might find that their topics of scholarship bounce around until the new frontier emerges. Such a process might take years to unfold, creating time constraints on the part of the Emerging Academic and the development of their own research program. Sometimes Emerging Academics self-select into "bouncing around" during their training, and produce pieces of scholarly work across a variety of burning questions. This process likely results in multiple pieces of scholarly work that have few discernable links to one another, an experience detailed in Anonymous Account 11.2.

> **Anonymous Account 11.2. The Job Talk**
>
> *Early Career Faculty*
>
> In graduate school, "narrowing down" on a specific research line was much less alluring than "opening up" to learning about new topics that seemed interesting to me. Thus, when I was preparing a job talk, I found it difficult to weave my various research experiences together with one common "thread." I developed a talk that focused on the projects that were most consistent with the work I planned to do in the future and then I practiced the talk (many, many times) in front of different audiences. Each time, I asked the audience to summarize my main research area and to tell me which parts of the talk were confusing or interesting. This feedback helped me to understand how well I was conveying my research interests and to hone down on the specific studies that were most engaging and memorable to the audience. In my later practice rounds, I began recording the talk, which helped me with time management and with feeling more comfortable and confident in delivery.

Other times, an Emerging Academic's training occurs within a specific line of the mentor's research. However, that line of research already includes many other Emerging Academics in the mentor's galaxy. For example, in many disciplines or broader fields Emerging Academics—in addition to their own independent scholarship—have to allocate time for "team scholarship." This form of scholarship might stem from a larger study run out of the mentoring environment. An example might include a grant-funded investigation run out of a mentor's large laboratory. These studies often take years, sometimes decades, to complete. Additionally, scholarship produced within these larger grant-funded studies might only tangentially relate to the research programs that any of the Emerging Academics involved in the studies eventually develop.

I highlight examples of mentoring environments that many Emerging Academics encounter because they speak to larger issues in mentored scholarship, namely control and time. As an Emerging Academic, you often have relatively little control over the confines of your scholarship. Over a relatively short time period, it's the mentoring environment that dictates whether the products of your scholarly work widen or narrow in scope. However, these constraints in both time and control do not dictate an inability to create a compelling research program—far from it. What these constraints reveal is the need to leverage tools that allow you to describe your research program with as few pieces of work as possible.

The Context Surrounding the Academic Job Talk, Revisited

To understand the minimum pieces of scholarship necessary to produce a compelling research program, we will return to themes discussed in Chapter 10, namely with regard to the context of the academic job talk. As mentioned previously, the audience at an academic job talk includes faculty members of the department or campus unit to which the job candidate applied to join. These faculty will ultimately decide whether the job candidate's scholarship passes threshold for hiring them onto the faculty. These decisions directly relate to how search committee members consume the work discussed by the job candidates interviewing for the faculty position. These search committee members review job applications, consume each interview candidate's job talk, and then based on this information, form a plan for advocating on behalf of the job candidate(s) they wish to hire. In Chapter 10 we reviewed the process that search committee members follow to screen job applicants and identify candidates to invite for on-campus interviews and academic job talks. After these screening and interview processes, the search committee members compose a plan to make hiring recommendations and present these recommendations for the full faculty to consider and cast a vote.

One element of this process that we have yet to consider in-depth involves the selection of scholarship to include in an academic job talk. Remember that in Chapter 10 I set a concrete value on the number of pieces of scholarship to incorporate into the talk—three. Setting this value on amount of scholarship has to do with key features of the context surrounding the academic job talk. In fact, beyond your ability to describe your research program, the audience of faculty at your talk will draw a variety of inferences about your approach to scholarship (Figure 11.1).

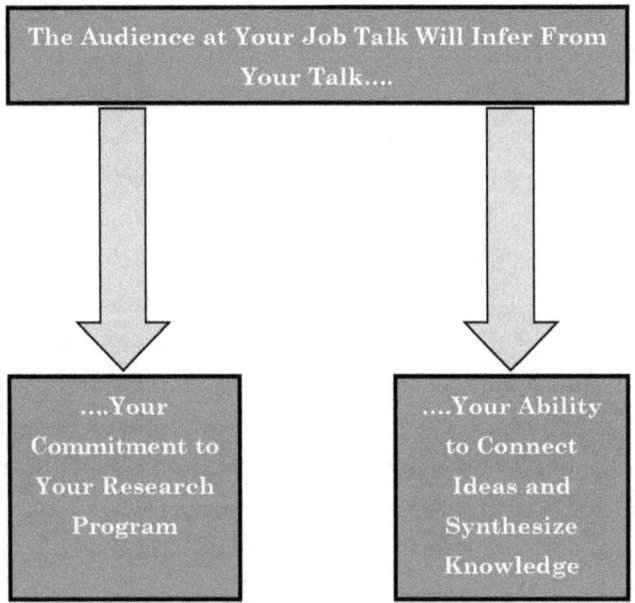

Figure 11.1. Inferences your audience will draw from your job talk.

At the broadest level, the audience will judge your commitment to your research program. Do you plan to stick to this research program, through good times and bad? The faculty at a job talk know the inherent difficulty in not only developing a research program, but also maintaining it. Your manuscript submissions will often encounter rejection. Your grant applications will often not receive funding. The faculty understand that academics undergo relentless exposures to failure. Thus, your talk has to have some history behind it. Chart a trajectory of work that allows you to demonstrate to the audience that with your research program, you are in it for the long haul.

To demonstrate your commitment to your research program, your talk must include, at minimum, more than one piece of scholarship. Another reason for including more than one piece of scholarship stems from a second inference the audience will draw from your talk. Faculty in the audience will infer from your talk the degree to which you can connect ideas and synthesize knowledge. Academics apply these tools to perform a number of core academic tasks, and as a member of the faculty you will be expected to perform them as well. At many job interviews, faculty will not have access to examples of how you carry out these tasks, and so they will use your talk to estimate your ability to carry out tasks that require connecting ideas and synthesizing knowledge.

What are some of the academic tasks that require connecting ideas and synthesizing knowledge? To work effectively in the classroom, an instructor needs to distill key principles from coursework readings, and deliver these principles to students for the purposes of critical thinking, consumption, and deliberation. Mentoring doctoral students involves teaching students how to dive into a body of literature. They need to understand the key themes in that literature well enough to develop scholarship—scholarship that incrementally contributes to that literature.

One cannot lead a class lecture or mentor doctoral students in their scholarly work if they cannot synthesize knowledge from disparate sources (i.e., multiple pieces of scholarship). Faculty at a job talk make judgments as to whether the speaker has acquired this tool. Do you know who has acquired this tool and wields it to an impressive degree? The author of Anonymous Account 11.3. Focus on this scholar's approach to synthesis and storytelling. In particular, review how they connect disparate scholarly works to their burning question. Study their methods for "test driving" their stories with people who have little background in their work. Without ever seeing this scholar in the classroom, I can guess that the students in their classroom can follow and comprehend the lectures they deliver in class.

Anonymous Account 11.3. The Job Talk	
Early Career Faculty	Academics are bludgeoned with the advice to "tell a story." It's good advice—people enjoy hearing stories and they help with memory—but I frequently ask myself "what *is* the story am I trying to tell?" For job talks, the pressure to craft a compelling story is magnified. People want to know the researcher you are and the researcher that you are to become. While I was preparing my job talk, I spent a lot of time pondering my "story." In truth, I worked on a lot of random projects in grad school. My CV spans several topics, methodologies, and populations. Breadth is good; too much breadth is not. I was right on that border. I knew much of my "story" would be post-hoc narration. Heeding the advice of a wise mentor, my goal was to boil down my research program to a single sentence (specifically, a question my research tries to answer). Two things helped me get there. • **Draw bubbles (preferably outside).** Researchers get trapped in restrictive spaces. We are trained to follow linear paths: idea generation, hypotheses, study

execution, and so on. We usually do this at our desk in front of our computers. When crafting your story, go outside (no excuses—I did this in Boston in January) and draw out a conceptual map of your research. Which topics do you study? Which projects fall into which topics? How does one project build on the next? Eventually, the smattering of bubbles and arrows and words will start to take shape.
- **Talk to strangers.** Most of the audience during your job talk will not be familiar with the topics you study. Your job is to talk to them like humans, not researchers. Use language someone with no training in your discipline would understand. One way to tell if you've sufficiently trimmed your jargon is to talk to strangers about what you study. I had several flights scheduled while I was preparing for my job talk. Apologies to my travel weary middle seat companions, but on each flight, I tried to strike up a conversation that led us to discussing what we do for work (not difficult in our culture, fortunately or not). When they asked, I tried to describe my research in three sentences that anyone would understand. I failed most of the time. I rambled. I clammed up. I relied on academic terms that have little to no meaning to 99.97% of humanity. Most conversations were awkward. But getting these kinks out on the streets helped smooth out my story and distill language I eventually used in my talk.

At this point, I ought to mention that a speaker might reveal an inability to synthesize knowledge if they include too much scholarship in a job talk. Do you recall that "one-slide studies" speaker from Chapter 10? The "not wow" speaker? Speakers who follow this approach tend to include many, many studies. At the same time, their talks often fail to connect those studies to form a coherent story. The one-slide studies approach typically results in a double-whammy of both T.M.I (too much information) and T.L.S. (too little story). Consequently, the Trilogy tool facilitates composing a job talk—and by extension a research program—that avoids problems arising from too few and too many pieces of scholarly work.

How the Trilogy Tool "Fits" Into Your Research Program

In building your research program, curation of pieces of scholarship should remain paramount. Too little scholarship and the faculty might have insufficient data to judge your commitment to your research program. Too much scholarship and the faculty might experience information overload at best, and at worst, they might judge you incapable of synthesizing knowledge across multiple sources. What this means is that your research program has to land on a "Goldilocks zone" of scholarship. In astrobiology, the Goldilocks zone—technically the habitable zone—consists of the array of orbits around a star that a planet might follow which, given the appropriate atmospheric pressure, results in a planetary surface that allows for the presence of liquid water (Huang, 1959; Kopparapu, 2013). Your research program's Goldilocks zone is that "just right" amount of scholarly work that allows you to tell a compelling story about your work, without the need to have a couple decades' worth of scholarship under your belt to tell that story. How do you ensure that your research program sits in that Goldilocks zone? By learning our Trilogy tool. If you have been to the theater in the last several decades, the Trilogy tool will definitely carry a ring of familiarity for you. We are about to embark on the last leg of our journey toward composing a compelling research program that fits your lived experiences as an Emerging Academic. It is time to come back to Earth. You have a trilogy to produce!

CHAPTER 12
The Trilogy Tool

Sixty-four: the number of Academy Awards® ceremonies held by the Academy of Motion Picture Arts and Sciences, before the producers of a horror film—*The Silence of the Lambs* (Bozman, Saxon, Utt, & Demme, 1991)—received the award for *Best Picture* (Academy of Motion Picture Arts and Sciences, 2019). Horror films seldom receive recognition. Yet, some filmmakers in the horror film genre know plenty about telling compelling stories. In fact, I drew inspiration for the Trilogy tool from a master storyteller in this genre: Wes Craven. We begin this chapter by reviewing Craven's *bona fides* as a storyteller. We then use elements of his storytelling background and approach to reveal guidelines for building your research program.

A Storytelling Philosophy So Like Your Own

Are you familiar with the term *polymath*? Before preparing this book, I knew about the gendered version of this term, *Renaissance man*, but in any event the term polymath refers to "[a] person of wide knowledge or learning" (Oxford, 2019). Among horror filmmakers, the late Wes Craven came as close as one could to living like a polymath. Craven first discovered a calling for filmmaking while on faculty at Clarkson College, where he taught courses on such subjects as Drama, Art, Literature, and English (Wooley, 2011). He built an expertise in these areas based on his graduate work at Johns Hopkins University—where he earned a Master's of Arts in Philosophy and Writing—and his undergraduate work at Wheaton College, where he earned a Bachelor of Arts with a double major in English and Psychology. Craven's educational background reveals a profile of someone who appears ill-prepared to devote a

195

career to writing, directing, and producing horror films. Yet, this background serves as a firm foundation for masterful storytelling. To tell compelling stories is to understand how people behave and how they react to stories. Craven's undergraduate coursework in Psychology likely facilitated his developing a profound insight into how people behave in group settings, like theaters. Craven's films reveal a deep appreciation for not only the power of captivating stories, but also the symbiotic relationship between the story and the audience bearing witness to it. In particular, Craven understood that the audience that consumes horror films does so with a great deal of agency. Audience members do not merely watch a horror film; they interact with it. In some ways, audience members bond with the other people watching the film, an idea clearly demonstrated in an excerpt from an interview of Craven by Walkuski (2013):

> I think the experience of going to a theater and seeing a movie with a lot of people is still part of the transformational power of the film....if you scream and everyone else in the audience screams, you realize that your fears are not just within yourself, they're in other people as well, and that's strangely releasing.

Two key elements underlying Craven's insight—indeed, his storytelling philosophy—have direct relevance to your use of the Trilogy tool when composing your research program. First, you are the storyteller at your job talk. To tell a compelling story is to evoke emotions from your audience. An academic job talk should evoke positive emotions from the audience. When faculty in the audience react positively to your talk, they engage in critical thinking, actively consume the scholarly material you discuss, and pose thoughtful questions during and after the talk.

Second, recall that in Chapter 10 we discussed that a key goal of your talk should be to motivate faculty on the search committee to advocate for hiring you. Thus, your mission involves motivating the audience at your talk to root for you; to become your biggest fans. You may encounter challenges with soliciting your audience for support. As noted in Chapter 10, audience members will vary in their familiarity with your research program. Audience members may even be rooting for other job candidates scheduled to interview for the faculty position to which you applied. All of this calls for strategic use of Craven's storytelling philosophy.

With clear parameters set for your job talk, we still have to contend with how you motivate the audience of faculty to support you and the prospect of you joining the faculty. Recall that in Chapter 11 we built a rationale for curating pieces of scholarship for the talk that best represent your research program. Which pieces should you select for your talk? During your talk, in what order should you discuss this work? The section that follows includes guidelines for selecting and organizing scholarly work for your job talk.

Craven's Trilogy Guidelines

The job talk approach I describe calls for discussing exactly three pieces of scholarship during your talk, a value that conforms to the Trilogy tool. Oxford (2019) defines trilogy as "a group of three related, novels, plays, [or] films." Of course, this is just a definition of the term. To understand trilogy, one has to master the process underlying its use. In an effort to model mastery of this process, I describe Craven's use of the Trilogy tool when directing *Scream* (Konrad, Woods, & Craven, 1996), *Scream 2* (Craven, Konrad, & Maddalena, 1997), and *Scream 3* (Craven et al., 2000). Briefly, the *Scream* trilogy tells an interrelated set of stories about a young woman, Sidney Prescott (played by Neve Campbell). Across her time in high school (*Scream*), college (*Scream 2*), and early in her career (*Scream 3*), Sidney and her friends find themselves in a series of frightening confrontations with multiple villains. Although the villains change from film-to-film, each dons the same ghostly outfit as they stalk their victims.

An important element in the *Scream* trilogy is that each villain in these films harbors a thematic connection with either a previous villain in the film series or with Prescott herself. In her efforts to defeat these villains, the films' protagonist Prescott seeks and receives support from characters in the films who are also stalked by and/or fall victim to these villains. Craven uses these supporting characters to unveil key elements of the stories told in the films. One key supporting character—film aficionado Randy Meeks (played by Jaime Kennedy)—facilitates the execution of a specific portion of the story that Craven wanted to tell.

Throughout the *Scream* trilogy, Meeks advises Prescott and the films' other supporting characters as to the means and motives of the villains they confront. Meeks reveals that the villains function much like characters in a horror film trilogy. By building into the Meeks character an expertise in film, Craven pulled for the audience's attention whenever Meeks spoke. Craven used the Meeks character to educate the audience about the "rules" of film trilogies. In establishing these rules, the Meeks character created a conflict in the story that allowed its ending to provide a sense of resolution to the storytelling. Craven's use of the Meeks character both enhanced the compelling nature of the storytelling, and revealed *Trilogy Guidelines*. These guidelines will help you select work to discuss during your job talk. I graphically depict these guidelines in Figure 12.1, and describe them in the sections that follow.

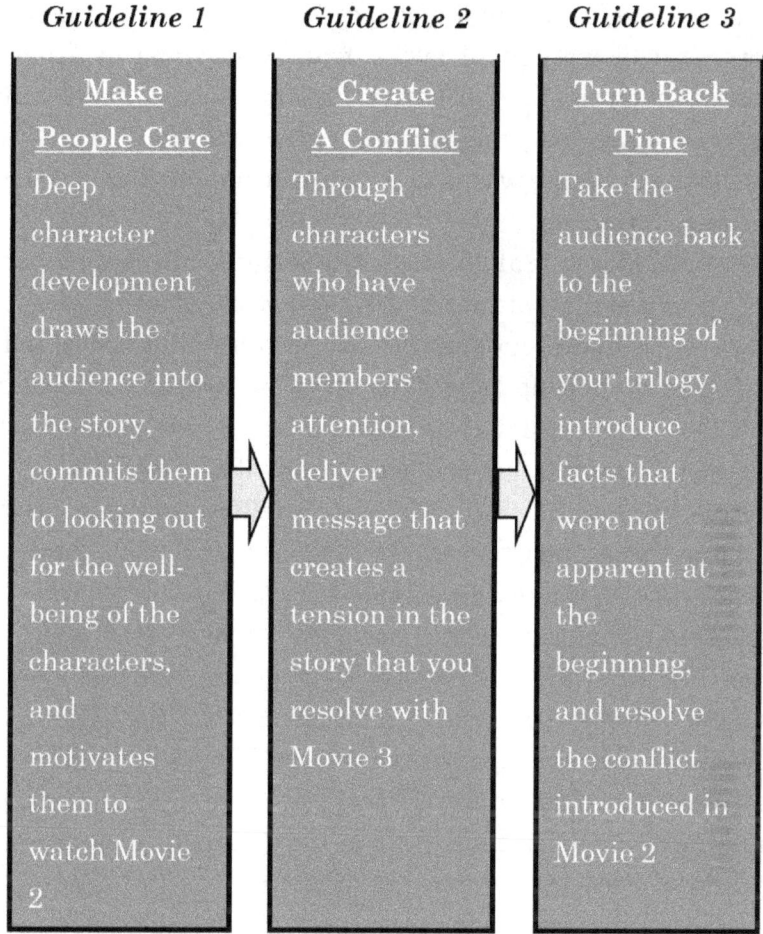

Figure 12.1. The trilogy guidelines.

Trilogy Guideline 1: Make People Care

Craven told compelling stories because he created protagonists who captured the audience's attention. His approach called for deep character development among his films' protagonists. When *Scream* opened in theaters, I recall reading a phrase describing Craven's approach, although in preparing this book I was unable to identify its source: *care before you scare*. Craven was a storyteller:

He wanted to do more than just scare people. During frightening scenes, Craven wanted to evoke fear and sympathy from the audience; that's the kind of horror film audience whose members want to continue following the story. As each beloved character perishes, the audience wants to continue watching and root for the remaining characters.

By motivating the audience to sympathize with the characters, Craven grabbed their attention. He needed to grab their attention. He had a story to tell, one that required a captive audience. In fact, Craven had a trick up his sleeve when he hooked his audience. Remember, a trilogy must tell three stories that connect to one another. To connect these stories, each film must "set up" the story told by the film that follows it. The first work you present from your trilogy has to tell a compelling story that *makes the audience care*. It has to also establish a plot line or progression in the narrative that leaves the door open for more stories. *Scream* sets up *Scream 2* by following the protagonist Prescott—who we first meet when she is in high school—into a later stage in her development, when we find her in college. This progression in the narrative allows Craven to use *Scream 2* to continue developing his main protagonist's character. In turn, this progression in the story allows Craven to create a conflict or "twist" in the plot line that he ultimately resolves in *Scream 3*. Creating a conflict is the key aim of Trilogy Guideline 2, and the key element you must execute with the second work in your trilogy.

Trilogy Guideline 2: Create a Conflict

Trilogy Guideline 2 reminds us of the versatility of story as a communication device. In Chapter 4, we learned how you can tell a compelling story in as little as one paragraph. This is because the components of a story—recall Olson's (2015) and-but-therefore storytelling template—require but a handful of sentences to deliver a message. However, you might have already noticed a key element of story: You can scale up use of this tool to tell an entire story, and you can even scale up the tool to connect separate stories into a cohesive narrative. These tools work to connect a trilogy of films. They also work to connect a trilogy of scholarly works in a research program.

In fact, in one film—*Scream*—Craven follows each of the Trilogy Guidelines discussed in this chapter. Here, I focus on the tools Craven leveraged in *Scream* for Trilogy Guideline 2: *Create a conflict*. By the point of the story in which Craven implements Trilogy Guideline 2, he has already hooked the audience with deep character development by using Trilogy Guideline 1. In particular, the Randy Meeks character I discussed previously serves the role of resident storyteller and horror film expert. Thus, by now audience members know that if they want to follow the story and get a sense of where the film is headed, they should listen to Meeks. This is where Craven creates a conflict for the audience, exemplified by a key scene, which I posted here: http://bit.ly/ECRToolboxChapter12TrilogyClip1. To be clear, at no point during these illustrations do I direct you to watching a frightening scene from these films; all of the scenes serve purely as narrative devices. With that said, I invite you to view the clip.

In this clip, we find Meeks attending a party. At this party, he lectures an audience of fellow party attendees about the "rules" of horror films. The rules all pertain to specific actions undertaken by a horror film character that signal their impending demise, such as consuming alcohol or illicit substances and engaging in sexual activity. Meeks tells the audience that horror films all follow a predictable narrative, thus creating a sense of safety. Yes, if a character breaks these rules, they will perish during the film, and that's bad. But at least you know all of that in advance, right? Doesn't knowing the horror film rules make for a safer, relatively palatable context to encounter frightening news? In the end, if a beloved horror film character breaks the rules, Craven tells the audience that at least they've been warned as to that character's fate. In doing so, Craven also tells the audience that *Scream* functions like any other horror film they have ever seen: frightening but predictable. And with this scene, Craven introduced the kind of conflict that the second film in a trilogy should execute. Indeed, later on in *Scream*, Craven introduces a fact that upends the audience: Prescott, the film's lead protagonist, breaks one of the horror film rules. Does this mean she too will encounter certain doom? With the tension created by executing Trilogy Guideline 2, Craven turns to Trilogy Guideline 3 to resolve this tension.

Trilogy Guideline 3: Turn Back Time

The third film in a trilogy is essentially the "therefore" in Olson's (2015) storytelling approach. The second film creates tension, and the third film resolves that tension. In executing Trilogy Guideline 3, Craven resolves tension. However, recall that the tension created by Craven had to do with the protagonist Prescott breaking the horror film rules used to execute Trilogy Guideline 2. In *Scream*, Craven created for the audience the impression that they were watching a standard horror film. *Scream* follows the predictable narrative of "characters who break the rules perish." Craven created this impression because he wanted to activate the audience's preconceived notions about horror films. He *turned back time* for the audience, and made them think about previous horror films they had seen. He turned back time for the audience to reveal elements of previous horror films that might not have been readily apparent to them before they saw *Scream*.

Yet, at the conclusion of *Scream* the audience learns that Craven deceived them. Not only did Prescott survive, she defeats the villains who have been after her the whole time. Trilogy

Guideline 3 allowed Craven to reveal his take-home message: A horror film can weave a compelling story if it violates the predictable elements of films in the horror genre. In Chapter 15, I expand upon this notion of using the third work in your trilogy to turn back time, but suffice to say that this chapter's discussion of Trilogy Guidelines 1, 2, and 3 reveals the key concepts for mastering the Trilogy tool.

Modeling Moments: The Next Three Chapters

I devote Chapters 13, 14, and 15 to Modeling Moments germane to use of our Trilogy tool. As with Chapter 4's Modeling Moment, I highlight specific pieces of scholarship to illustrate key issues regarding use of this tool. However, unlike Chapter 4, for the next three chapters I specifically focus on scholarship produced by the doctoral student in my laboratory—Bridget (http://bit.ly/ECRToolboxChapter3MakolCV)—about whom we learned in Chapter 3. Remember that I have no tricks up my sleeve regarding Bridget and her work. She produced the first work in her trilogy of stories before she began doctoral training in my laboratory (Makol & Polo, 2018). In Chapter 13, I use this work to illustrate the application of Trilogy Guideline 1, and how this work lays a foundation for the scholarship discussed in Chapter 14, which I use to illustrate execution of Trilogy Guideline 2. The two Modeling Moments in Chapters 13 and 14 then set the stage for Chapter 15, which I use to illustrate execution of Trilogy Guideline 3.

CHAPTER 13
Trilogy: Part 1

I begin this chapter as I will with Chapters 14 and 15, with short episodes from my days as an Emerging Academic. I use these episodes in particular, and Act III more broadly, to do with you what you should do with each piece of work in your job talk. In Act III, I turn back time: I go back to my beginnings in order to reveal a "hidden truth" about research programs that helps you build your own research program. So, pay close attention to the episode that opens up this chapter, and pay close attention to the episodes that open the two chapters that follow. These episodes not only lay the foundation for a hidden truth to be revealed later, they also lay the foundation for the Modeling Moment discussed in each chapter.

The episode in this chapter and those in Chapters 14 and 15 highlight considerations for selecting pieces of work that meet the Trilogy Guidelines described in Chapter 12. The first episode occurred at one of the first academic conferences I attended and at which I presented research (De Los Reyes, Berman, & Silverman, 2001), the Association for Advancement of Behavior Therapy (now named the Association for Behavioral and Cognitive Therapies). Here, I met a scholar who eventually became a consequential colleague, Mike Vasey. At the time, I found myself in the midst of preparing my graduate school applications, and working as a volunteer research assistant in the laboratory of Wendy Silverman, who served on the faculty at Florida International University. Wendy currently serves as Alfred A. Messer Professor in the Child Study Center and Professor of Psychology at Yale University. On Wendy's strong recommendation, one of the graduate programs to which I applied was the Clinical Psychology Doctoral Program at The Ohio State University. In my application I stated an interest in studying under Mike's mentorship, who then served as Professor of Psychology on their faculty as he does now. I took advantage of the conference to meet prospective mentors and get a sense of their current work, and I knew that Mike was on schedule to present research at that meeting.

I did not wind up studying under Mike, and I do not recall telling him this story before preparing this book, but he had a profound influence on me very early in my training. At this conference, I had the opportunity to speak with Mike and learn about his current research and future plans. One moment from this interaction not only buried itself in my memory, but also showed me firsthand an exciting element of what I thought I might like about academic work. I cannot remember what I said—and maybe Mike was just being nice—but I recall saying something in response to Mike's description of his current work. Before Mike responded, he shifted his eye gaze up and to the left. My first thought in observing Mike's reaction was one of complete and utter delight: *Whatever I just said, did I give Dr. Vasey an idea?* That moment solidified my commitment to academic work. Before the conference, I had about a couple years to observe my mentor Wendy and her day-to-day work in the laboratory. I learned that academia might be a viable career option, because it looked like Florida International University paid Wendy to think. And with my interaction with Mike I had a front-row seat to observing another element of the job: Academic work provides you with the opportunity to make other people think. Where do I sign up for that?

By the point in your talk at which you begin discussing your scholarship, you've already exposed your audience to a compelling description of your burning question. Hopefully, you presented your audience with new ideas and the theoretical framework you use to answer your burning question. You sufficiently aroused audience members' curiosity so that they want to hear more about what you do. They hopefully want to know: When you produce scholarship stemming from your burning question, how do you approach the work? How do you turn ideas into action?

With the first work in your trilogy, focus on one objective. You need to spark excitement among audience members, and motivate them to learn about the work you produce. This is very important. Ideas are one thing; countless people harbor the capacity for generating ideas. Any thoughtful person can come up with 100 burning questions in a day. Researchers go beyond generating burning questions. We researchers chase burning questions, and we cannot chase all questions at once. As an Emerging Academic, you definitely cannot chase multiple questions. During our training, we find just enough time to chase down a single burning question and disseminate scholarship about this question. With our research programs, we devise a plan to chase one burning question, and we commit to that chase. Thus, in the years filled with trials and tribulations, reading countless pieces of scholarship, and pushing your work through the peer review system, how do you chase your burning question?

What is the key piece of work in your record that motivates you to share your work with others? Do you believe this work motivates others to learn more about your research program? This kind of scholarship meets Trilogy Guideline 1, and this work can take many forms. It could be your first publication. It might also be the work that leads to an epiphany about your burning question, but that epiphany occurs later on in your training. Wherever on the timeline of your training you produced this work, it must (a) logically follow the timeline of your job talk and (b) "set up" the second work in your trilogy.

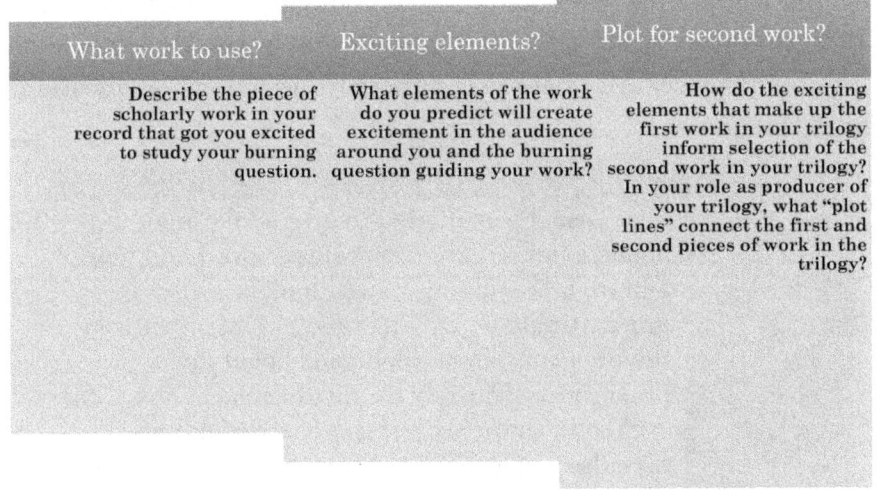

Figure 13.1. Story boards for selecting the first work in your trilogy.

In Figure 13.1, I graphically depict key considerations for selecting scholarship that meets Trilogy Guideline 1, in a "story board" format to facilitate use of these considerations. Complete the story boards in the figure, as you would if you were planning the "plot" to a film. Much like what *Scream*'s characters did for Craven, work that meets Trilogy Guideline 1 should grab your audience's attention. The attention-grabbing elements of the work might vary depending on your research program or norms of your discipline. In Psychology or Physics, it could take the form of an unexpected finding in your research program. In History, it could be some of your first observations of a key figure or event. In any case, work that meets Trilogy Guideline 1 should leave the door open to more scholarship. Specifically, the attention-grabbing elements of your first work should continue to appear in the second work in your trilogy, to create a sense of progression in the narrative of your work. As you select the first work in your trilogy, envision how your audience might react to the work. As detailed by the compelling narratives in Anonymous Accounts 13.1 and 13.2, thinking about your audience may help you decide how to frame your work and help you anticipate reactions or questions from the audience.

Anonymous Account 13.1. Unclear Talks	
Early Career Faculty	Last year, I was invited to give a talk in a department with faculty whose work I had long admired. Despite my usual tendencies to procrastinate on writing talks, I had prioritized the presentation and felt good about my preparation. The day for my talk came, and I was excited to share my latest research findings. I was also eager to get the audience's feedback and input on a new study I was planning. About halfway into the talk, an audience member stopped me to ask a question. That *question*, however, turned out to be a veiled attack of my work, and when I tried to offer some pieces of data to alleviate this person's skepticism, he interrupted me and continued on with his arguments. I was stuck. I wasn't sure how to pivot from what was no longer a productive discussion, and I wasn't sure how much of the audience was now viewing my work with this same skeptical lens. I was also a little rattled, and I totally lost the groove I had been in. I waited for him to finish his point, paused, and thanked him for raising good concerns that I would need to think about some more. I continued on and eventually finished my presentation, significantly less confident and excited about the work I was sharing. Although the experience was frustrating and a sour note for a visit I had been excited about for months, I learned a really valuable lesson in that moment. Now, in nearly every talk I give on my research,

fairly early on I raise some possible "alternative explanations" for what else could explain the phenomenon I study, and I try to spend just a couple minutes explaining why these alternatives are plausible but don't fully explain the effects (and what evidence we use to make these conclusions). This one additional slide, presented within the first 5-10 minutes of my talk, seems to put people at ease. Now, although skeptical audience members might not agree with my perspective, they feel like their points are acknowledged and validated upfront. If you work in a research area that has some controversy or differences in opinion, I recommend addressing those issues early on in your talk, perhaps with a note that you would be happy to discuss these debates in more detail at the end of your presentation.

Anonymous Account 13.2. Unclear Talks

Early Career Faculty

As a new professor who is developing new courses in a graduate program that is very different from the program at which I received doctoral training, I often fear that I might lose my audience during classroom lectures, and, sometimes, I have. This usually becomes clear to me when students do not know how to answer discussion questions that I pose. In addition to including content-focused discussion questions after a lecture, I frequently ask students to reflect on the lecture and identify the point or points they found most confusing or unclear. I hope that asking all students to do this helps to normalize the idea that some topics can be difficult to grasp and that it's important to seek clarity on those areas. This student feedback helps me plan for allocating review time in the next class. It also helps me proactively plan to spend more time on these topics in future semesters.

Modeling Moment: Trilogy Guideline 1

For Bridget's first work, we focus on one of her first articles; the published version of her master's thesis from DePaul University (Makol & Polo, 2018). Recall that in Chapter 3, I noted that academics in Psychology build their research program based on work published in peer review journals. Further, the key work that Bridget must discuss during her job talk involves research conducted where she served as the lead- or first-author. In Psychology, Emerging Academics demonstrate the ability to carry out independent research by publishing scholarship as the first author listed among other authors. Thus, all of Bridget's scholarship highlighted in these Modeling Moments will consist of first-author, peer review journal articles.

With each article described in the Modeling Moment in this chapter and in Chapters 14 and 15, I will present the article's abstract. I do this to summarize the main aims and findings of the article and highlight connections between each article and the burning question described in Chapter 4's Modeling Moment. Further, the abstract allows us to see how the article meets Trilogy Guideline 1. The following text reports the abstract from Makol and Polo (2018):

> Depression is one of the most common mental health problems among U.S. adolescents, particularly among Latinos. Parent-child ratings of the presence and severity of child depressive symptoms show only low-to-moderate agreement. However, research has failed to examine discrepancies in populations with the highest levels of unmet need and little is known about patterns and predictors of parent-child agreement in ratings of depressive symptoms among ethnic minority families in community settings. Using a sample of 184 low-income, predominantly Latino, 5th through 7th grade students (63.6% female) at chronic risk for depression, this study utilized

exploratory Latent Class Analysis (LCA) to uncover patterns of parent-child endorsement of core diagnostic depressive symptoms. Overall, children reported higher levels of core (i.e., depressed mood, anhedonia, irritability) and secondary (e.g., sleep disturbances) depressive symptoms relative to their parents. The three latent classes identified include a low endorsement and high agreement class (LH), high endorsement and high agreement class (HH), and high child endorsement and low agreement class (HCL). Multinomial regression models revealed that previous mental health service use and higher externalizing problems were associated with HH class membership, relative to HCL class membership. Findings provide evidence that a substantial number of children may have depressive symptoms that go undetected by their parents. Access to services among children at-risk for depression may be increased with psychoeducation to improve parental awareness and stigma reduction.

Modeling Moment: Debrief

Why use this article for the first work in Bridget's trilogy? Recall the burning question described in Chapter 4's Modeling Moment: *We are very curious about why different people often perceive the same behaviors in different ways*. Further, recall the answer to the burning question: *People lead complex lives*. Bridget's article directly flows from both this burning question and the theoretical framework used to answer it. Specifically, clinicians rely on people to provide reports about youth depression; hereafter we refer to these people as *informants*. The informants typically consist of the youth and significant others in their lives, like parents and teachers. The reports informants complete consist of ratings about behaviors indicative of youth depression, like feeling down, losing interest in hobbies, and difficulty concentrating. The informants providing these reports often disagree on whether they perceive the youth being assessed as displaying behaviors indicative of depression. Further, there may be some good reasons why they disagree, in particular the reality that youth may behave differently depending on the context or where they are, like home, school, or with their peers. Thus, Bridget's scholarship takes a conceptually grounded look at discrepant perceptions of behavior as they manifest in informants' reports about youth depression.

We can clearly link Bridget's first work to Chapter 4's burning question. But does this scholarship fit Trilogy Guideline 1? That is, can Bridget use this scholarship to engage the audience at a job talk? I'm a little biased here, but I think she can. With mental health research, the informants used to assess youth depressive symptoms most often include self-reports from youth and the reports of their parents, who initiate care on their behalf (Hunsley & Mash, 2007). Further, when a youth and their parent provide reports about the youth's depressive symptoms, their reports frequently yield different conclusions (De Los Reyes & Kazdin, 2005). Observations in the empirical literature of disagreements between parent and youth reports of youth mental health trace back to the late 1950s (Lapouse & Monk, 1958). Further, over several decades researchers consistently observed these disagreements manifest between informants' reports of depressive symptoms and every other mental health domain assessed in youth (Achenbach, McConaughy, & Howell, 1987; De Los Reyes et al., 2019a). As with other mental health concerns (e.g., anxiety, attention and hyperactivity, disruptive behavior; De Los Reyes & Kazdin, 2006a; Hawley & Weisz, 2003), these disagreements among informants' reports create considerable uncertainty in the clinic and laboratory. In fact, the answer to whether treatments targeting youth depressive symptoms improve youth functioning varies considerably depending on the informant(s) used to estimate treatment effects (e.g., Eckshtain et al., 2020; Weisz, McCarty, & Valeri, 2006).

Up until Bridget's paper we knew little about the basic composition or patterns of parent and youth reports about youth depressive symptoms (De Los Reyes et al., 2015). Clinically, my colleagues and I could point to cases in which youth would report depressive symptoms that went uncorroborated by reports taken from their parents, and vice versa. Stated another way, although disagreements often manifested between youth and parent reports, these disagreements did not "behave" the same way for all youth-parent pairs. In fact, sometimes we assessed youth-parent pairs that agreed quite well on the presence of youth depressive symptoms. Yet, we did not know if we could reliably detect these reporting patterns. Up until recently, many believed these reporting disagreements stemmed from one or both informants providing unreliable or biased reports (De Los Reyes, 2011; De Los Reyes, Thomas, Goodman, & Kundey, 2013).

Three things excite me about Bridget's first work. I predict these same things would excite a job talk audience. First, in a large sample of youth at risk for depression, Bridget found that she could leverage sophisticated statistical techniques to reliably identify a variety of youth-parent reporting patterns. These patterns ranged from youth-parent pairs who agreed on the presence of depressive symptoms to those who disagreed a great deal. This first element of Bridget's work speaks to the veracity of the informants' reports themselves. That is, if youth and parents provide imprecise, inaccurate reports about youth depressive symptoms, then Bridget would find it quite difficult to reliably detect patterns in disagreements between these same reports. In contrast, Bridget reliably detected these patterns, which bodes well for future work in her trilogy.

Second, as noted in the abstract, Bridget linked these reporting patterns to youth-level characteristics germane to assessing and treating depression. These characteristics included history of mental health service use and the need for services for mental health concerns beyond depression, such as aggressive behavior and hyperactivity. This element of Bridget's first work in her trilogy also bodes well for further exploring the reporting patterns she identified. Specifically, understanding clinical characteristics germane to youth depression could assist clinicians with key elements of clinical decision-making, including determining which treatments or services might best fit the needs of the youth who require care. Further, as mentioned previously youth and parent reports often factor prominently in the decisions made by clinicians regarding care for youth depression. Thus, if one could use these patterns of youth-parent reports to understand characteristics germane to youth depression, then one can boost the cost-efficiency and utility of these commonly utilized clinical instruments.

Third and more broadly, by selecting work from her record that clearly links back to a burning question and theoretical framework, Bridget begins her trilogy by demonstrating that she knows how to take abstract ideas and turn them into a concrete piece of work. As detailed in Anonymous Account 13.3, your audience will expect your talk to have focus; a discernable structure. What better way to accomplish this task than to carefully curate the work you discuss during the talk, and link it to the burning question that motivates your work?

Anonymous Account 13.3. Unclear Talks

Post-Doctoral Fellow

During my first year as a postdoctoral fellow, I was asked to give a 30-minute presentation to my department about my previous and current research as well as my plans for a grant submission. In the weeks prior to my talk, I spent quite a bit of time planning for it, preparing my slides, and practicing my delivery. Although I did not realize it at the time, I was making the mistake of trying to cover entirely too much material during this brief amount of time. I had completed and was currently working on studies in several distinct, but related, areas, and I incorrectly believed it was important to discuss them all; this left me with too little time to discuss my idea for a grant submission. Given my preparation, I thought my delivery of the talk went well. It was not until I reached the 15 minutes that were set aside for questions and feedback that I realized the mistake I had made. One faculty member pointed out that in my overview of my grant, I had not clearly outlined my study aims and hypotheses. Another faculty member noted that although my content was good, my presentation could use "a bit more focus." I received similar feedback in the written evaluations of my presentation. Honestly, I felt somewhat defensive about this at first, but I recognized that this reaction mostly stemmed from embarrassment. Since that time, I have realized the importance of telling a clear, coherent story and that it is more important to present a few studies in more detail than to try to cover all of your work in one talk.

Next Steps

By now, you might have gathered that these disagreements among informants' reports about youth mental health occur not just with depression but within assessments of myriad mental health domains, including other emotional states like anxiety (De Los Reyes & Makol, 2019). Further, these disagreements manifest in a host of assessments used for purposes of screening, diagnosis, and treatment, and in clinical settings as diverse as schools, community mental health centers, and outpatient clinics (De Los Reyes & Kazdin, 2005). They also occur in inpatient settings (e.g., Prinstein, Nock, Spirito, & Grapentine, 2001), and for assessments of behaviors as severe as those that indicate suicide risk, such as suicidal thoughts and suicide attempts (Jones et al., 2019). Think about this: The assessment process in an inpatient setting begins at the point at which one seeks admission to this setting. Many times, the reason for this admission revolves around the person being assessed as posing imminent danger to themselves or other people (Reynolds et al., 2018). Even in clinical contexts in which the reason for the assessments includes quite severe, even life-threatening behaviors, one encounters disagreements between informants' reports about youth mental health. What if Bridget's work with assessing at-risk youth could inform clinical decision-making within assessments of youth at acute risk for severe mental health concerns? Clearly, we want to see what's next in Bridget's trilogy!

CHAPTER 14
Trilogy: Part 2

Recall that the episode described at the opening of Chapter 13 took place before I began doctoral training. I focused on elements of this episode dealing with sparking curiosity and engaging your audience; key objectives for selecting scholarship to address Trilogy Guideline 1. For this chapter's episode, I fast-forward to around the mid-point of my doctoral training. My doctoral mentor Alan and I had only recently received the first set of reviews on a manuscript that I had written under his supervision. This manuscript became the article discussed in Chapter 2, the one involving Alan's use of modeling to shape my behavior (De Los Reyes & Kazdin, 2005).

At the time of this episode, Alan and I found the reviews to be favorable. It appeared that, with some revision, the editor would eventually accept this manuscript for publication in the *Psychological Bulletin*, perhaps the most widely read review journal in Psychology (Albarracín, 2015; Sternberg, 1991). My 2005 article with Alan was the third article I had published up until then. Further, the previous two articles I had published addressed related topics (De Los Reyes & Kazdin, 2004; De Los Reyes & Prinstein, 2004). At the time, I thought I was onto something with work in this general area of study. Thankfully, Alan created a conflict in the narrative of my doctoral training, a key piece to consider in selecting scholarship for Trilogy Guideline 2.

I will spoil the ending to this episode: Alan's conflict eventually became an article I published under his supervision in the *Psychological Review* (De Los Reyes & Kazdin, 2006a). Let's get to the important part, the conflict. Although we both experienced excitement about the prospect of our paper appearing in the *Psychological Bulletin,* Alan expressed concern about whether his colleagues would care much about the topics addressed in the paper. In fact, Alan proclaimed that the only evidence we had at the time of anyone caring is that we both were interested enough to write the paper, and the editor handling the paper and the reviewers selected to evaluate it probably liked it as well. Alan presented me with an objective for our next project: Make people care about the stuff you care about. Alan created a conflict in my "training story" that I had to resolve. Conflicts in scholarly work occur often: It's typically up to us as individual scholars to figure out how to resolve them. The narrative in Anonymous Account 14.1 serves as a good example. Similarly, the second work in your trilogy creates a conflict in the story that you resolve with the third work in your trilogy.

Anonymous Account 14.1. Challenging Questions	
Doctoral Student	I really enjoy giving talks and disseminating science. I find discussing and communicating your work with others to be one of the core facets of scientific study—but that means it can also be incredibly challenging. One of the hardest things for me in a presentation is getting asked about specific stats or specific analyses. Typically, when I present on a paper or ongoing project, I try to focus on the primary aims and analyses and then discuss implications and future directions. But almost ALWAYS I will get questions like, "did you look at the data this way?", or "what about an interaction between this and that?" Having a slide deck at the end of my talk with ALL analyses—primary and supplementary—helps ease my anxiety about getting asked specific statistical questions or analytical questions and not providing answers or remembering. I will have graphics, tables, and screenshots of results that I think people may ask about. This allows me to focus my attention on arguably the even harder questions about theory, implications, and limitations.

In Figure 14.1, I graphically depict key considerations for selecting scholarship that meets Trilogy Guideline 2, using the story board format from Chapter 13. When deciding on the second work in your talk, keep two objectives in mind. First, as we learned in Chapter 13, the first work should be focused on a key theme that you expect will "hook" your audience and compel them to follow you along your journey across your research program. Now that you have your audience hooked, you need to keep that motivation going with the second work in your trilogy. The second work should elaborate upon the central theme or "plot" of the first work. As with considerations I raised in Chapter 13, your research program or norms of your discipline likely dictate what form your second work takes. In the sciences, the second work might take the form of a follow-up study of a key finding made in the first work. Perhaps scholarship norms in your discipline mean that your own scholarship does not take the form of articles in peer review journals, but in a single work like a book. Under these circumstances, the first work might have taken the form of one of the first few chapters of the book, and the second work takes place in a chapter located somewhere in the middle of the book. In any case, keep your audience engaged by connecting the plot from your first work to the plot explored in your second work.

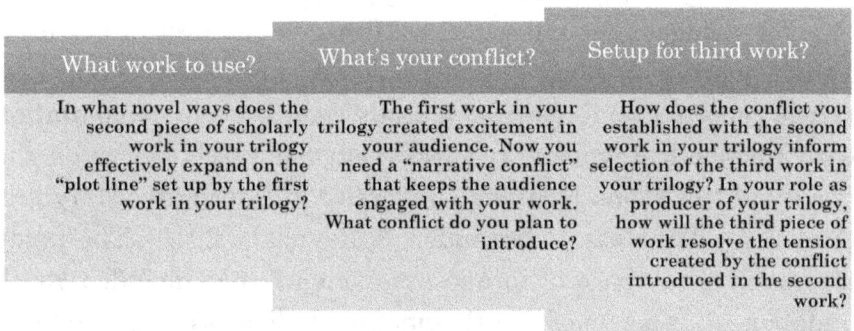

Figure 14.1. **Story boards for selecting the second work in your trilogy.**

Equally important as your first objective is the second. Recall how Craven leveraged his Meeks character in *Scream*. With his expertise in film, Meeks compels the audience to listen to his rules of horror films. In the process, the character lays the foundation for a conflict in the narrative; the key protagonist winds up breaking these rules. In creating this conflict, Craven "sets up" the resolution to the film. For Craven, the resolution (i.e., Trilogy Guideline 3) involves turning back time and forcing the audience to think about their preconceived notions about horror films. By activating these preconceived notions, Craven facilitates bringing about the resolution of the film: The rule-breaking protagonist survives and defeats the villains. Similarly, with the second work in your trilogy, keep the audience engaged in your storytelling. At the same time, create a conflict in the narrative that lays the foundation for the third work in your trilogy. Note that you do not have to make this conflict in your narrative explicit when describing the second work in your trilogy. Rather, the point is to select a piece of work that both keeps your audience engaged and includes an element upon which you can capitalize as a conflict in your narrative—a conflict that you will eventually resolve when you describe the third work in your trilogy.

Modeling Moment: Trilogy Guideline 2

For Bridget's second work, we focus on the first of her first-author journal articles published under my supervision. This article reported findings from a study completed in collaboration with Elizabeth Reynolds and Rick Ostrander, who serve on the faculty of the Johns Hopkins University in Baltimore, Maryland (Makol, De Los Reyes, Ostrander, & Reynolds, 2019). The study leveraged a database of intake assessments that included youth and parent reports of youth emotional distress (e.g., anxiety and depression). Staff collected these intake assessments for youth admitted to care at a 12-bed inpatient unit located at the Bloomberg Children's Center, a medical center affiliated with the Johns Hopkins University that services youth ages 5-17 years for acute treatment and hospitalization.

In Chapter 13, I noted that the same statistical tools Bridget used in the first work in her trilogy (Makol & Polo, 2018) to identify patterns of reports in risk assessments of youth depressive symptoms might be applicable to other assessment contexts. In particular, these tools might apply to assessments of emotional concerns beyond depression, like anxiety. These tools might also apply to assessments delivered as part of services geared toward relatively severe patient populations, like assessments used to inform services for youth admitted to inpatient care. Bridget might leverage these tools to identify coherent patterns of reports about youth admitted to inpatient care, and in a way that allows staff to use the patterns to predict how youth will respond to inpatient care. The following text reports the abstract from Makol et al. (2019):

> When compared to one another, multiple informants' reports of adolescent internalizing problems often reveal low convergence. This creates challenges in the delivery of clinical services, particularly for severe outcomes linked to internalizing problems, namely suicidal thoughts and behaviors. Clinicians would benefit from methods that facilitate interpretation of multi-informant reports, particularly in inpatient settings typified by high-cost care and high-stakes decision-making. 765 adolescent inpatients (70.3% female; M_{age} = 14.7) and their parents completed measures of adolescent internalizing problems. We obtained baseline clinical and treatment characteristics from electronic medical records. Latent class analyses revealed four reporting patterns: Parent-Adolescent Low (LL; 49.0%),

Parent Low-Adolescent High (PL-AH; 11.5%), Parent High-Adolescent Low (PH-AL; 21.8%), Parent-Adolescent High (HH; 17.6%). Relative to the LL class, adolescents in the PH-AL and PL-AH classes were more likely to be admitted with suicidality. In terms of treatment characteristics and relative to the LL class, HH and PH-AL adolescents were more likely to receive standing antipsychotics, PH-AL adolescents were more likely to be in seclusion, and HH adolescents had longer hospital stays. At discharge and relative to the LL class, HH, PH-AL, and PL-AH adolescents were more likely to receive an anxiety disorder diagnosis. Further, HH, PH-AL, and PL-AH adolescents were more likely to receive partial hospitalization or care in another restrictive environment after inpatient treatment, relative to the LL class. This naturalistic study informs clinical decision-making by aiding our understanding of how multi-informant reports facilitate interpretations of adolescents' clinical presentations as well as predictions about treatment characteristics.

Modeling Moment: Debrief

The second work in your trilogy should continue engaging the audience with a novel take on the first work's plot. However, in continuing to engage the audience with the second work in your trilogy, you have to create a conflict in the story that lays the foundation for the third work in your trilogy. Bridget quite effectively meets these objectives with her second work.

Several characteristics of assessments conducted in inpatient settings and the nature of the setting itself makes this article a compelling follow-up to the article that Bridget showcased in the first work in her trilogy. Indeed, mental health care providers working in youth inpatient settings deliver services to a particularly vulnerable, high-risk population. The decisions service providers make within inpatient settings can be life-or-death decisions. These settings need accurate instruments that facilitate sound decision-making (see also Friedman et al., 2011).

Yet, inpatient settings encounter unique challenges in acquiring and implementing instruments that facilitate sound decision-making. Inpatient settings often cannot afford high-quality instruments and must turn to freely available instruments (Beidas et al., 2015). The time-intensive nature of care in inpatient settings also calls for instruments that can be delivered efficiently and hold prognostic value, or the capability of predicting key outcomes in inpatient care, such as length of hospital stay or risk of readmission (Reynolds et al., 2018).

All of these characteristics fit the cost- and time-efficient nature of many of the measures completed by informants like youth and parents. However, scholars and health care providers have long called into question the veracity of data gleaned from these reports when collected in inpatient settings. As mentioned previously, adolescents in inpatient settings often report suicidal thoughts and behaviors that go uncorroborated by parents (Klaus, Mobilio, & King, 2009), and at times parents report that their children display suicidal thoughts even when children themselves do not confirm having these thoughts (Thompson et al., 2006). Questions about these disagreements take on an enhanced importance in inpatient settings, because many interpret the disagreements as arising from youth downplaying their concerns so as to avoid inpatient admission (Nock et al., 2010; Busch et al., 2003). Importantly, beliefs about the accuracy of informants' reports may lead those collecting and interpreting them to discard reports they deem questionable. Thus, Bridget's second work allowed her to put these questions about the veracity of youth and parent reports to the test. Testing her burning question with a study about informants' reports collected in an inpatient setting resulted in a very conservative test of this question. If she can apply her approach to an inpatient setting and draw meaningful findings from youth and parent reports in this setting, the results could be quite influential. Indeed, her work might result in the ability of inpatient settings to improve clinical decision-making by boosting the predictive power of the instruments gathered in these settings.

Next Steps

By continuing to engage the audience, key elements of Bridget's second work allow her to create a conflict in her narrative that she resolves with the third work of her trilogy. She accentuates the inpatient setting and the high-risk youth population it serves. She cites research indicating that the informants tasked to report about youth inpatients may provide inaccurate reports. The audience listens in with intrigue as she reports data indicating that not only can she reliably identify coherent patterns of reports about youth anxiety and depression taken from youth and parents, but these patterns have prognostic value. Bridget leverages these reporting patterns to identify youth patients at risk for longer hospital stays. The patterns allow her to predict which youth will require relatively intensive clinical services during inpatient care. Bridget's work broke new ground by demonstrating that patterns of reports completed on relatively short and cost-efficient instruments allow one to predict key characteristics of service delivery in youth inpatient settings. By showcasing this study as the second work in her trilogy, Bridget leads the audience to reasonably suspect that the same approach she used for the first two works in her trilogy has finally solved a riddle about assessment that, for decades, has plagued clinical decision-making. As we discuss in Chapter 15, Bridget is about to reveal a key element of her work that upends all of these expectations. In doing so, the second work in her trilogy allowed Bridget to grab her audience's attention, create a conflict, and lay the foundation for the third and final work in her trilogy, where she will focus on a study that resolves the conflict set up by the second work.

CHAPTER 15
Trilogy: Part 3

As detailed in Anonymous Account 15.1, episodes from doctoral training have a profound influence on our development as scholars. Consequently, it's no surprise that I used episodes from my training to open Chapters 13 and 14. In Chapter 13, I took you to before I began my doctoral training to illustrate concepts surrounding engaging your audience, the key consideration for selecting work that meets Trilogy Guideline 1. In Chapter 14, we reviewed an episode at the mid-point of my doctoral training to illustrate the need to create a conflict, which informs selection of work that meets Trilogy Guideline 2. In this chapter, we will focus on the culmination of your efforts in selecting scholarship for the preceding stories in your trilogy, and selecting the third work in your trilogy, thus meeting Trilogy Guideline 3.

> **Anonymous Account 15.1. Seeing a Great Talk**
>
> *Post-Doctoral Fellow*
>
> In my first or second year of graduate school, I saw a talk that has shaped my development as a scientist more than any other. It was a practice talk. There were probably about eight or nine of us at the lab meeting—research assistants, graduate students, and postdocs—watching a professor practice a talk she was preparing for a lay audience. The professor was not my mentor and it was not my primary lab. The topic (which had something to do with behavioral economics) was not one that I was especially passionate about. It was a Monday evening. I was tired. I was prepared to watch the practice talk and share my feedback, and then to go home and eat

dinner. I was not expecting to be influenced by—or even especially interested in—this talk. Even the professor giving the talk conveyed that she was not particularly excited about it, but had agreed to give the talk because she wanted to support the organization that had invited her. But, as the professor began her talk, it felt more like a story than any lecture, seminar, brown bag, or conference talk I had ever attended. She set up and eventually solved a compelling puzzle—a riddle about human behavior. She included photos, diagrams, charts, cartoons, and even memes—but very few words on her slides, so that the experience was one of watching and listening to her tell a story. The talk flew by. I was riveted. Now, years later, I still think of that talk any time that I have to give a talk myself. I barely remember the content of the talk, but the style and structure seem to be permanently etched in my brain. I have learned to love communicating about my work and have found that when I present it as a critically important story—a riddle that I can pose and then answer—it is engaging and fun for me, as well as (I hope) for my audience.

For this chapter's episode, we find ourselves around the same point of my doctoral training as the episode that opened Chapter 14. At the time, Will Corbin, a faculty member in the Clinical Psychology program at Yale University, served as the program's Director of Clinical Training or administrative head. Will now serves as Professor of Psychology at Arizona State University. Will asked for a meeting with me to discuss issues surrounding my training. Aside from the issues that prompted the meeting, during this meeting Will provided me with an insight about academic work that ultimately proved invaluable to my pursuit of a research career. I withheld discussing this episode until now to highlight a key theme of the third work in a trilogy.

Here was Will's insight: When he began composing the application materials that landed him his first faculty job, the submission guidelines for the job openings to which he applied prompted him to discuss his research program. You will encounter similar guidelines for the job openings to which you will submit applications. At this meeting, Will disclosed to me that as he began the application process, he honestly did not know how to articulate his research program. In fact, he admitted that at the outset, he did not know whether he had a research program. He had to review the work he had produced during years of doctoral and post-doctoral training to piece together his research program, in reverse. This is a faculty member at Yale University, disclosing to me, an Emerging Academic, that scholars land their first faculty jobs based on research programs that only become apparent to them when they are about to look for work.

Recall what we learned in Chapter 4: An Emerging Academic displays very little control over their research program. Emerging Academics pursue scholarship at the discretion of their mentors. In fact, the episode from Chapter 14 detailed my pursuits with scholarly work, which occurred under the supervision of my mentor Alan. Further, Alan's advice to me obviously stemmed from his own ideas, resources, and larger research program. All of the boundary conditions that Emerging Academics encounter during training make it nearly impossible for them to have their research program figured out years in advance of looking for that first academic job.

Now recall the last time you saw an academic job talk. In particular, think about a talk that you found masterfully delivered by a fellow Emerging Academic near the end of their doctoral or post-doctoral training. In all likelihood, the speaker composed a cogent, compelling story of their scholarship. More importantly, the speaker likely composed this story just a few months before their talk, while they were putting together the rest of their application materials. I do not know about you, but that element of the academic job talk process hits me like a wave of comfort. Like I just exited a spa. The final version of an Emerging Academic's masterfully delivered job talk looks like the speaker took years to purposefully craft their research program. For the grand majority of us currently employed as faculty at academic institutions, when we were Emerging Academics looking for our first job, we crafted our research programs months—not years—in advance of the talks that landed us our first jobs. Further, we composed our research programs post-hoc, and based on pieces of scholarship that chronologically displayed a pattern that bore little resemblance to the timeline of our job talks. The post-hoc nature of the academic job talk process might not have been clear to you at the start of reading this book. In reality, this book is all about giving you guidance on how to compose a "research program in reverse." This process of composing a trilogy of scholarship is a completely normal part of pursuing your first faculty job.

    Let's probe your reactions to reading the last three paragraphs. Doing so will help crystalize your objectives with selecting your third work. Did you find Will's revelation about storytelling in reverse mind-blowing? Perhaps you felt that this idea existed "under the radar" this whole time, but seeing it out in the open took you by surprise? That's the feeling you must pull from the audience with the third work in your trilogy.

    To return to our discussion of the *Scream* trilogy in Chapter 12, a scene from *Scream 3* nails the main points with the third work in a trilogy: http://bit.ly/ECRToolboxChapter15TrilogyClip2. Take a moment to view the clip. In line with this clip, in Figure

15.1, I graphically depict the key considerations for selecting scholarship that meets Trilogy Guideline 3. This figure follows the story board format from Chapters 13 and 14. What does the clip reveal? As with the first clip we viewed in Chapter 12, we see our film expert Randy Meeks discussing rules about filmmaking, only here he focuses on the rules of film trilogies. Craven uses the Meeks character to contextualize the progression of narratives in film trilogies. An audience member should feel that elements in the plot of *Scream 3* were unapparent to them from the first two stories in the trilogy. That feeling comes from the storyteller turning back time on the audience, and revealing a "hidden truth" in the narrative that helps to create a resolution to the collection of stories told during the trilogy. Across the films in his trilogy, Craven engaged his audience in *Scream*, created a conflict in *Scream 2* that kept the audience engaged with the storytelling, and turned back time in the storytelling in *Scream 3* to reveal a "hidden truth" that facilitates resolving *Scream 2*'s conflict.

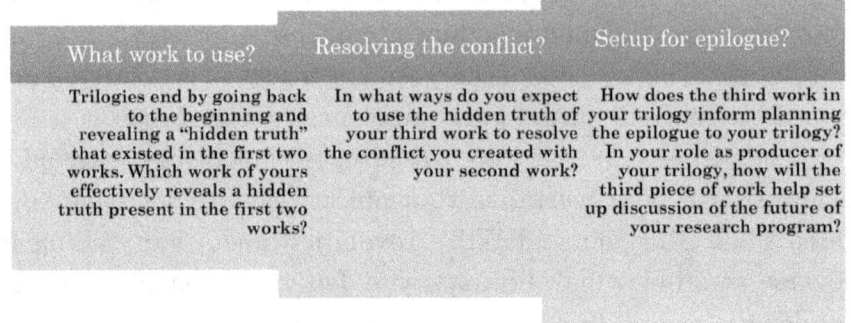

Figure 15.1. Story boards for selecting the third work in your trilogy.

In *Scream 3*, Craven turns back time and takes the audience to an earlier point in the narrative. He does so to reveal new information about the protagonist Sidney Prescott, namely information surrounding her mother; a key character in the narrative of the film trilogy. Craven took his audience back to before Prescott was born to reveal aspects of her family history to which the audience had yet to be exposed. Craven turned back time, and in doing so lay the foundation for *Scream 3*'s narrative in a way that resolved the tension created by *Scream 2*. And that's your mission with Trilogy Guideline 3. Your key objective with selecting scholarship for the third work in your trilogy is to position this story in way that turns back time, and takes your audience back to the beginning of the story of your research program.

The purpose of turning back time is to reveal insights to your research program that the audience was incapable of seeing at the outset of your trilogy. The effect should be similar to using a rearview mirror while driving. Picture yourself driving on the highway. You look into the rearview mirror and see a vehicle on the road, but it's a vehicle you did not see a few moments ago. Your third work is a version of this rearview mirror effect. Direct your audience's attention to ideas present earlier in your narrative that could only be seen from the vantage point of having already reviewed the first two works in your trilogy. As with Trilogy Guidelines 1 and 2, work that meets Trilogy Guideline 3 can take many forms. For those in science, perhaps sometime during your training you discovered an important limitation of your general approach to scholarship. Perhaps this limitation was a key component of the research design of the studies comprising your first two pieces of work. The third work in your trilogy might be a study that addresses this limitation head-on, and provides the audience with a new appreciation of the previous two studies you described. For those in disciplines where the scholarship takes the form of a book, the third work in your trilogy might be a chapter in the book that reveals a little-known fact or innovative interpretation of the events or historical figures explored in the book. In these and other cases, the objective remains the same, as Randy Meeks states in *Scream 3*: "[T]rue trilogies are all about going back to the beginning, and discovering something that wasn't true from the get-go."

Modeling Moment: Trilogy Guideline 3

Bridget's third work consists of a study she presented in 2018 at the same national conference referenced in the episode that opened Chapter 13 (Makol, Glenn, Youngstrom, & De Los Reyes, 2018). Bridget prepared a first-author manuscript based on this project, and the manuscript is currently under review for publication in a peer review journal (Makol et al., 2020). For her project she made use of a database from my archives, consisting of a sample of adolescents whose parents had contacted my laboratory to either seek an evaluation of their adolescent for possible concerns with social anxiety, or participate in a non-clinic study of how adolescents interact with their parents (Glenn et al., 2019). All adolescents in the sample completed a series of laboratory tasks designed to mimic social interactions with same-age, unfamiliar peers (Deros et al., 2018). Each adolescent, their parent, and the unfamiliar peer with whom they interacted all provided reports on measures of the adolescent's social anxiety. Further, trained staff independently observed each adolescent's behavior within the social interactions to make ratings of the adolescent's social anxiety during these interactions.

Toward the end of Chapter 14, I hinted that Bridget's third work would allow her to turn back time and reveal a hidden truth that brings a resolution to her trilogy. This revelation would be one that the audience could only see from the "rearview mirror" after exposure to the first two pieces of work in Bridget's trilogy. In fact, elements of the study design noted previously and in the study's abstract below factor prominently in the revelations made during Bridget's third work. The following text reports the abstract from Makol et al. (2020):

Assessing youth psychopathology involves collecting multiple informants' reports. Yet, multi-informant reports often disagree, necessitating integrative strategies that optimize predictive power. The *Trait* score approach leverages principal components analysis (PCA) to account for the context and perspective from which informants provide reports. This approach may boost the predictive power of multi-informant reports and thus warrants rigorous testing. We tested the *Trait* score using multi-informant reports of adolescent social anxiety in a mixed clinical/community sample of adolescents ($n=127$). The *Trait* score incrementally predicted observed social anxiety (βs: .47-.67) and referral status (*OR*s: 2.66-6.53), above-and-beyond individual informants' reports and a composite of informants' reports. The *Trait* score predicted observed behavior at magnitudes well above those typically observed for individual informants' reports of internalizing psychopathology (i.e., rs=.01-.15). Findings demonstrate the ability of the *Trait* score to improve prediction of clinical indices, and potentially transform widely used practices in multi-informant assessments.

Modeling Moment: Debrief

Recall that in Chapters 10, 11, and 12, I emphasized the crucial need to prepare your job talk with your audience in mind. This theme takes center stage when delivering the third work in your trilogy. Picture Bridget at this moment in her talk. She has her audience wrapped around her finger. Following her second work people listen with intrigue to see the progression of her trilogy. Now, Bridget turns back time to set up a compelling resolution to her trilogy. If I were in Bridget's place, I would start off the third work with a metaphor. As detailed in the abstract above, Bridget's third work draws heavily from a brilliant article published by Helena Kraemer and colleagues (2003). Kraemer currently serves as Emeritus Faculty in the Department of Psychiatry and Behavioral Sciences at Stanford University. In this article, Kraemer reveals an important insight about selecting, interpreting, and integrating information from multiple informants' reports about youth mental health.

As detailed previously, mental health care providers and researchers alike commonly observe disagreements among the reports that informants provide about youth mental health; 50 years of research attest to this observation (De Los Reyes et al. 2015). These disagreements manifest in mental health clinics and laboratories all over the world (De Los Reyes et al., 2019a). They also introduce uncertainties into decisions surrounding mental health services and research, particularly when assessors cannot determine why informants' reports disagree (De Los Reyes et al., 2013). If those conducting these assessments know these disagreements occur often and hinder clinical decision-making, then what can an assessor do to make these disagreements work for the assessment process rather than against it? Here is Kraemer's insight: Force the informants to disagree with one another by treating them like satellites triangulating on a target.

The satellite metaphor works perfectly here. Picture Bridget asking the audience members to take out their phones. She drops her satellite metaphor:

> Have you ever used the maps application on your phone to direct you to a restaurant or some other place, and along the way you walk under an obstruction like an overpass and your "map app" loses you? You know you're standing right here, but the app says you're standing way over there? Why does that happen? It happens because your phone emits a signal tracked by a global positioning system (GPS). The map app uses that signal and the GPS to pinpoint your location and

use it as a reference point from which it sends you directions to wherever you wish to go. The GPS system uses multiple satellites to track your phone's signal at any given moment. The system works great when all satellites get to track you at once. However, if you encounter a barrier between you and a portion of the sky, the GPS loses data. Less data means less power to estimate your location. And there lies the big problem with mental health assessments. In the end, we use multiple informants because no one informant provides us all the data we need. We use multiple informants in the hopes that their reports get us closer to the data we need to make accurate decisions in the clinic and laboratory. But all too often we relinquish control over who provides us these reports. Sometimes, it's because we approach the assessment passively and rely only on the informants who come to us, like the parent who initiates care on their child's behalf. Other times we actively exclude informants from our assessments because we believe them to be "bad reporters." Sometimes we label an informant a "bad reporter" because they tell us things that other informants do not. But think about those satellites again. The GPS successfully tracks your phone not only because it leverages multiple satellites, but multiple strategically placed satellites. They form a perimeter around you and lock on your position from different points in space. My first two studies revealed the potential for patterns of multiple informants' reports to inform clinical services and research. My third study reveals that optimizing the information we obtain from these reporting patterns involves strategically selecting informants to create predictable reporting patterns. I pick two informants who could not disagree with each other more if they tried. I pick a third informant whose data sits in between that of the first two informants. My informants disagree with one another and from the get-go I can tell you why. This triad of informants becomes the satellites in my measurement positioning system. They sit in three different points in space, and triangulate on the "mental health position" of the people I assess. Now, I will walk you through who these informants are, why I picked them, and how I leverage their data to optimize the predictive power of multi-informant assessments.

Next Steps

Bridget's satellite metaphor allows her to connect themes from each of the works in her trilogy, and reveal a "hidden truth" in clinical assessments. The audience could not see this truth until they made it to the point in the talk in which she introduced the satellite metaphor. Using the first two works in her trilogy, Bridget got the audience excited about these assessments, and created a conflict in the story. Building on the excitement and conflict, Bridget leveraged the third work in her trilogy to turn back time and reveal a novel insight about these assessments. This novel insight allowed her to resolve the conflict in her narrative. In this way, Bridget's third work becomes the kind of "mic drop moment" you want to have near the end of your talk. More broadly, Bridget effectively wove a story across three pieces of work. What effect does good storytelling have on an audience? To address this question, I close this chapter with Anonymous Accounts 15.2, 15.3, and 15.4.

Anonymous Account 15.2. Seeing a Great Talk

Early Career Faculty

I sometimes am concerned that the longer I stay in the ivory tower, the harder it becomes to speak to people outside of it. In particular, to be able to have a discussion that children have needs beyond making sure that they are fed, clothed, and have shelter, is not always met warmly. I was extremely inspired by hearing a mentor of mine speak about children's emotional needs to a broad audience. I think in part it helped that he was an older, White man who did not send a signal that he was a particularly touchy-feely kind of guy. It was just a set of facts, laid out with evidence, and nice figures of the brain and pretty charts of data, that showed that kids need warm and responsive caregiving. I truly believe he convinced everyone there to shift their mindset, at least a little bit to consider kids as in need of nurturance. I suspect people went home and held their little ones a bit tighter, called their grown children and grandchildren, and started considering how better to account for the role of the caregiving environment in their own research. I want to channel that when I talk to audiences about my work—to show them with data that caregiving matters—and remind them that they can apply this information immediately to their daily lives.

Anonymous Account 15.3. Seeing a Great Talk

Doctoral Student

I had the privilege of attending a masterfully crafted talk about responding to peer review at a conference. I walked into the talk expecting to learn a few tips on writing response letters. I walked out not only with a lot of practical advice, but also with renewed motivation towards my scholarly work, and newfound enthusiasm towards the peer review process. The talk had many elements of a great presentation: a clearly identified topic and scope, structure, use of accessible metaphors, inclusion of personal and relatable anecdotes and concrete examples, humor, and inspirational stories. The talk fundamentally changed my approach to peer review. Before attending that talk, whenever I would receive a revise-and-resubmit decision, I would drag my feet for weeks before reluctantly working on the response letter. However, when I received a revise-and-resubmit decision on a manuscript a few weeks after attending that talk, I felt grateful to the peer review process for improving my manuscript, and was genuinely excited to dive into writing a response letter. A great talk is one that not only captivates you in the moment, but also delivers a powerful message that helps you grow as a researcher.

Anonymous Account 15.4. Seeing a Great Talk

Early Career Faculty

Talks are exhausting. We, as audience members, are forced to sit still for minutes to hours and passively absorb content that we might not understand or care about. I gauge a good talk based on my net energy: do I leave the talk feeling more or less energized than how I felt when the talk started? One talk sticks out as especially net positive. The speaker started with a story about his young daughter. One morning as he was walking downstairs to start his day, he saw his daughter and her friend covered in blood. They were holding a knife. He rushed towards them to help, but as he got closer to the kitchen, he noticed they were laughing. Their gashes couldn't have been too painful...? Turns out, the girls were working on a school project that, oddly enough, involved carving a piece of (animal) meat. The blood wasn't theirs. The speaker spent the next several minutes explaining how this story illustrated the power of infusing curiosity in our everyday lives. The story, while intentionally dramatic and extreme (most parents would respond this way to a bleeding child!), was an example of how we rapidly make assumptions about situations and respond reactively. He then drew a contrast of approaching situations with curiosity, slightly pausing to garner alternative explanations for the knife + child + blood + laughter. He posed provocative questions that challenged us to explore other ways to approach this situation. He broke up the talk with an interactive group exercise that pulled for perspective-taking via real world scenarios. He was a captivating storyteller, he tailored the talk to the audience, and he prompted us to engage directly with the content.

CHAPTER 16
Trilogy: Epilogue

At the end of Chapter 15, I alluded to "mic drop moments." You may be tempted to end your talk with the "bang" that is your third work. Indeed, it marks a powerful moment in your talk. The concluding story of your trilogy enthralled the audience just as you planned. Why not end your talk at such a climactic moment? Recall Chapter 11, and in particular the inferences that the job talk audience draws from the speaker (Figure 11.1). One key inference we learned was that of your commitment to your research program. Your audience will infer a great deal from the chronology of stories in your talk, and in particular, the years you spent composing the scholarship you used to describe your research program. Thus, the end portion of your talk is not a portion to be taken lightly. Indeed, recall one of the ways in which job talks go wrong. In particular, recall our discussion in Chapter 10 about talks with "one-slide studies." Faculty at job talks might find this format irksome, in part, because in reeling off study after study, the speaker risks losing the audience by reciting findings. They should be captivating audience members with the narrative that connects those findings. However, recall that an equally appalling element of the one-slide study method revolves around the underlying rationale for its use: a futile attempt to out-do other job candidates with mere scholarly productivity. If the speaker's focus is to impress with productivity, where does a job talk like that go? Taken to its logical conclusion, this approach, almost without exception, results in job talks for which the clock runs out before the speaker gets to the "next steps" of their research program. Needless to say, if you wish to deliver a compelling account about your work, you must carve out time in the talk to discuss where you see your work headed. Discussing your next steps allows you to build connections with your audience, and you may gain colleagues in the process (Anonymous Account 16.1).

> **Anonymous Account 16.1. Influential Questions**
>
> **Early Career Faculty**
>
> During a job talk, I discussed an ongoing study and how I envisioned continuing the study at the University where I was interviewing. One audience member asked a question about a key component of the study. I shared some of my initial thoughts in response to the question and mentioned that I would love to talk with her more about this topic, since I knew that the question stemmed from her primary area of research. The audience member is now one of my most valued colleagues. We have had several discussions about research and have already collaborated on some initiatives within our department. In addition to presenting an opportunity to clarify information about research, I think questions can also present opportunities to build collaborations and to learn from the audience.

Fortunately, the Trilogy tool facilitates conceptualizing the end of your talk. The key reason why your audience wants to see evidence of your commitment to your research program is to make predictions about your future. Do you plan to commit to your research program, through good times and bad, in sickness and in health? How do you convince the audience that your work has many more years ahead and stories to look forward to? Following the work that concludes your trilogy, you have your audience's attention. Now, they want to understand where you might take your research program if you join their faculty. You have a unique opportunity to make this part of the decision-making process easy for them. Give the audience an epilogue to your trilogy. In Figure 16.1, I graphically depict key areas of focus to use when discussing the epilogue to your trilogy of scholarship. This figure follows the story board format from Chapters 13, 14, and 15.

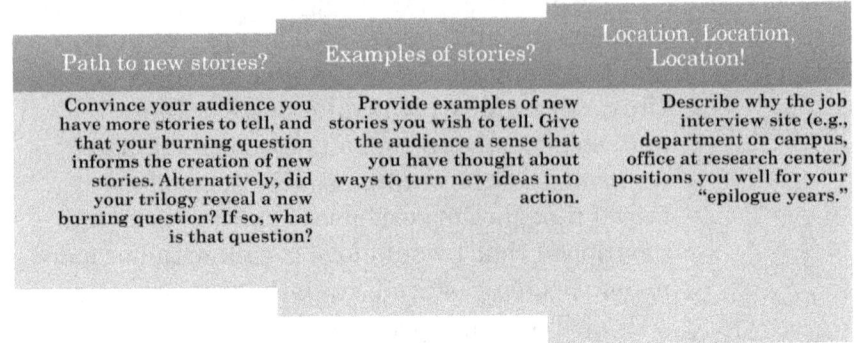

Figure 16.1. Story boards for planning the epilogue to your trilogy.

In storytelling, an *Epilogue* is "a section or speech at the end of a book or play that serves as a comment on or a conclusion to what has happened" (Oxford, 2019). The epilogue to a job talk is more comment than conclusion. That is, your epilogue sets the stage for your commentary on the future of your research program. In fact, the epilogue is what sets trilogies in job talks apart from film trilogies. In the third film of a trilogy, the filmmaker typically seeks to resolve the series of stories, and in fact the filmmaker tends to close the door to future storytelling. Instead, following the third work in your trilogy, leave the door open for more stories.

In scholarly work, what might "leaving the door open for more stories" look like? The answer to this question likely varies across disciplines. For some talks, the third work in a trilogy naturally leads to unanswered questions that beg for more inquiry. For other talks, a key conceptual limitation of the work or limitation in study design might cut across all of the scholarly work discussed during the talk. Addressing these limitations head-on might be a useful next step for scholarly work. As I describe below, often in Clinical Psychology tightly controlled or standardized basic research conducted in university laboratories marks the origin for scholarly work conducted in relatively uncontrolled, unstandardized applied settings like community mental health centers, hospitals, or primary schools. Your goal with the epilogue to your trilogy is to convince your audience that you have more scholarship to produce, and you have a plan for what form your scholarship will take over the next few years.

Modeling Moment: Epilogue

I tell my students that the act of submitting an application to fund your scholarly work often yields tangible benefits, even when the application itself fails to receive funding. For example, one of my failed applications led to a series of discussions with a colleague that resulted in an article about alternative approaches to funding scholarly work (De Los Reyes & Wang, 2012). A series of failed applications motivated a colleague and me to produce a special issue in a journal, to boost the relevance of our work in the eyes of grant reviewers (De Los Reyes & Ohannessian, 2016). More recently, portions of a grant application that, after years of revisions and resubmissions, finally received funding inspired an article focused on the next few years of our newly funded research agenda (De Los Reyes, Cook, Gresham, Makol, and Wang, 2019b).

In Bridget's case, she recently submitted a revised version of her predoctoral training grant application to the National Institutes of Health (Makol, 2019). Training grants submitted to the National Institutes of Health receive evaluations for not just the research proposed in the application but also for the training plan. Within this plan, the applicant describes the path through which they will become immersed in their specific research literature of interest, and learn the methods used to execute the proposed research. Bridget's first submission received a favorable score and I believe that the revised submission may very well receive funding for the research and training plan proposed in the application. I also believe that, even if ultimately unsuccessful in funding, key ideas in Bridget's National Institutes of Health training grant application inform the epilogue to her job talk (Makol, 2019). In particular, one passage of text in her application focuses on what Bridget envisions to be the next steps in her career following the execution of the research and training plan she proposed. I modified this passage of text slightly for the purposes of modeling the delivery of the epilogue portion of the job talk:

> The work I discussed today sets the stage for an innovative program of research designed to optimize use of behavioral data to improve the basic science of affective disorders and enhance the precision of clinical decision-making. For basic research, my work reveals insights on strategies for integrating multivariate data beyond survey reports, such as multi-method, dimensional data in experimental psychopathology, or the units of analysis in the National Institute of Mental Health's Research Domain Criteria initiative. For applied research, my work informs the development of methods for tailoring evaluations to the unique assessment needs of youth, and to ultimately improve the precision of clinical decision-making and intervention outcomes.

Modeling Moment: Debrief

One key element of National Institutes of Health training grant applications helps to contextualize this chapter's Modeling Moment. Like making hiring decisions for faculty positions, reviewers for these training grant applications focus as much on the applicant as they do on the proposed research and training plan. In particular, reviewers keenly focus on the applicant's future. That is, beyond the proposed funding period—which ranges anywhere from one year to no more than five years—does the applicant provide any evidence that they seek a future in research focused on improving public health? If so and assuming that work conducted during the funding period yields interesting research findings that inform future research plans, what might that future look like for this applicant? In this way, funding applicants and job talks both necessitate the delivery of an epilogue.

In the case of Bridget's job talk, she executes her epilogue using a two-pronged approach. One prong focuses on basic research, and the potential for the work she discussed in her talk to inform paradigms for integrating research modalities beyond subjective reports. In fact, one finds low correspondence among modalities used to directly assess biological functioning (De Los Reyes & Aldao, 2015). Thus, Bridget's work may have direct relevance to research supported by the National Institutes of Health and recent initiatives in clinical neuroscience (e.g., Sanislow et al., 2010). An audience member might envision Bridget seeking out collaborative opportunities that involve working with colleagues in clinical neuroscience. These collaborations might take the form of Bridget applying the paradigm she described and tested in the third work of her trilogy for use in integrating neurobiological measures. Efforts at integrating these measures might improve their ability to predict important clinical indices like treatment response or diagnosis.

The second prong of Bridget's approach to her epilogue speaks to the versatility or adaptability of her research program. Indeed, in discussing how her research program also informs applied research, Bridget allows the audience to see her work go down a different path. This path might involve collaborating with colleagues in more applied settings to see how her paradigm optimizes the ability of assessments used in these settings to inform service delivery for clients receiving mental health care. As I discuss below, how Bridget crafts her epilogue factors prominently in how her audience will react to her work and importantly, in the questions she will field from the audience. In this respect, and as detailed in Anonymous Account 16.2, the speaker has a profound influence on questions posed by the audience.

Anonymous Account 16.2. Influential Questions	
Early Career Faculty	Once an audience member was trying to catch me in what he seemingly perceived as overly casual language. I used the word "consulting" in describing work I had done, and once the talk concluded—after interrupting me twice during my talk—he asked me to specify what "exactly" I had done as a consultant. Luckily, I was prepared with an answer. One thing I learned from this experience: be prepared to defend anything that you mention during your talk. If you cite prior work, know what the researchers did and why they did it; if you present a certain analysis, know why you chose it and what it says about the constructs. When I used the word "consulting," I was prepared to describe specific consulting projects. It was tough to balance answering his question accurately and comprehensively without sounding defensive, especially given his tone and behavior earlier in the talk. I remembered that when I'm answering one person's question, I am speaking to the entire audience. Research *should* be challenged, and researchers should be prepared to respond to criticism—even when it feels personal—with openness and curiosity.

Bridget's epilogue points to factors involved in hiring faculty that often go unnoticed by those new to the decision-making process. Faculty positions in academia have seen a long downward decline in availability and thus increased competition for these positions (e.g., Jaschik, 2017; Xue & Larson, 2015). Thus, when a department or academic unit receives a faculty opening, everyone involved wants to maximize the utility of the opening. They want a lot of bang for their buck, so to speak. What better way to play to these motivations than to convey to the audience:

- *I can see my work extending to research conducted across multiple disciplines;*
- *I enjoy creating excuses to work with colleagues from diverse disciplines; and thus*
- *I see myself having many productive conversations with multiple faculty members in this room!*

Next Steps

At the conclusion to her epilogue, Bridget sets herself up for a productive end to her job talk. At this point, these talks typically transition to a large "question and answer" period in which faculty ask the speaker questions that arose for them during the talk. If Bridget frames the end of her talk as laid out previously, she gets a unique opportunity to field questions not only from audience members who share a great deal of overlap in research programs, but also questions from members who have built research programs quite distinct from hers.

A related component of post-epilogue talks warrants discussion. Specifically, a common phenomenon of this portion of the talk involves audience members asking questions regarding areas of scholarship or scholarly topics that the speaker has yet to pursue. Audience members ask these questions not to stump speakers; usually the questioner would know in advance that the speaker has yet to study the topics about which they focused their question. Rather, the purpose of these questions revolves around assessing the speaker's abilities to conceptually link their research program to the programs of academics from other scholarly universes. In this sense, speakers often find value in using the epilogue to focus on linking the content of scholarship discussed during the talk to areas of scholarship outside the scope of the talk. In fact, sometimes these epilogues have a way of "pulling" for questions within a scope that falls out of the speaker's comfort zone, but not too far out where they encounter difficulty addressing questions from the audience. And these kinds of epilogues have a way of giving speakers practice with connecting the stories they tell about their research program to the programs of other scholars—a focal point of discussion in the final chapter of this book.

CHAPTER 17
How Your Research Program Serves You and Your Scholarly Universe

Anonymous Account 17.1. Experiencing Awe

Early Career Faculty

Growing up, I studied to be a classical pianist. The excitement of creating something from nothing—from taking singular sounds and combining them to build something beautiful—was, to me, the coolest experience in the world. Chasing that feeling kept me practicing for two hours a day for nearly a decade! For most of that time, I was unconvinced that any other career path (outside of music) could generate that same awe and satisfaction as when you finally "brought a piece to life:" When you heard its component parts suddenly make sense as a cohesive whole. At the same time, I struggled with the idea that a classical music career was unlikely to allow me to contribute to solving pressing, real-world problems—something I hoped to be able to do, though I wasn't sure how. So when it came time to choose a college, I opted for a liberal arts education instead of conservatory. In my first year, during a psychology class I hadn't even intended to take, I learned about the concept of "clinical research" for the first time. None of my family members are in healthcare or science (most did not finish college), and my high school chemistry course felt frustratingly divorced from real-world issues—so the notion of "applied science" was totally new to me. But learning that theory and statistics could be used to *create previously non-existent solutions to major public health challenges* was an eye-opener. Using data-points to build new depression interventions, for instance, seemed a lot like learning a Chopin étude, one measure at a time...but with tangible benefits for people in need. In the following ten years, I got as much applied, clinical research experience as I could. I'm grateful every day to be in a career that not only allows people to help solve serious health challenges, but that actually offers—both through independent work and collaborations with incredible colleagues—that same "awe" feeling I once assumed was singular to music.

I opened the closing chapter of this book with a brilliant narrative detailed in Anonymous Account 17.1. The author of this account describes in lucid detail an element of academic work that many encounter but few discuss. Scholarly work has the potential to inspire awe. Many elements of a research career make it worth pursuing. It's these moments of awe that keep you going when work gets challenging. I want to use this chapter and the Anonymous Accounts contained herein to motivate action on your part. To push you to take your research career to new heights. Academics in your scholarly universe have a lot riding on you. They are counting on you. They want you to join them on a mission: to keep your scholarly universe spinning on. Don't let them down. Identify your star, the burning question that drives your research. Your colleagues wait with anxious anticipation to see you build a thought-provoking research program. They all know the difficult path one follows to build a research program. Are you ready for peer review? Do you have the tools and fortitude needed to navigate this system? To conquer this system and publish your work? This book prepared you to answer these questions.

THE EARLY CAREER RESEARCHER'S TOOLBOX

In Chapter 1, I noted my frustration that so many Emerging Academics like you find the academic tasks one needs to master to start a research career mystifying. In reading this book, you acquired tools to facilitate mastery of academic tasks, in an effort to demystify them. Throughout the book, I hinted at another frustration that motivated me to describe and model for you the academic tools you now possess. This core frustration has to do with the accessibility of the tools you need to begin a research career. I acquired some of the tools in my toolbox by consulting some great resources available to all of us (Silvia, 2007, 2018; Olson, 2015). Yet, I carry a toolbox containing many, many other tools that I acquired by consulting a supportive network of colleagues and mentors. I find this part of academia to be grossly unfair: The price of admission to accessing academic tools should not be who you know. The price of admission should be your willingness to learn the tools presented to you, and do the hard work needed to master their use. To learn from your experiences and expose yourself to contexts that allow you to test whether the learning paid off (Anonymous Account 17.2).

Anonymous Account 17.2. Experiencing Awe

Early Career Faculty

I strongly identify as a researcher first, and perhaps a somewhat reluctant clinician second. I have, however, gained the most insight into my most passionate research questions by engaging clinical training. I started a practicum placement that did not share the theoretical model in which my academic department trained its students. Initially, I would watch interactions between parents and children from a behavioral perspective—seeing some parents who were trying to interact with their kids as being on-track and effortful. However, my supervisors and co-students would speak at length about the experience of the child in those

interactions as being intruded upon, and in a way not valued. It was a shift in perspective that took some time to see, and now I am amazed at how that shift has helped shape my own research. My "awe" was realizing that I was missing something so important all along, and that it would have been so easy for me to have missed this valuable training opportunity. I now spend more time reflecting on the experiences of children, particularly those who cannot yet advocate for themselves, and what messages they get from their caregivers and broader structures that surround them about their worth, their value, and their independence.

I wrote this book to right a wrong that we see across the expanse of all our scholarly universes. I wrote this book to make accessible the tools that, historically, one attained only if they grew up in a supportive mentoring environment. We spent the entire book learning and mastering tools to address the three questions presented in Chapter 1; the questions you must answer affirmatively to successfully land a faculty job and begin your career:

- *Where do you fit within academia, and what burning question drives your work?*
- *On the path to publishing your work, how do you respond to reviews of your work?*
- *How do you connect pieces of your work to build a research program?*

The tail end of this book dealt with the third question. We learned and mastered tools for integrating multiple scholarly products into a coherent, compelling research program. It's this final set of academic tools that dictates the knowledge that spreads not just from your work but from all of the work in your scholarly universe. In your universe, ideas do not dictate the spread of knowledge to you and your colleagues. Nor does knowledge spread via the mere accumulation of scholarship reflected in years' and decades' worth of scholarly books and journal articles. Knowledge spreads with stories. The three-act structure of storytelling that we commonly see in film also functions as your universe's scholarship equation for storytelling. This structure allows you to communicate your work to others and others to communicate theirs to you. Why do we spread knowledge through stories? We use stories because neither you nor any other colleague in your scholarly universe harbors the capability to learn all one needs to learn of every subject matter that warrants scholarly inquiry. You rely on the expertise of your colleagues—and your colleagues rely on your expertise—to build your universe's collective base of knowledge. This base of knowledge can only be built with effort and trust. You and your colleagues must put forth effort to master the tools of story to share knowledge with each other. Your audience needs to hear the story of your scholarship told in ways so clear that anyone in that audience, regardless of their familiarity with your work, has the opportunity to comprehend and learn.

The greater the efforts you and your colleagues place in leveraging story to communicate with one another, the easier it becomes to trust in your collective abilities to move knowledge forward. This trust begets so many of the things that make a research career a worthwhile, fruitful pursuit. So much of scholarship takes place in solitude. We toil away on our lonesome reading the scholarship of others. We read to compile the knowledge and ideas that inspire our own ideas and generation of scholarly products. We generate knowledge, and we share this knowledge with our colleagues. And when we share knowledge with colleagues, and we not only understand story but master its inner workings, we learn the most profound lesson of all: *We do not have to produce knowledge in solitude* (Anonymous Account 17.3).

Anonymous Account 17.3. Experiencing Awe

Early Career Faculty

A well-known science organization approached our lab with a project idea. They wanted us to write a book on the human mind. Their instructions were essentially: "We'd like you to write a book about the psychology of human thought and behavior. Feel free to include anything that is scientifically supported and might be of interest to our readers. Hardcover book, around 300 pages. Good luck!" I was in my second year of graduate school. The proposition was overwhelming. Consolidate the most important scientific findings across all of psychology, make it interesting, and hurry up! Tick tock. My advisor and I needed some creativity, and fast. We met in a park the following Friday afternoon. We brought a single notebook (and some snacks). We had no idea where to start… so we didn't choose a starting point. We threw out whatever popped into our head—papers we had read recently, prominent researchers, intriguing findings, applications for interventions, horrible research ideas that no one should ever pursue, and so on. It was nonlinear and it was messy. I didn't say it at the time, but I was feeling increasingly overwhelmed (and frankly, hopeless) as our conversation meandered on. After two hours of "brainstorming"—maybe just storming—I looked down at our notebook and it hit me: we had an entire outline of our 10-chapter book. Two hours! We could already see the pieces of each chapter unfolding. In the moment, I felt the magic of creation. In what felt like a haphazard food fight, we created something from nothing. The extra layer: we knew in advance that thousands of copies of the book would be published. We had the power to potentially influence thousands of lives. In a field that most people enter to help others, I felt that, for the first time, my work might actually do so.

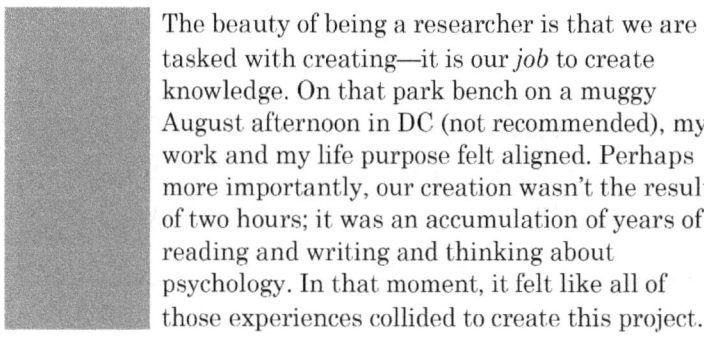

> The beauty of being a researcher is that we are tasked with creating—it is our *job* to create knowledge. On that park bench on a muggy August afternoon in DC (not recommended), my work and my life purpose felt aligned. Perhaps more importantly, our creation wasn't the result of two hours; it was an accumulation of years of reading and writing and thinking about psychology. In that moment, it felt like all of those experiences collided to create this project.

Through story you learn that some of your colleagues harbor burning questions similar to your own. Not only do your solar systems reside in the same universe, but only a short distance separates them from each other. The tools of story dictate your capacity for seeing not only the distance between your solar system and those of your colleagues but also the connections between the stars and planets of these solar systems. Story helps you perceive your universe without time. With the power of story, time evaporates. Story allows you to lean on the expertise of your colleagues, and vice versa. Story helps you bend space. With story, you close gaps in space between solar systems. You facilitate the ability to build collaborations with like-minded scholars where none previously existed. By evaporating time and bending space, you and your colleagues discover new opportunities for connecting the scholarship produced among solar systems. Story helps you learn from others, and story helps you grow with others.

As we end our time together, I have one request: Use your new tools to facilitate working with other scholars. Create excuses to work with like-minded scholars in your universe. Take risks. Form connections with scholars in universes to which no one in your own universe has traveled previously. Make colleagues. Form collaborations. Expand your scholarly universe, and ensure that it spins on.

Glossary

And-But-Therefore: An approach developed by Olson (2015) to distill principles of narrative structure for the purposes of improving the ability of researchers to communicate their work.

Bias: In **Peer Review**, a factor in **Evaluators'** reviews of scholarly work that directly impacts measurement validity or accuracy in measurement, or instances in which their judgments systematically reflect characteristics of the evaluated work other than its quality.

Burning Question: The abstract idea around which the whole of a program of scholarly work revolves (see also **Star**).

Collaborator: A colleague with whom a scholar shares previous scholarship and/or ongoing scholarly pursuits.

Editor: In **Peer Review**, an established figure in a specific discipline or field who leads the evaluation of work submitted for publication in a scholarly outlet (e.g., academic journal).

Editorial Consultant: In **Peer Review**, scholars who **Editors** invite to independently evaluate work submitted for publication in scholarly outlets, and submit their evaluations of the strengths and weaknesses of the work (see also **Evaluator**).

Emerging Academic: Someone with the potential to consume, critique, and add to the knowledge base of a specific area of scholarly interest, but who has yet to demonstrate the ability to produce scholarly work outside of the confines of a supervisory relationship with an experienced academic tasked with serving as their **Mentor** during key points of their academic training (e.g., doctoral or post-doctoral study).

Epilogue: Metaphorical device embedded in the **Trilogy Tool** to represent the portion of an academic job talk in which the speaker outlines their directions for future scholarly work.

Evaluator: A colleague with whom a scholar has yet to collaborate but who nonetheless harbors the necessary expertise to understand and interpret the scholar's work (see also **Peer Review**).

Galaxy: Metaphorical device embedded in the **Shared Universe Tool** to represent an experienced scholar's program of scholarly work (see also **Mentor**), as well as the scholarly environment in which an **Emerging Academic** receives training.

Gravitational Force: Metaphorical device embedded in the **Shared Universe Tool** to represent the theoretical framework used to explain an abstract topic or idea. Essentially, the Gravitational Force binds an idea to the individual pieces of scholarly work created in pursuit of that idea (see also **Solar System**).

Inter-Rater Reliability: In **Peer Review**, a test of the degree to which two or more **Evaluators** converge on their reviews of the same scholarly work.

Mentor: An experienced professional who provides an **Emerging Academic** with supervised training designed to develop their capability to pursue an independent research career.

Peer Review: An evaluative system implemented and sustained by scholars to ensure quality control of work published in scholarly literatures (see also **Evaluator**).

Planet: Metaphorical device embedded in the **Shared Universe Tool** to represent the concrete pieces of scholarship (e.g., books, journal articles) produced within a line of scholarly work or larger program of scholarly work (see also **Solar System**).

Psychometrics: A sub-discipline of Psychology focused on understanding and in some cases improving measurements of mental processes and related domains.

Research Program: A compelling story or account of an academic's area of expertise or body of scholarly work.

Revise and Resubmit (R&R): A phrase used to describe a type of editorial decision about a manuscript that is submitted for publication in a scholarly journal (see also **Peer Review**). Following receipt of comments about that manuscript by an independent set of scholars (see also **Evaluator**), the **Editor** does not reject the manuscript for publication, and instead, invites the authors of that manuscript to make revisions in response to commentary, and resubmit the revised version of the manuscript for further consideration.

Shared Universe Tool: An academic tool described in this book, focused on conceptualizing the relationship between the **Emerging Academic**, their **Mentor**, and the colleagues with whom the Mentor shares related scholarly interests.

Solar System: Metaphorical device embedded in the **Shared Universe Tool** to represent a line of scholarly work consisting of a core idea (i.e., **Star**) that drives the work, concrete pieces of scholarship (i.e., **Planets**) stemming from that core idea, and a theoretical framework (i.e., **Gravitational Force**) designed to bind or connect the core idea and pieces of scholarly work.

Star: Metaphorical device embedded in the **Shared Universe Tool** to represent the abstract idea around which the whole of one's **Research Program** revolves (see also **Solar System**).

Trilogy Tool: An academic tool described in this book, focused on conceptualizing the integration of multiple pieces of a scholar's academic work into a cohesive, compelling **Research Program**.

Universe: Metaphorical device embedded in the **Shared Universe Tool** to represent a network of scholars who devote their academic work to pursuing interconnected ideas or scholarly pursuits (see also **Burning Question**).

About the Author

Andres De Los Reyes received his Ph.D. in 2008 from Yale University. He began his career as an Assistant Professor at the University of Maryland at College Park. Within 10 years he was promoted up the ranks to Full Professor with tenure. He serves as Director of the Comprehensive Assessment and Intervention Program (www.caipumd.weebly.com), where he has provided research training to hundreds of undergraduate and graduate students. Dr. De Los Reyes has over 100 publications, many in career-defining peer review journals in Psychology such as the *Psychological Bulletin, Psychological Review, Psychological Assessment*, and *Annual Review of Clinical Psychology*. He has received over $1.5 million in research funding from the Institute of Education Sciences, National Science Foundation, and National Institutes of Health. His service record reveals his passion for education and professional development. In 2019, Dr. De Los Reyes served as Chair of the Board of Educational Affairs (www.apa.org/ed/governance/bea/) of the American Psychological Association, Psychology's largest organization with over 100,000 members. He serves as Editor for the *Journal of Clinical Child and Adolescent Psychology* (2017-2025), a top-tier journal with subscriptions at institutions in over 30 countries. He also founded and serves as Program Chair for the *Future Directions Forum* (www.jccapfuturedirectionsforum.com). This annual event offers professional development workshops and small-group and one-on-one consultations on all aspects of scholarly work. He has received a number of honors, including the American Psychological Association's *Distinguished Scientific Award for an Early Career Contribution to Psychology*, and Fellow status at the American Psychological Association and Association for Psychological Science.

References

Abbot, D.S., & Switzer, E.R. (2011). The Steppenwolf: a proposal for a habitable planet in interstellar space. *The Astrophysical Journal Letters, 735*, L27. doi: 10.1088/2041-8205/735/2/L27

Academy of Motion Picture Arts and Sciences (2019). The official Academy Awards® database [Online searchable database]. Retrieved from http://awardsdatabase.oscars.org/.

Achenbach, T.M., McConaughy, S.H., & Howell, C.T. (1987). Child/adolescent behavioral and emotional problems: Implications of cross-informant correlations for situational specificity. *Psychological Bulletin, 101*, 213-232. doi: 10.1037/0033-2909.101.2.213

Adler, S. (2008). Exclusive: Spike Lee says 'I'll take the Obama high road' in Clint Eastwood argument. *MTV News*. Retrieved from http://www.mtv.com/news/2430190/exclusive-spike-lee-says-ill-take-the-obama-high-road-in-clint-eastwood-argument/.

Albarracín, D. (2015). Editorial. *Psychological Bulletin, 141*, 1-5. doi: 10.1037/bul0000007

Arad, A. (Producer), Feige, K. (Producer), & Favreau, J. (Director) (2008). *Iron man* [Motion picture]. United States: Paramount Pictures.

Beidas, R.S., Stewart, R.E., Walsh, L., Lucas, S., Downey, M.M., Jackson, K., Fernandez, T., & Mandell, D.S. (2015). Free, brief, and validated: Standardized instruments for low-resource mental health settings. *Cognitive and Behavioral Practice, 22*, 5-19. doi: 10.1016/j.cbpra.2014.02.002

Benner, A. (2018). Adolescence. In M. Bornstein (Ed.), *The SAGE encyclopedia of lifespan human development* (Vols. 1-5). Thousand Oaks, CA: SAGE Publications, Inc. doi: 10.4135/9781506307633

Bornmann, L. (2008) An analysis of the peer review process from the perspective of sociology of science theories. *Human Architecture: Journal of the Sociology of Self Knowledge, 6*, 23-38. Retrieved from https://scholarworks.umb.edu/humanarchitecture/vol6/iss2/3

Borsboom, D. (2005). *Measuring the mind.* New York: Cambridge University Press.

Bozman, R. (Producer), Saxon, E. (Producer), Utt, K. (Producer), & Demme, J. (Director) (1991). *The silence of the lambs* [Motion picture]. United States: Orion Pictures.

Busch, K.A., Fawcett, J., & Jacobs, D.G. (2003). Clinical correlates of inpatient suicide. *The Journal of Clinical Psychiatry, 64,* 14-19. doi: 10.4088/JCP.v64n0105

Cicchetti, D.V. (1991). The reliability of peer review for manuscript and grant submissions: A cross-disciplinary investigation. *Behavioral and Brain Sciences, 14,* 119-135. doi: 10.1017/S0140525X00065675

Craven, W. (Producer and Director), Konrad, C. (Producer), & Maddalena, M. (2000). *Scream 3* [Motion picture]. United States: Dimension Films.

Craven, W. (Producer and Director), Konrad, C. (Producer), & Maddalena, M. (Producer) (1997). *Scream 2* [Motion picture]. United States: Dimension Films.

De Los Reyes, A. (2018a, January). *Become the most prolific writer you know: Evidence-based strategies for boosting productivity in your academic writing.* Workshop conducted at the American Psychological Association's Academic Career Education Series webcast,

Washington, DC. Retrieved from https://www.apa.org/education/ce/pdp0027.

De Los Reyes, A. (2018b, June). *The (gross) anatomy of responding to peer review commentary.* Workshop conducted at the Future Directions Forum, Washington, DC. Retrieved from http://bit.ly/ECRToolboxChapter9PersistandProceed.

De Los Reyes, A. (2017). Inaugural Editorial: Making the *Journal of Clinical Child and Adolescent Psychology* your "home journal". *Journal of Clinical Child and Adolescent Psychology, 46,* 1-10. doi: 10.1080/15374416.2016.1266649

De Los Reyes, A. (2011). Introduction to the special section: More than measurement error: Discovering meaning behind informant discrepancies in clinical assessments of children and adolescents. *Journal of Clinical Child and Adolescent Psychology, 40,* 1-9. doi: 10.1080/15374416.2011.533405

De Los Reyes, A., & Aldao, A. (2015). Introduction to the special issue: Toward implementing physiological measures in clinical child and adolescent assessments. *Journal of Clinical Child and Adolescent Psychology, 44,* 221-237. doi: 10.1080/15374416.2014.891227

De Los Reyes, A., Augenstein, T.M., & Aldao, A. (2017). Assessment issues in child and adolescent psychotherapy. In J.R. Weisz and A.E. Kazdin (Eds.), *Evidence-based psychotherapies for children and adolescents* (3rd ed., pp. 537-554). New York: Guilford.

De Los Reyes, A., Augenstein, T.M., Wang, M., Thomas, S.A., Drabick, D.A.G., Burgers, D., & Rabinowitz, J. (2015). The validity of the multi-informant approach to assessing child and adolescent mental health.

Psychological Bulletin, 141, 858-900. doi: 10.1037/a0038498

De Los Reyes, A., Goodman, K.L., Kliewer, W., & Reid-Quiñones, K.R. (2010). The longitudinal consistency of mother-child reporting discrepancies of parental monitoring and their ability to predict child delinquent behaviors two years later. *Journal of Youth and Adolescence, 39,* 1417-1430. doi: 10.1007/s10964-009-9496-7

De Los Reyes, A., Henry, D.B., Tolan, P.H., & Wakschlag, L.S. (2009). Linking informant discrepancies to observed variations in young children's disruptive behavior. *Journal of Abnormal Child Psychology, 37,* 637-652. doi: 10.1007/s10802-009-9307-3

De Los Reyes, A., & Kazdin, A.E. (2004). Measuring informant discrepancies in clinical child research. *Psychological Assessment, 16,* 330-334. doi: 10.1037/1040-3590.16.3.330

De Los Reyes, A., & Kazdin, A.E. (2005). Informant discrepancies in the assessment of childhood psychopathology: A critical review, theoretical framework, and recommendations for further study. *Psychological Bulletin, 131,* 483-509. doi: 10.1037/0033-2909.131.4.483

De Los Reyes, A., & Kazdin, A.E. (2006a). Conceptualizing changes in behavior in intervention research: The range of possible changes model. *Psychological Review, 113,* 554-583. doi: 10.1037/0033-295X.113.3.554

De Los Reyes, A., & Kazdin, A.E. (2006b). Informant discrepancies in assessing child dysfunction relate to dysfunction within mother-child interactions. *Journal of Child and Family Studies, 15,* 645-663. doi: 10.1007/s10826-006-9031-3

De Los Reyes, A., Lerner, M.D., Keeley, L.M., Weber, R., Drabick, D.A.G., Rabinowitz, J., & Goodman, K.L. (2019a). Improving interpretability of subjective assessments about psychological phenomena: A review and cross-cultural meta-analysis. *Review of General Psychology, 23*, 293-319. doi: 10.1177/1089268019837064

De Los Reyes, A., Cook, C.R., Gresham, F.M., Makol, B.A., & Wang, M. (2019b). Informant discrepancies in assessments of psychosocial functioning in school-based services and research: Review and directions for future research. *Journal of School Psychology, 74*, 74-89. doi: 10.1016/j.jsp.2019.05.005

De Los Reyes, A., & Makol, B.A. (2019). Evidence-based assessment. In T.H. Ollendick, L. Farrell, and P. Muris (Eds.), *Innovations in CBT for childhood anxiety, OCD, and PTSD: Improving access and outcomes* (pp. 28-51). New York: Cambridge.

De Los Reyes, A., & Ohannessian, C.M., (2016). Introduction to the special issue: Discrepancies in adolescent-parent perceptions of the family and adolescent adjustment. *Journal of Youth and Adolescence, 45*, 1957-1972. doi: 10.1007/s10964-016-0533-z

De Los Reyes, A., & Prinstein, M.J. (2004). Applying depression-distortion hypotheses to the assessment of peer victimization in adolescents. *Journal of Clinical Child and Adolescent Psychology, 33*, 325-335. doi: 10.1207/s15374424jccp3302_14

De Los Reyes, A., Berman, S.L., & Silverman, W.K. (2001, November). *Anxiety, depression, and fear and its influence on parent over-reporting of child anxiety and fear.* Poster presented at the annual meeting of the Association for Advancement of Behavior Therapy, Philadelphia, PA.

De Los Reyes, A., Thomas, S.A., Goodman, K.L., & Kundey, S.M.A. (2013). Principles underlying the use of multiple informants' reports. *Annual Review of Clinical Psychology, 9,* 123-149. doi: 10.1146/annurev-clinpsy-050212-185617

De Los Reyes, A., & Wang, M. (2012). Applying psychometric theory and research to developing a continuously distributed approach to making research funding decisions. *Review of General Psychology, 16,* 298-304. doi: 10.1037/a0027250

Deros, D.E., Racz, S.J., Lipton, M.F., Augenstein, T.M., Karp, J.N., Keeley, L.M., . . . De Los Reyes, A. (2018). Multi-informant assessments of adolescent social anxiety: Adding clarity by leveraging reports from unfamiliar peer confederates. *Behavior Therapy, 49,* 84-98. doi: 10.1016/j.beth.2017.05.001

De Vries, D.R., Marschall, E.A., & Stein, R.A. (2009): Exploring the peer review process: What is it, does it work, and can it be improved? *Fisheries, 34,* 270-279. doi: 10.1577/1548-8446-34.6.270

Eckshtain, D., Kuppens, S., Ugueto, A., Ng, M.Y., Vaughn-Coaxum, R., Corteselli, K., & Weisz, J.R. (2020). Meta-analysis: 13-year follow-up of psychotherapy effects on youth depression. *Journal of the American Academy of Child and Adolescent Psychiatry, 59,* 45-63. doi: 10.1016/j.jaac.2019.04.002

Epilogue (2019). In *Oxford's living dictionary.* Retrieved from https://en.oxforddictionaries.com/definition/epilogue.

Faust, B.P. (Producer), Golin, S. (Producer), Rocklin, N. (Producer), Sugar, M. (Producer), & McCarthy, T.

(Director) (2015). *Spotlight* [Motion picture]. United States: Open Road Films.

Feige, K. (Producer), & Black, S. (Director) (2013). *Iron man 3* [Motion picture]. United States: Walt Disney Studios Motion Pictures.

Feige, K. (Producer), & Branagh, K. (Director) (2011). *Thor* [Motion picture]. United States: Paramount Pictures.

Feige, K. (Producer), & Favreau, J. (Director) (2010). *Iron man 2* [Motion picture]. United States: Paramount Pictures.

Feige, K. (Producer), & Johnston, J. (Director) (2011). *Captain America: The first avenger* [Motion picture]. United States: Paramount Pictures.

Feige, K. (Producer), & Whedon, J. (Director) (2015). *Avengers: Age of Ultron* [Motion picture]. United States: Walt Disney Studios Motion Pictures.

Feige, K. (Producer), Russo, A. (Director), & Russo, J. (Director) (2019). *Avengers: Endgame* [Motion picture]. United States: Walt Disney Studios Motion Pictures.

Feige, K. (Producer), Russo, A. (Director), & Russo, J. (Director) (2018). *Avengers: Infinity war* [Motion picture]. United States: Walt Disney Studios Motion Pictures.

Feige, K. (Producer), Russo, A. (Director), & Russo, J. (Director) (2016). *Captain America: Civil war* [Motion picture]. United States: Walt Disney Studios Motion Pictures.

Feige, K. (Producer), Russo, A. (Director), & Russo, J. (Director) (2014). *Captain America: The winter soldier* [Motion picture]. United States: Walt Disney Studios Motion Pictures.

Feige, K. (Producer), & Taylor, A. (Director) (2013). *Thor: The dark world* [Motion picture]. United States: Walt Disney Studios Motion Pictures.

Feige, K. (Producer), & Waititi, A. (Director) (2017). *Thor: Ragnarok* [Motion picture]. United States: Walt Disney Studios Motion Pictures.

Feige, K. (Producer), & Whedon, J. (Director) (2012). *The avengers* [Motion picture]. United States: Walt Disney Studios Motion Pictures.

Fincham, F.D., & Lucier-Greer, M. (2018). Emerging adulthood. In M. Bornstein (Ed.), *The SAGE encyclopedia of lifespan human development* (Vols. 1-5). Thousand Oaks, CA: SAGE Publications, Inc. doi: 10.4135/9781506307633

Friedman, B., Berdahl, T., Simpson, L.A., McCormick, M.C., Owens, P.L., Andrews, R., & Romano, P.S. (2011). Annual report on health care for children and youth in the United States: Focus on trends in hospital use and quality. *Academic Pediatrics, 11*, 263-279. doi: 10.1016/j.acap.2011.04.002

Glenn, L.E., Keeley, L.M., Szollos, S., Okuno, H., Wang, X., Rausch, E., . . . De Los Reyes, A. (2019). Trained observers' ratings of adolescents' social anxiety and social skills within controlled, cross-contextual social interactions with unfamiliar peer confederates. *Journal of Psychopathology and Behavioral Assessment, 41*, 1-15. doi: 10.1007/s10862-018-9676-4

Grazer, B. (Producer), & Lee, S. (Director) (2006). *Inside man* [Motion picture]. United States: Universal Pictures.

Hasson, U., Furman, O., Clark, D., Dudai, Y., & Davachi, L. (2008). Enhanced intersubject correlations during movie viewing correlate with successful episodic encoding. *Neuron, 57*, 452-462. doi: 10.1016/j.neuron.2007.12.009

Hawley, K.M., & Weisz, J.R. (2003). Child, parent, and therapist (dis)agreement on target problems in outpatient therapy: The therapist's dilemma and its implications. *Journal of Consulting and Clinical Psychology, 71,* 62-70. doi: 10.1037/0022-006X.71.1.62

Huang, S.S. (1959). Occurrence of life in the universe. *American Scientist, 47,* 397-402. Retrieved from https://www.jstor.org/stable/27827376.

Hunsley, J., & Mash, E.J. (2007). Evidence-based assessment. *Annual Review of Clinical Psychology, 3,* 29-51. doi: 10.1146/annurev.clinpsy.3.022806.091419

Ioannidis, J.P., Tatsioni, A., & Karassa, F.B. (2010). Who is afraid of reviewers' comments? Or, why anything can be published and anything can be cited. *European Journal of Clinical Investigation, 40,* 285-287. doi: 10.1111/j.1365-2362.2010.02272.x

Jaschik, S. (2017). Another bad year for history jobs. *Inside Higher Ed.* Retrieved from https://www.insidehighered.com/news/2017/11/17/decrease-number-openings-history-faculty-jobs.

Johnson, D.R., & Hermanowicz, J.C. (2017). Peer review: From "sacred ideals" to "profane realities". In M.B. Paulsen (Ed.), *Higher education: Handbook of theory and research* (vol. 32, pp. 485-527). Cham, Switzerland: Springer.

Jones, J.D., Boyd, R.C., Calkins, M.E., Ahmed, A., Moore, T.M., Barzilay, R., Benton, T.D., & Gur, R.E. (2019). Parent-adolescent agreement about adolescents' suicidal thoughts. *Pediatrics, 143,* 1-12. doi: 10.1542/peds.2018-1771

Juran, J.M., & Godfrey, A.B. (1999). *Juran's quality handbook* (5th ed.). New York: McGraw-Hill.

Kazdin, A.E. (2012). *Behavior modification in applied settings* (7th ed.). Long Grove, IL: Waveland.

Kazdin, A.E. (2007). Mediators and mechanisms of change in psychotherapy research. *Annual Review of Clinical Psychology, 3*, 1-27. doi: 10.1146/annurev.clinpsy.3.022806.091432

Kazdin, A.E. (1987). Treatment of antisocial behavior in children: Current status and future directions. *Psychological Bulletin, 102*, 187-203. doi: 10.1037/0033-2909.102.2.187

Ki, J.J., Kelly, S.P., & Parra, L.C. (2016). Attention strongly modulates reliability of neural responses to naturalistic narrative stimuli. *Journal of Neuroscience, 36*, 3092-3101. doi: 10.1523/JNEUROSCI.2942-15.2016

Kinberg, S. (Producer), Reynolds, R. (Producer), Shuler Donner, L. (Producer), & Miller, T. (Director) (2016). *Deadpool* [Motion picture]. United States: 20th Century Fox.

Klaus, N.M., Mobilio, A., & King, C.A. (2009). Parent-adolescent agreement concerning adolescents' suicidal thoughts and behaviors. *Journal of Clinical Child and Adolescent Psychology, 38*, 245-255. doi: 10.1080/15374410802698412

Konrad, C. (Producer), Woods, C. (Producer), & Craven, W. (1996). *Scream* [Motion picture]. United States: Dimension Films.

Kopparapu, R.K. (2013). A revised estimate of the occurrence rate of terrestrial planets in the habitable zones around Kepler M-dwarfs. *The Astrophysical Journal Letters, 767*, L8. doi: 10.1088/2041-8205/767/1/L8

Kraemer, H.C., Measelle, J.R., Ablow, J.C., Essex, M.J., Boyce, W.T., & Kupfer, D.J. (2003). A new approach to integrating data from multiple informants in psychiatric assessment and research: Mixing and matching contexts and perspectives. *The American Journal of Psychiatry, 160,* 1566-1577. doi: 10.1176/appi.ajp.160.9.1566

Kurtz, G. (Producer), & Lucas, G. (Director) (1977). *Star wars: Episode IV – A new hope* [Motion picture]. United States: 20th Century Fox.

Lapouse, R., & Monk, M.A. (1958). An epidemiologic study of behavior characteristics in children. *American Journal of Public Health, 48,* 1134-1144. doi:10.2105/AJPH.48.9.1134

Laughlin, G., & Adams, F.C. (2000). The frozen Earth: Binary scattering events and the fate of the Solar System. *Icarus, 145,* 614-627. doi: 10.1006/icar.2000.6355

Laursen, B., Coy, K.C., & Collins, W.A. (1998). Reconsidering changes in parent–child conflict across adolescence: A meta-analysis. *Child Development, 69,* 817-832. doi: 10.1111/j.1467-8624.1998.tb06245.x

Lennon, J., & McCartney, P. (1967). With a little help from my friends [Recorded by the Beatles]. On Sgt. Pepper's Lonely Hearts Club Band [multitrack tape]. London: Parlophone.

Lipworth, W.L., Kerridge, I.H., Carter, S.M., & Little, M. (2011). Journal peer review in context: A qualitative study of the social and subjective dimensions of manuscript review in biomedical publishing. *Social Science and Medicine, 72,* 1056-1063. doi: 10.1016/j.socscimed.2011.02.002

Lissauer, J.J. (1987). Timescales for planetary accretion and the structure of the protoplanetary disk. *Icarus, 69,* 249-265. doi: 10.1016/0019-1035(87)90104-7

Makol, B.A. (2019). *From basic science to clinical decision-making: A theoretically grounded, integrative approach for optimizing multi-informant assessments of youth affective symptoms.* Grant application.

Makol, B.A., De Los Reyes, A., Ostrander, R., & Reynolds, E.K. (2019). Parent-youth divergence (and convergence) in reports of youth internalizing problems in psychiatric inpatient care. *Journal of Abnormal Child Psychology, 47,* 1677-1689. doi: 10.1007/s10802-019-00540-7

Makol, B.A., Glenn, L.E., Youngstrom, E.A., & De Los Reyes, A. (2018, November). *Optimizing adolescent, parent, and peer confederate reports in evidence-based assessment of adolescent social anxiety.* Poster presented at the annual meeting of the Association for Behavioral and Cognitive Therapies, Washington, DC.

Makol, B.A., Youngstrom, E.A., Racz, S.J., Qasmieh, N., Glenn, L.E., & De Los Reyes, A. (2020). *Integrating multiple informants' reports: How conceptual and measurement models may address long-standing problems in clinical decision-making.* Manuscript submitted for publication.

Makol, B.A. & Polo, A.J. (2018). Parent-child endorsement discrepancies among youth at chronic-risk for depression. *Journal of Abnormal Child Psychology, 46,* 1077-1088. doi: 10.1007/s10802-017-0360-z

Makol, B.A., Sajwani, A., Grocochinski, M., Reeb, S., & Polo, A.J. (2015, November). *"My child holds her sad feelings in." Youth emotion inhibition as a predictor of parent-child report discrepancies of core youth depressive symptoms.* Poster presented at the 49th Annual Convention of the Association of Behavioral and Cognitive Therapies, Chicago, IL.

MarineParents.com, LLC (2019). What's after Boot™: School of infantry. Retrieved from http://whatsafterboot.com/soi.asp.

Marsh, H.W., Jayasinghe, U.W., & Bond, N.W. (2008). Improving the peer-review process for grant applications: reliability, validity, bias, and generalizability. *American Psychologist, 63*, 160-168. doi: 10.1037/0003-066X.63.3.160

McCormick, C.B., & Barnes, B.J. (2008). Getting started in academia: A guide for educational psychologists. *Educational Psychology Review, 20*, 5-18. doi: 10.1007/s10648-007-9058-z

National Science Foundation, National Center for Science and Engineering Statistics (2018). *Full-time graduate enrollment in science and engineering continues to grow in 2016 due to increased enrollment by foreign students on temporary visas.* Retrieved from https://www.nsf.gov/statistics/2018/nsf18307/.

Nock, M.K., Park, J.M., Finn, C.T., Deliberto, T.L., Dour, H.J., & Banaji, M.R. (2010). Measuring the suicidal mind: Implicit cognition predicts suicidal behavior. *Psychological Science, 21*, 511-517. doi: 10.1177/0956797610364762

Nunnally, J.C., & Bernstein, I.H. (1994). *Psychometric theory* (3rd ed.). New York, NY: McGraw-Hill.

Okahana, H., & Zhou, E. (2018). *Graduate enrollment and degrees: 2007 to 2017.* Washington, DC: Council of Graduate Schools.

Olson, R. (2015). *Houston, we have a narrative: Why science needs story.* Chicago, IL: University of Chicago Press.

Paus, T., Keshavan, M., & Giedd, J. N. (2008). Why do many psychiatric disorders emerge during adolescence? *Nature Reviews Neuroscience, 9*, 947-957. doi: 10.1038/nrn2513

Pier, E. L., Brauer, M., Filut, A., Kaatz, A., Raclaw, J., Nathan, M. J., ... & Carnes, M. (2018). Low agreement among reviewers evaluating the same NIH grant applications. *Proceedings of the National Academy of Sciences, 115,* 2952-2957. doi: 10.1073/pnas.1714379115

Polymath (2019). In *Oxford's living dictionary.* Retrieved from https://en.oxforddictionaries.com/definition/polymath.

Prinstein, M.J., & Patterson, M.D. (Eds.). (2013). *The portable mentor: Expert guide to a successful career in psychology* (2nd ed.). New York: Springer.

Prinstein, M.J., Nock, M.K., Spirito, A., & Grapentine, W.L. (2001). Multimethod assessment of suicidality in adolescent psychiatric in-patients: Preliminary results. *Journal of the American Academy of Child & Adolescent Psychiatry, 40,* 1053-1061. doi: 10.1097/00004583-200109000-00014

Rao, N., & Wong, J.M.S. (2018). Early child development. In M. Bornstein (Ed.), *The SAGE encyclopedia of lifespan human development* (Vols. 1-5). Thousand Oaks, CA: SAGE Publications, Inc. doi: 10.4135/9781506307633

Resch, K., Ernst, E., & Garrow, J. (2000). A randomized controlled study of reviewer bias against an unconventional therapy. *Journal of the Royal Society of Medicine, 93,* 164-167. doi: 10.1177/014107680009300402

Reynolds, E.K., Silver, A.A., Morris, A., Hankinson, J.C., Perry-Parish, C., Specht, M.W., & Ostrander, R. (2018). Factors associated with length of youth inpatient psychiatric hospitalization. *Adolescent Psychiatric, 8,* 111-120. doi: 10.2174/2210676608666180508125157

Rota, J. (Producer) (2003). *Legendary nights: The tale of Hagler-Hearns*. [Documentary]. United States: Home Box Office.

Roven, C. (Producer), Snyder, D. (Producer), & Snyder, Z. (Director) (2016). *Batman v. Superman: Dawn of justice* [Motion picture]. United States: Warner Brothers Pictures.

Samsung. (2017, January 23). Galaxy Note 7: What we discovered [Press release]. Retrieved from https://news.samsung.com/global/infographic-galaxy-note7-what-we-discovered.

Sanislow, C.A., Pine, D.S., Quinn, K.J., Kozak, M.J., Garvey, M.A., Heinssen, R.K., . . . Cuthbert, B.N. (2010). Developing constructs for psychopathology research: Research domain criteria. *Journal of Abnormal Psychology, 119*, 631-639. doi:10.1037/a0020909

Schekman, R. (2016). Introduction: The challenge of reproducibility. *Annual Review of Cell and Developmental Biology*, 32. doi: 10.1146/annurev-cb-32-100316-100001

Schmidt, S. (2009). Shall we really do it again? The powerful concept of replication is neglected in the social sciences. *Review of General Psychology, 13*, 90-100. doi: 10.1037/a0015108

Shapiro, L. (2015). The author who thinks 'South Park' can help save science. *Huffington Post*. Retrieved from https://www.huffingtonpost.com/entry/randy-olson-science-narrative_us_56312db4e4b063179910afb4.

Silvia, P.J. (2007). *How to write a lot: A practical guide to productive academic writing*. Washington, DC: American Psychological Association.

Silvia, P.J. (2018). *How to write a lot: A practical guide to productive academic writing* (2nd ed.). Washington, DC: American Psychological Association.

Smetana, J., & Gaines, C. (1999). Adolescent-parent conflict in middleclass African American families. *Child Development, 70,* 1447-1463. doi: 10.1111/1467-8624.00105

Smith, R. (2006). Peer review: a flawed process at the heart of science and journals. *Journal of the Royal Society of Medicine, 99,* 178-182. doi: 10.1258/jrsm.99.4.178

Spier, R. (2002). The history of the peer-review process. *TRENDS in Biotechnology, 20,* 357-358. doi: 10.1016/S0167-7799(02)01985-6

Steinberg, L. (2005). Cognitive and affective development in adolescence. *Trends in Cognitive Sciences, 9,* 69-74. doi: 10.1016/j.tics.2004.12.005

Sternberg, R.J. (1991). Editorial. *Psychological Bulletin, 109,* 3-4. doi: 10.1037/h0092473

Tennyson, A.L. (1833). *Ulysses.* Retrieved from https://www.poetryfoundation.org/poems/45392/ulysses.

Thompson, R., Dubowitz, H., English, D.J., Nooner, K.B., Wike, T., Bangdiwala, S.I., Runyan, D.K., & Briggs, E.C. (2006). Parents' and teachers' concordance with children's self-ratings of suicidality: Findings from a high-risk sample. *Suicide and Life-threatening Behavior, 36,* 167-181. doi: 10.1521/suli.2006.36.2.167

Trilogy (2019). In *Oxford's living dictionary.* Retrieved from https://en.oxforddictionaries.com/definition/trilogy.

Trower, C.A. (2012). *Success on the tenure track: Five keys to faculty job satisfaction.* Baltimore: Johns Hopkins University Press.

United States Marine Corps (2015). *Military topographic map I B170229XQ student handout.* Retrieved from https://www.trngcmd.marines.mil/Portals/207/Site%20 Images/TBS/B170229XQ%20Military%20 Topographic%20Map%20I.pdf?ver=2015-10-13-090146-213.

Walkuski, E. (2013). Exclusive interview: Wes Craven talks Yeah TV, Nightmare on Elm Street and his future. *Arrow in the Head.* Retrieved from https://www.joblo.com/horror-movies/news/exclusive-interview-wes-craven-talks-yeah-tv-nightmare-on-elm-street-and-his-future.

Weisz, J.R., McCarty, C.A., & Valeri, S.M. (2006). Effects of psychotherapy for depression in children and adolescents: A meta-analysis. *Psychological Bulletin, 132,* 132-149. doi: 10.1037/0033-2909.132.1.132

Wilson, M.G. (Producer), Broccoli, B. (Producer), & Mendes, S. (Director) (2012). *Skyfall* [Motion picture]. United Kingdom & United States: Sony Pictures Releasing.

Wooley, J. (2011). *Wes Craven: The man and his nightmares.* Hoboken, NJ: John Wiley & Sons.

Xue, Y., & Larson, R.C. (2015). STEM crisis or STEM surplus? Yes and yes. *Monthly Labor Review, 2015.* doi: 10.21916/mlr.2015.14

Index

abstract ideas, 54, 59
academics
   failures/successes in, 41–43, 130–131
   finding work, 7, 81–82, 175–183
   See also Anonymous Accounts; Emerging Academics; job talks
academic toolbox
   Modeling Moments
   burning questions, 54–59
   feedback, 158–159
   illustrated, 13–14
   mentors, 26–29
   peer review tools, 135–137, 159
   research programs, 54–57
   Trilogy epilogue, 243–246
   Trilogy guideline 1, 210–214
   Trilogy guideline 2, 220–223
   Trilogy guideline 3, 232–236
tools
   adapting tools, 18
   attention to detail, 137
   battle of attrition approach, 137
   comment discrepancies, 159–161
   defined, 7
   evaluators, 135–137, 159, 166–169
   filmmaking, 8–13
   harsh feedback, 159, 161–165
   of mentors, 73
   methodological, 42
   perform peer reviews, 137
   publication outlets, 135
   revise and resubmit, 136–137, 142–152
   seek advice, 137
   Shared Universe tool, 12, 13, 18, 24–26, 62, 96, 186
   Trilogy tools, 12–13, 177–178, 185–186, 199–203, 207, 210–214, 219–223
active ingredients, 9, 168–169
ambient films, 22, 24–26
and-but-therefore, 45–47, 200–202
Anonymous Accounts
   defined, 14–15
   experiencing awe
      17.1, 249–250
      17.2, 251–252

17.3, 254–255
feedback
  8.1, 133–134
  8.2, 143
  9.1, 157–158
  9.2, 162–163
graduate school, applying
  5.1, 62–63
  5.2, 69–70
  5.3, 82
  5.4, 93–94
job market
  10.1, 175–176
  10.2, 176–177
job talks
  11.1, 185–186
  11.2, 188
  11.3, 192–193
  13.1, 208–209
  13.2, 209
  13.3, 215
  15.1, 226–227
  15.2, 237
  15.3, 238
  15.4, 239
meeting mentors
  3.1, 31
  3.2, 32–33
  3.3, 36–37
  3.4, 38–39
questions, challenging/influential

14.1, 218
16.1, 241
16.2, 246
rejection
  7.1, 115–116
  7.2, 125–126
weaknesses
  4.1, 43–44
  4.2, 47–48
writing schedules
  2.1, 19
  2.2, 21
  2.3, 23
attrition, 131, 137, 153–155
author resources, 128

back-up plans, 125–127
barriers, structural, 117–126
Batman, 40–41
biases, 117, 123–126, 159, 166–169
  See also evaluators; peer reviews
burning questions
  defined, 16
  journals and, 77–78
  Me and My Mentor's Galaxy, 98
  mentors and, 50, 66, 72–73, 76–80
  Modeling Moments, 54–59
  sneak previews, 58

solar system and, 51–54

Captain America, 24–26
collaborating, 64, 99–100, 112–113, 245–246
co-mentors, 99, 102–104
conflict(s)
   of interest, 113
   key, 59
   storytelling and, 200–202, 219, 232–236
Craven, Wes, 195–203, 220, 231–232

Deadpool, 40

editors/editorial consultants
   evaluator selection and, 151
   as helpful tools, 159–169
   listings of, 127–128
   roles of, 114–115
   subjective evaluation and, 118–120
Emerging Academics
   core mission of, 51–54
   defined, 4–6
   imposter syndrome, 25
   mentors and
      expectations, 5–6, 32, 49, 96, 101
      inhospitable galaxies, 104–107
      interdependency, 51–52
      research programs, 99–101
      Shared Universe, 24–29
   mentor selection and
      burning questions, 50, 66, 76–80, 99
      co-mentors, 99, 102–104
      compatibility, 62–65
      galaxies and, 31–32, 67–69, 76, 85, 104–107, 188–189
      grad programs and, 79–81
      Me and My Mentor's Galaxy, 98
      other students and, 88–91, 105
      planets and, 76
      quantity–efficiency, 71–72
      questions to ask, 75–91
      resources, 33, 73–74, 102
      scholarly works, 12, 30, 72–73, 86, 188–189
      Shared Universe, 12–13, 18, 24–26, 62, 96
      "siblings," 65
      STAR factors, 99
      time constraints, 70–72, 88–90

trade-offs, 75, 83–85
peer review and, 116–117
scholarship/scholarly works, 187
as Spiderman, 24–26
structural barriers and, 117–126
structural supports and, 126–131
unworthiness and, 25
emerging adulthood, 4–5
employment
difficulties of finding, 7
interviews, 81–82
job talks and, 175–183
evaluators
biases of, 117, 123–126, 159, 166–169
comments of, 142, 145
consensus and, 112, 119–124
empathy and, 125–126, 133–137, 147–148
peer reviews and, 118–119, 161–165
reasons to serve as, 155–156
recommendations and, 135, 138–140
selecting, 128–129, 151
expectations
Emerging Academics and, 5–6, 32, 49, 96, 101
imposter syndrome, 25

failures, 41–43, 130–131
See also Anonymous Accounts
feedback
Modeling Moments, 158–159
peer reviews and, 141–143
perspective of evaluator, 136–137
See also Anonymous Accounts; peer reviews
filmmaking, 8–13
finances, 82, 103
focus groups, 11
frameworks, 53–54, 59, 67–75, 83, 87, 101–102
Future Directions Forum, 18

galaxies
defined, 16
vs. grad programs, 63–65
inhospitable, 104–107
Me and My Mentor's Galaxy, 98
of mentors, 31–32, 67–69, 72–73, 76, 85, 104–107, 188–189
multiple, 102–104
research programs and,

49–52, 72–73, 87, 99–101
Shared Universe tool, 12–13, 18, 24–26, 62, 96
solar system metaphor, 49–52
"Goldilocks zone," 194
graduate school, 63–65, 79–82, 90
   See also Anonymous Accounts
gravitational force, 53–54, 59

health challenges, 93–94
high quantity–low efficiency, 71–72

imposter syndrome, 25
intellect, 131
interconnection, 30, 75
interest, conflict of, 113
inter-raters, 119–124, 126, 149, 160
   See also evaluators
interviews, 81–82, 178
Iron Man, 24–26, 40

job talks
   audience of, 189–190
   conflict/hook of, 219
   context of, 177–183
   epilogues, 242–243, 247
   masterful, 227–229
   motivation and, 196–197, 206
   "one-slide studies," 193–194, 239–240
   storytelling and, 196–197, 200–202
   Trilogy tools and, 226–227, 230
   See also Anonymous Accounts; employment
journals, 77–78

Kazdin, Alan, 27–28, 65, 217–218
key conflict, 59

learning environments, 31–32, 68–73
   See also galaxies
letters
   cover templates/examples, 135–137, 148, 154, 156, 159, 168–169
   response example/template, 145, 161, 164–165
low quantity–high efficiency, 71–72

Makol, Bridget, 33–36, 210–214, 220–224, 232–236, 243–244
Marvel Cinematic Universe,

24–26
Me and My Mentor's Galaxy, 98
mentors
  Alan Kazdin, 27–28, 65, 217–218
  burning questions, 50, 66, 76–80, 99
  collaborators and, 112
  co-mentors, 99, 102–104
  environments/galaxies of, 31–32, 68–69, 72–73, 76, 85, 103–107, 188–189
  evaluators and, 112–114
  expectations and, 30, 32, 49, 96, 101
  influence of, 31
  interdependency and, 49, 51–52
  as Iron Man, 24–26, 40
  job talks and, 186
  Laurie Wakschlag, 95
  research programs and, 26–29, 99–101
  resources of, 73–74, 102
  selection of
    burning questions and, 50, 66, 76–79, 99
    compatibility and, 62–65
    galaxies and, 31–32, 67–69, 72–73, 76, 85, 104–107, 188–189
    grad programs and, 79–81
    Me and My Mentor's Galaxy, 98
    other students and, 88–91, 105
    planets and, 76
    quantity–efficiency and, 71–72
    questions to ask, 75–91
    resources, 33, 73–74, 102
    scholarly works and, 12, 30, 72–73, 86, 188–189
    Shared Universe, 12–13, 18, 24–26, 62, 96
    time constraints, 70–72, 88–90
    trade-offs, 75, 83–85
  "siblings," 65
  STAR factors, 99
  See also Anonymous Accounts; Emerging Academics
methodologies, 42
Modeling Moments
  applied, 135–137
  Bridget Makol and, 210–214, 220–224, 232–236, 243–244
  burning questions, 54–59
  failures, 41–43
  feedback, 158–159

illustrated, 13–14
mentors, 26–29
peer review tools, 135–137, 159
research programs and, 54–57
Trilogy epilogue, 243–246
Trilogy guideline 1, 210–214
Trilogy guideline 2, 220–223
Trilogy guideline 3, 232–236
motivation, 102, 144, 196–200, 206–208, 219, 247

narratives
  and-but-therefore, 45–47
  incorporating, 42
  peer reviews and, 114
  storytelling and, 200–202
  Trilogy tools and, 230
  See also Anonymous Accounts
networks, 24, 65, 175–176, 251
Nock, Matthew, 65

"one-slide studies," 179–180, 193–194

peer reviews

and attrition, 131, 137, 153–155
empathy and, 125–126, 133–137, 147–148
evaluator bias, 159
feedback and, 157–158, 162–163
inter-raters and, 119–124, 126, 149, 160
purpose of, 117–118
quality control and, 113–116
reasons to serve, 155–156
revise and resubmit (R&R)
  action plan, 145–152
  attention to detail, 152–153
  letter templates/examples, 135–137, 145, 159, 161
  making revisions, 148–150
  options, 126
  process of, 129–130
  seeking advice, 151–152
persistence, 130–131, 154–155, 170–171
perspective, 135–137, 147–148
  See also Anonymous Accounts
planets, 30, 51, 59, 76
plans B–E, 125–127

psychology, 115–116
psychometrics, 120, 123–124
publication outlets
  choosing wisely, 138–140
  evaluators and, 156
  information available, 127–129
  online material, 135
  roles within, 114

quality control, 113, 117–119
quantity–efficiency, 71–72

rater biases, 117–119, 123–126, 159, 166–169
real estate, 74, 83
rejection
  Modeling Moments, 158–159
  peer reviews and, 141–143
  perspective of evaluator, 136–137
  research/research programs, 115–116, 125–126
  See also Anonymous Accounts; peer reviews
relationships
  co-mentors and, 99, 102–104
  difficulties within, 104–107
  mentors and Emerging

Academics, 24–29
Shared Universe, 12, 18, 62
time constraints, 70–72, 88–90
research/research programs
  articulating, 228
  awe and, 249–252, 254–255
  building, 62, 85–87, 99–102, 107
  burning question script, 55–57
  career decisions, 8, 107
  galaxies/solar systems, 49–52, 99–107
  "Goldilocks zone" and, 194
  job talks and, 177, 190
  Me and My Mentor's Galaxy, 98
  mentors and, 26–27, 91, 99–101, 105
  Modeling Moments and, 54–57
  rejection and, 115–116, 125–126
  See also Anonymous Accounts; scholarship/scholarly works
resources, 33, 73, 102, 128
revise and resubmit (R&R)
  action plan, 145–152
  attention to detail, 152–153
  defined, 116–117

letter templates/examples, 135–137, 145, 154, 156, 159, 161, 168–169
making revisions, 148–150
options, 126
process of, 129–130
seeking advice, 151–152

satellites, 234–236
schedules, 19–23, 145–147
   See also Anonymous Accounts
scholarship/scholarly works
   awe within, 249–250, 251–252
   burning question script, 55–57
   and evaluator recommendations, 138–140
   expectations and, 49
   feedback and, 133–134, 157–158, 162–163
   framework of, 52–54
   galaxies and, 72–73, 87, 99–101
   "Goldilocks zone" and, 194
   inter-raters and, 119–124, 126, 149, 160
   journals, 77–78
   mentors and, 12, 30, 72–73, 86, 188–189
   multiple outlets, 126–127
   "one-slide studies," 179–180, 193–194
   and persistence, 130–131, 154–155, 170–171
   and planets, 51, 59
   public and private issues, 41–42
   publication outlets and, 138–140
   quality control and, 113, 117–119
   research programs and, 7–9, 54, 99–101, 228
   solar system and, 52–54
   storytelling and, 207–208
   structure of, 87–88
   team scholarship and, 188–189
   themes of, 36
   Trilogy tools and, 196–199
   un/fair segments, 117–130
   universe of, 30, 64, 113
   See also job talks; peer reviews; revise and resubmit (R&R)
Scream trilogy, 198–202
serendipity, 38–39
Shared Universe tool
   and Captain America, 24–26
   galaxy and, 12–13, 96, 186
   origins of, 18

and selecting mentor, 62
solar systems
   burning question and, 52–54
   defined, 50–51
   and mentors, 76
   research programs and, 49–52
Spiderman, 24–26
STAR factors
   burning questions, 99
   defined, 67–73
   intersectionality of, 75
   Me and My Mentor's Galaxy, 98
   real estate and, 74, 83
stars, 51–53, 59
storytelling
   academic toolbox and, 8–13
   benefits of, 255
   and-but-therefore, 45–47
   conflicts and, 200–202, 219, 232–236
   filmmaking and, 9–11
   "Goldilocks zone" and, 194
   motivational, 196–199, 207, 219
   narratives, 42, 45–47, 200–201
   scholarly works and, 207–208
   story boards, 207, 219, 230, 242
   three-act structure and, 11
   trilogy tools and, 199–203
   Wes Craven, 195–203, 220, 231–232
   See also Anonymous Accounts
strengths, 41–42
structural barriers, 117–126
structural supports, 126–131
successes, 41–43, 130–131
   See also weaknesses
summary judgments, 114–115
superheroes
   Batman, 40–41
   Captain America, 24–26
   Deadpool, 40
   Iron Man, 24–26, 40
   Spiderman, 24–26
   tenured professors as, 25–26
supports, structural, 126–131

tenure, 25–26, 44
theoretical framework, 53–54, 59, 87, 101–102
three-act structure, 11
time-management, 19–23, 43, 145–147
toolbox
   Modeling Moments
      burning questions,

54–59
feedback, 158–159
illustrated, 13–14
mentors, 26–29
peer review tools, 135–137, 159
research programs and, 54–57
Trilogy epilogue, 243–246
Trilogy guideline 1, 210–214
Trilogy guideline 2, 220–223
Trilogy guideline 3, 232–236

tools
adapting tools, 18
attention to detail, 137
battle of attrition approach, 137
comment discrepancies, 159–161
defined, 7
evaluators, 135–137, 159, 166–169
filmmaking, 8–13
harsh feedback, 159, 161–165
of mentors, 73
methodological, 42
perform peer reviews, 137
publication outlets, 135
revise and resubmit, 136–137, 142–152
seek advice, 137
Shared Universe tool, 12, 13, 18, 24–26, 62, 96, 186
Trilogy tools, 12–13, 177–178, 185–186, 199–203, 207, 210–214, 219–223

Trilogy tools
conflict/hook, 219
defined, 177–178, 185–186
guidelines, 199–203, 210–214, 220–223, 232–236
motivation, 196–199
story boards, 207, 219, 230, 242

universe
components, 117
fair segments, 126–131
planets, 30, 50–51, 54, 95
scholarly, 64, 113
unfair segments, 117–126
unworthiness, 25

Wakschlag, Laurie, 95
weaknesses, 41–43, 130–131
See also Anonymous

THE EARLY CAREER RESEARCHER'S TOOLBOX

Accounts
worksheet, Me and My Mentor's Galaxy, 98
writing, 19–23

Index written by Heather Pendley

CPSIA information can be obtained
at www.ICGtesting.com
Printed in the USA
LVHW012043190720
661016LV00001B/81